COMPARATIVE POLITICS

Losers' Consent

COMPARATIVE POLITICS

Comparative Politics is a series for students and teachers of political science
that deals with contemporary issues in comparative government and politics.
As Comparative European Politics it has produced a series of high quality books since its
foundation in 1990, but now takes on a new form and new title for the new
millennium—Comparative Politics. As the process of globalization proceeds, and as
Europe becomes ever more enmeshed in world trends and events, so it is necessary to
broaden the scope of the series. The General Editors are Professor Alfio Mastropaolo,
University of Turin and Kenneth Newton, University of Southampton and
Wissenschaftszentrum Berlin. The series is published in association with the European
Consortium for Political Research.

OTHER TITLES IN THIS SERIES

Party Politics in New Democracies
Edited by Paul Webb and Stephen White

Citizens, Democracy, and Markets Around the Pacific Rim
Edited by Russell J. Dalton and Doh Chull Shin

The Performance of Democracies
Edeltraud Roller

Democratic Challenges, Democratic Choices
Russell J. Dalton

Democracy Transformed?
Edited by Bruce E. Cain, Russell J. Dalton, and Susan E. Scarrow

Environmental Protest in Western Europe
Edited by Christopher Rootes

Social Movements and Networks
Edited by Mario Diani and Doug McAdam

Delegation and Accountability in Parliamentary Democracies
Edited by Kaare Strøm, Wolfgang C. Müller, and Torbjörn Bergman

The Presidentialization of Politics
Edited by Thomas Paguntke and Paul Webb

Elections, Parties, Democracy
Michael D. McDonald and Ian Budge

Losers' Consent: Elections and Democratic Legitimacy

CHRISTOPHER J. ANDERSON, ANDRÉ BLAIS,
SHAUN BOWLER, TODD DONOVAN, and
OLA LISTHAUG

UNIVERSITY PRESS

OXFORD

UNIVERSITY PRESS

Great Clarendon Street, Oxford OX2 6DP

Oxford University Press is a department of the University of Oxford.
It furthers the University's objective of excellence in research, scholarship,
and education by publishing worldwide in

Oxford New York

Auckland Bangkok Buenos Aires Cape Town Chennai
Dar es Salaam Delhi Hong Kong Istanbul Karachi Kolkata
Kuala Lumpur Madrid Melbourne Mexico City Mumbai Nairobi
São Paulo Shanghai Taipei Tokyo Toronto

Oxford is a registered trade mark of Oxford University Press
in the UK and in certain other countries

Published in the United States
by Oxford University Press Inc., New York

British Library Cataloguing in Publication Data

Data available

Library of Congress Cataloging in Publication Data

Data available

ISBN 978–0–19–927638–7 (Hbk.)
978–0–19–923200–0 (Pbk.)

1 3 5 7 9 10 8 6 4 2

Typeset by SPI Publisher Services, Pondicherry, India
Printed in Great Britain
by
Biddles Ltd., King's Lynn, Norfolk

Preface

Democracy is based on the idea that elections are the principal vehicle for popular influence in government. And while democracy strives for equality in citizens' opportunities to participate in electoral contests, it also is designed to create unequal outcomes: for some to win, others have to lose. We argue that this inequality matters for political legitimacy because it generates ambivalent attitudes towards political authorities on the part of the losers. This book examines the causes and consequences of this ambivalence for the legitimacy of democratic institutions. While it should not come as a surprise that winners support the processes that make them successful, it should perhaps be more surprising that the losers, instead of refusing to accept the outcome and undermine the system, are frequently willing to consent to being governed by the winners. Because the efficacy of democratic regimes can be seriously threatened if the losers do not consent to their loss, the central themes of this book focus on losing: how institutions shape losing, and how losers respond to their loss. And this, we argue, is critical for understanding how democracy works since being able to accept losing is one of the central, if not the central, requirement of democracy.

While all of us have been working on questions related to the theme of the book for some time, the book has its most immediate origins in a conference organized in October 2002 by Chris Anderson with the help of the Center on Democratic Performance and the Department of Political Science at Binghamton University (SUNY). We are grateful to Ned McMahon (then Director of CDP) and Grace Schulman for helping to organize the conference and the *George L. Hinman Fund for Public Policy* for providing the necessary resources for bringing together the group of authors as well as a number of conference participants.

We would like to thank the following individuals for participating in the conference and providing thoughtful and constructive feedback during the sessions: Tom Brunell, Gretchen Casper, David Cingranelli, Lucy Goodhart, Will Heller, Rick Hofferbert, Bonnie Meguid, Dick Niemi, Jonas Pontusson, Bing Powell, David Rueda, Chris Way, and Antoine Yoshinaka. Portions of the book also were presented as papers at the Midwest Political Science Association National Conference, Chicago, April 3–6, 2003. Many thanks to Jeff Karp and the panel audience for providing stimulating comments and to Carol Mershon for allowing us to meet in so congenial an environment.

In addition, Chris Anderson is grateful to the National Science Foundation, which supported this research through grant SES-9818525. He also would like to thank the colleagues and students in the Binghamton University Political Science Department, where much of the work was done, as well as the Maxwell School of Syracuse University where the book was completed. He also is grateful to various collaborators who have helped shape this work over the years by reading drafts, working on papers, or simply listening to and commenting on ideas: Kathleen O'Connor, Silvia Mendes, Michael McDonald, Yuliya Tverdova, David Rueda, Aida Paskeviciute, Gretchen Casper, Karl Kaltenthaler, and Herbert Kitschelt. Thanks also to seminar participants at the University of Oxford (Nuffield College), Columbia University (biannual seminar on political psychology), and Cornell University (Department of Government and Johnson Graduate School of Management) for providing helpful feedback.

André Blais thanks Peter Loewen and Marc-André Bodet for their research assistance, and the Social Sciences and Humanities Research Council of Canada for its financial support.

Shaun Bowler is grateful to the Academic Senate UC Riverside for financial support and colleagues at UC Riverside, Jon Hiskey, Martin Johnson, and John Williams, for feedback and helpful comments.

Todd Donovan thanks political science faculty and graduate students at Rice University and Texas Tech University for helpful feedback on parts of this research. He is grateful to the Research Advisory Council and Bureau of Faculty Research at Western Washington University for their financial support.

Ola Listhaug thanks Loek Halman and the Norwegian Social Science Data Services for providing him with EVS 1999 data, Catherine Netjes, Aida Paskeviciute, Elena Sandovici, and Yuliya Tverdova for help with the classification of parties, and Lars Grønflaten, Jo Jakobsen, and Robert Ekle for excellent research assistance.

The authors also would like to thank the following for permission to reproduce published material: Fagbokforlaget (Figure 4.1); University of California Press (Table 9.6); Elsevier (Table 9.7); Auckland University Press (Table 9.8).

The authors would like to thank the editorial staff at Oxford University Press for their expert work on this book. We are particularly grateful to Claire Croft at OUP and Rosamund Davies of Ashwell Enterprises for their efficient, excellent, and cheerful contributions to the book.

Contents

List of Figures

List of Tables

About the Authors

Christopher J. Anderson is Professor of Government at Cornell University. His research examines the micro-foundations of democracy and political economy in comparative perspective. He is the author of *Blaming the Government: Citizens and the Economy in Five European Democracies*, and numerous articles on citizen politics in contemporary democracies. Anderson is the winner of the American Political Science Association's *Heinz Eulau Award* for the best article published in the *American Political Science Review* and the recipient of the *Emerging Scholar Award* given by the APSA Organized Section on Elections, Public Opinion, and Voting Behavior to the top young scholar in the field.

André Blais is Professor in the Department of Political Science at the Université de Montreal, a research fellow with the Centre interuniversitaire de recherche en économic quantitative (CIREQ), and holds a Canada Research Chair in Electoral Studies. His research interests are voting and elections, electoral systems, public opinion, and research methodology. Professor Blais also is the principal coinvestigator of the Canadian Election Study. He has published more than 100 articles in journals such as the *American Journal of Political Science, British Journal of Political Science, Political Studies, European Journal of Political Science, Revue française de science politique, Canadian Journal of Political Science, Comparative Political Studies, Public Opinion Quarterly, Electoral Studies, Political Behavior, Party Politics,* and *Quality and Quantity.* His most recent books are: *Establishing the Rules of the Game: Election Laws in Democracies* (University of Toronto Press, 2004, with Louis Massicotte and Antoine Yoshinaka), Anatomy of a Liberal Victory: Making Sense of the Vote in the 2000 Canadian Election (Broadview Press, 2002, with Elisabeth Gidengil, Richard Nadeau and Neil Nevitte), and *To Vote Or Not To Vote? The Merits and Limits of Rational Choice Theory* (University of Pittsburgh Press, 2000).

Shaun Bowler is Professor of Political Science at the University of California, Riverside. Professor Bowler's research interests include comparative electoral systems and voting behavior. His work examines the relationship between institutional arrangements and voter choice in a variety of settings ranging from the Republic of Ireland to California's initiative process. Professor Bowler is the author and editor of six books on elections and political behavior, including *Demanding Choices: Opinion Voting and Direct Democracy* with Todd Donovan (University of Michigan Press, 1998). He has published numerous articles in the leading journals of political science, including the *American Political Science Review, American Journal of Political Science, Journal of Politics,* and the *British Journal of Political Science.*

Todd Donovan is a Professor in the Political Science Department at Western Washington University, in Bellingham, WA. He has published dozens of articles in academic journals, including the *American Journal of Political Science, British Journal of Political Science, Journal of Politics,* and *Electoral Studies.* He has also co-authored five books, including two on direct democracy: *Demanding Choices: Opinion and Voting in Direct Democracy* (University of Michigan Press, 1998, with Shaun Bowler), and *Citizens as Legislators: Direct Democracy in the United States* (Ohio State University Press, 1998, co-edited with S. Bowler and C. Tolbert). His latest books include *Electoral Reform and Minority Representation* (Ohio State University Press, 2003, with Bowler), a study of semi-proportional representation elections in the United States, and *Reforming the Republic: Democratic Institutions for the New America* (Prentice Hall, 2004 with Bowler). Donovan's primary academic expertise is in the areas of American state politics, direct democracy, election systems, and representation. He has received grants to study electoral politics and direct democracy in the United States, Australia, Canada, and New Zealand.

Ola Listhaug is Professor of Political Science and Chairman in the Department of Sociology and Political Science at The Norwegian University of Science and Technology, and leader of the working group on Values and Violence at the Centre for the Study of Civil War, PRIO. He has published widely in the fields of political behavior, comparative politics, and comparative sociology in journals such as the *American Political Science Review, Journal of Politics, British Journal of Political Science, Comparative Political Studies, European Journal of Political Research, Acta Sociologica,* and *Scandinavian Political Studies.* He has been a visiting scholar at the University of Michigan, the University of Iowa, and the University of North Carolina, Chapel Hill. His involvement in international research projects includes participation in the *European Values Study* and the *Beliefs in Government* study of the European Science Foundation. Listhaug is the winner of the *Franklin L. Burdette Pi Sigma Alpha Award* and the *Heinz Eulau Award* of the American Political Science Association (both with Stuart Elaine Macdonald and George Rabinowitz).

Winning Isn't Everything: Losers' Consent and Democratic Legitimacy

Winning isn't everything, it's the only thing.

Vince Lombardi

The dynamics of politics is in the hands of the losers. It is they who decide when and how and whether to fight on.

William Riker (1983)

Maybe Vince Lombardi was right and Bill Riker's concern with political losers hopelessly romantic. After all, over the years, political scientists and football coaches alike have tended to pay more attention to the winners than the losers. It seems to be a natural impulse since humans compete to win and because the taste of victory is sweet. Given that winning and winners are almost universally celebrated in today's world, while losers are frequently forgotten, it is perhaps not surprising that football coaches in particular have long perceived the world around them through the lens of winning and losing. And it appears that many students of democratic politics would agree with Lombardi as well. Perhaps this is not unexpected either, given that, in the world of democratic politics, candidates and parties compete for votes, and elections determine who has the right to choose the country's direction and who has to await another day.

And where better to look for winners than on game day in the case of football or election-day in a democracy? And what better to explain than how the triumphant party won and, consequently, how winning can be achieved next time around? Perhaps because of this, political scientists have spent considerable energy trying to understand election outcomes—that is, how winners are produced. In fact, the study of why elections come out as they do and why voters make the choices they do is one of the great success stories in the modern history of political science, spawning a veritable industry of scholars, research institutes, poll takers, training programs, and, in recent years, even computer programmers (Scarbrough 2003).

Yet, however interesting and exciting winners and winning are, they represent only one side of the coin when it comes to understanding political life. In fact, we contend that understanding winning is no more relevant than understanding losers insofar as the study of political systems is concerned, given that the attitudes and behaviors of losers determine whether the game will go on in the first place and whether it will continue to be played in the long run. Put simply, then, given that the consent of the losers is one of the central, if not *the* central, requirements of the democratic bargain, Lombardi may have a point, but as Riker rightly observes, without the losers we do not get to play the game.

Political science has often overlooked the reactions and behavior of political losers in order to focus on the whos, whys, and hows of winning. To rectify this, and to put the proper emphasis on the importance of losers' behavior in producing stable and legitimate democratic rule, the central themes of this book focus on losing and its consequences—that is, how institutions shape losing, how losers respond to their loss, and how losers' consent affects the legitimacy and viability of democratic institutions. Because these are central questions in the study of democracy, we start by first explaining why we think losers matter; we then provide an overview of the investigation we undertake in this book.

ELECTION OUTCOMES AND DEMOCRATIC LEGITIMACY

In what follows, we are primarily concerned with people's attitudes toward the functioning of government, also commonly referred to as political legitimacy. Citizen attitudes toward the political system have long played a central role in theories of political behavior, and they usually are viewed as important indicators of a healthy civic and democratic political culture (cf. Putnam 1993; see also Kornberg and Clarke 1992). And there is plenty of anecdotal evidence to support this view: throughout the twentieth century, examples abound of countries whose democratic political systems have faltered because they lacked the critical ingredient of a supportive citizenry. Put another way, political scientists care about citizens' attitudes toward government and political institutions because they have long suspected that low levels of citizen support pose a threat to democratic systems (Lipset 1959; Powell 1982). In fact, to say that both the functioning and the maintenance of democratic polities are intimately linked with what and how citizens think about democratic governance is perilously close to stating a tautology.

The assumption that democracies are more likely to last or function well if citizens have positive opinions about government is commonly made both for systems undergoing democratic transitions as well as presumably more stable democratic systems (though the latter have yet to see the actual breakdown of a long-standing democratic order; cf. Bermeo 2003). While questions of popular support for democratic governance are of practical and immediate relevance for the continued stability of emerging democratic institutions (Mishler and Rose 1997), citizens' approval of democratic governance is believed to be important for understanding challenges aimed at reforming mature democratic institutions as well (Dalton 2004). Thus, what citizens think about democratic political institutions is important for theoreticians and policy-makers alike and relevant for both older and newer democracies.

Below, we examine how the experience of being among the winners and losers in electoral contests affects people's beliefs about the political system. Focusing on winning and losing in democratic elections is appropriate because democracy is, at its core, based on the idea that the political process ought to be routinely and necessarily responsive to what citizens want, and that elections are the principal vehicle for popular influence in government by determining who gets to rule: 'the essential democratic institution is the ballot box and all that goes with it' (Riker 1965: 25). It is thus no surprise that elections usually are a main ingredient in the definition of a democracy (Riker 1965; Dahl 1971; Huntington 1991) because they are the mechanism by which the power to determine the authoritative allocation of values (Easton 1953) is allocated or, to use Harold Lasswell's famous phrase, who gets to decide 'who gets what, when, and how' (Lasswell 1953).

However, although democracy strives for equality in opportunity to participate in electoral contests, it also is unavoidably unequal in the outcomes it produces. Elections reward or punish individual voters' choices through the much publicized consequences of the collective choice of all voters over competing political programs. That is, casting one's ballot for a party or candidate does not automatically turn voters into winners and losers; it is only through the compilation of all voters' choices on the basis of an agreed-upon formula that a president or legislators are elected and a government is thereafter formed, and that the electorate can be subsequently divided into those on the winning and those on the losing side.[1] Political winning and losing thus directly connects micro-decisions and macro-outcomes; wins and losses are individually experienced but collectively determined. As importantly, we argue that the experience of winning and losing and becoming part of the majority and minority leads people to adopt a lens through which they view political life.

If we consider, for a moment, reactions after an election, we should not be surprised to find the winners to be happy and content with the outcome. While becoming a winner may be difficult, being the winner, in fact, is easy. After all, the ideas and interests of the winners will now be reflected in policy outputs for the next few years (this assumes, of course, that the winners' preferences will be enacted). For citizens and elites alike, winning an election means getting a greater share of preferred policies, and there is no reason to expect many regrets about such an outcome or, more importantly, the process that produced it (see also Miller and Listhaug 1999).

---

[1] This rendering of the democratic process is necessarily incomplete, as a number of democratic systems manufacture winners and losers after an election has been held through elite bargaining. We will address these distinctions in a later chapter.

This is not the case for losers who could, quite reasonably, be expected to be discouraged and displeased both with the outcome of the election and the process that produced it. The morning after the ballots are tallied is not nearly so pleasant for the losers. In fact, we can expect the losers to work hard at using all legal and defensible means to thwart the efforts of the winners to pursue their desired policies. In a real way, then, democratic design envisions the losers' job to consist of making life difficult for the winners.

Yet, if democratic procedures are to continue in the long run, then the losers must, somehow, overcome any bitterness and resentment and be willing, first, to accept the decision of the election and, second, to play again next time. That they would do either is not altogether obvious. After all, 'Consenting to a process is not the same thing as consenting to the outcomes of the process.' (Coleman 1989: 197; cited in Przeworski 1991: 14; see also Lipset 1959; Habermas 1975). Thus, to use a memorable phrase of one of the more important studies of losing, the continuation of democratic systems depends, in part, on the 'losers' consent' (Nadeau and Blais 1993). As Nadeau and Blais note 'losers' reactions are absolutely critical' (p. 553). Winners are likely to be happy with the system but losers' support for the system 'is less obvious' since that support 'requires the recognition of the legitimacy of a procedure that has produced an outcome deemed to be undesirable. In the end, the viability of electoral democracy depends on its ability to secure the support of a substantial proportion of individuals who are displeased with the outcome of an election' (Nadeau and Blais 1993: 553).

And while losing once may not be so difficult, in some circumstances the question becomes whether the losers really are willing to compete in democratic elections next time but also, if they lose again, the time after that and the time after that. It is possible that, at some point, the losers could simply decide not to bother to play at all and stay at home on election-day. And there is plenty of evidence from around the globe that this is frequently what losers do. Other reactions could be a little less passive. Perhaps the losers could organize a boycott of a process they believe to be stacked against them or, more extreme still, could actively work to overthrow what they see as an unfair system. The central question concerning the durability of democracy thus is this: 'How does it happen that political forces that lose in contestation comply with the outcomes and continue to participate rather than subvert democratic institutions?' (Przeworski 1991: 15).

There are many examples of leaders and citizens who refuse to accept loss, even in countries whose similarly situated neighbors have successfully made the democratic transition. In fact, in extreme cases losers' reactions may also lead to conditions that contribute to civil war. In the case of Spain, for example, the narrow victory of the Popular Front in the election of February 1936 started a series of events leading to the civil war that broke out in July the same year. But there are just as many examples of leaders who simply concede and get on with life. Richard Nixon in 1960 and Al Gore in 2000 are two famous examples of American leaders who arguably lost by the narrowest of margins and quite possibly in a less than fair way. Yet both peacefully and gracefully conceded defeat. On December 13, 2000, after the United States Supreme Court had, in effect, ruled that George W. Bush was the rightful winner of the presidential election, Gore said in a nationally televised address:

Now the U.S. Supreme Court has spoken. Let there be no doubt: While I strongly disagree with the court's decision, I accept it. I accept the finality of this outcome, which will be ratified next Monday in the Electoral College. And tonight, for the sake of our unity of the people and the strength of our democracy, I offer my concession. I also accept my responsibility, which I will discharge unconditionally, to honor the new president-elect and do everything possible to help him bring Americans together in fulfillment of the great vision that our Declaration of Independence defines and that our Constitution affirms and defends.

What was astounding to many about Gore's gracious concession was his willingness to accept the outcome given that, according to Gallup polls taken at the time, 97 percent of those who had voted for him believed that he was the rightful President of the United States.

Some might argue that this is only what one would expect from a politician who knows he may get another chance to play the game and in a country with the longest-functioning system of electoral democracy. After all, it is a well-known fact that winning is the precursor of losing and losing the precursor of winning, as parties that win an election tend to lose votes already at the next election (Paldam and Skott 1995). But this is not necessarily what one would expect in countries like Ghana and Senegal. Yet there, too, the losers of the 2000 presidential elections bowed out gracefully. This was particularly remarkable in Senegal, where Abdou Diouf, who had been President for nineteen years, lost to Abdoylaye Wade, who had been the opposition leader for twenty-six years. On March 19, 2000, Diouf conceded graciously, saying

I am full of vigor to continue, but if the people decide otherwise, I will thank the Senegalese people for having placed their faith in me for so many years and I will congratulate the winner. The most important thing for me is that Senegal shows the world it is a democratic country, a country where the law is upheld and human rights are respected.

Such sentiments and the behavior that goes with it are clearly different from the behavior we frequently observe around the world, where losers are unwilling to admit defeat. Robert Mugabe's behavior in Zimbabwe after the March 2002 election, for example, stands in stark contrast to de Klerk in South Africa. Similarly, Ukraine and Belorussia provide different examples to the Baltic states and even that of Russia. We also see examples of countries where people refuse to participate in elections or referendums because to do so (in an election they know they would lose) would give legitimacy to what they see as an objectionable process. Some of the religious parties in Pakistan, for example, boycotted the 2002 referendum called by President Musharaff, Northern Irish Catholics have periodically boycotted elections in Northern Ireland as have people in Central America in the immediate period of transition.

To be sure, sometimes losers refuse to concede for good reason, in particular when the election turns out to be less than fair. Thus, following the October 2003 Azerbajan election in which the son of the ailing President Geidar Aliev won election to succeed his father, opposition leaders and observers from the European Union and the Organization for Security and Cooperation in Europe charged that there had been widespread violations during the balloting. In the election's aftermath, 174 people were arrested and at least one person died after police clashed with protesters.

Perhaps among the more spectacular examples in recent memory of losers' unwillingness to consent to a process they found objectionable were the presidential elections in Peru in 2000 and 2001, when the incumbent President Fujimori ran for a (contested) third term in office. In the 2000 election, the main challenger Alejandro Toledo withdrew from the May 28 run-off and urged electoral officials to postpone the election to ensure the fairness of the electoral process. He also urged his supporters to boycott the election. By virtue of Toledo's boycott of the run-off, Fujimori won a third term. Yet, on September 16, 2000, the incumbent president announced early elections in which he would not take part, leading to the election of Toledo in June 2001.

THE IMPORTANCE OF LOSERS' CONSENT FOR DEMOCRATIC LEGITIMACY

What is key, then, is how people react to loss; in particular, how rebellious or how apathetic a reaction is invoked. In part, losers' consent is critical for democratic systems to function because losers are numerous; in part, it is important because of the incentives that losing creates. Fundamentally, people prefer winning over losing, and losses tend to weigh more heavily than gains (Tversky and Kahneman 1992). Positive political theorists have long recognized this insight and built their theoretical apparatus around the notion that players will employ a variety of strategies (such as strategic voting, agenda manipulation, or vote trading, for example) that maximize gains and avoid losses (Riker 1982, 1983). As a result, the optimal strategic choice usually is the one that provides the highest probability that losses are avoided and, conversely, that wins are achieved.

Winning and losing are not simply conditions. Associated with those conditions are differing incentives and of particular importance are incentives in relation to the status quo. Current institutions result from distributional conflicts in society—that is, the result of bargains over acceptable wins and losses.

These also will change when such wins and losses are no longer socially acceptable (Knight 1992). Winning and losing thus matter because the stability and
continued functioning of political systems depend on actors' incentives for
institutional change. As William Riker pointed out some twenty years ago,
today's losers thus are the 'instigators of political change' (Riker 1983: 64),
and today's winners have the greatest incentive to avoid such change (see also
Shepsle 2003).[2]

In this way, then, the winner–loser distinction not only provides a general
framework that is consistent with understanding political behavior more generally, it also has implications for the long-run stability and longevity of a political
system. Specifically, the continued existence of the system depends to a larger
extent on the consent of the losers than the consent of the winners. And if
system stability and maintenance are important long-run goals for democrat-
ically organized polities—as, we would argue, they should be—losers are the
crucial veto players of democratic governance. Studying winners and losers
thus provides theoretical leverage for understanding the behaviors and attitudes of individuals, but also provides insight into the resilience and fragility
of the political system as a whole.

AN ALTERNATIVE VIEW OF DEMOCRATIC ELECTIONS

Traditionally, scholars of political behavior have focused on understanding
and explaining the outcomes of elections rather than how these outcomes
affect political behavior. Such an approach carries with it an unstated, but
important assumption, namely that it is the winners of elections that are worthy
of study because winners have the power to make policy. While this approach
is indispensable for understanding the nature of voters' choices in democratic
systems, it is of limited use for understanding how democracies come to be
and remain stable in the first place. That is, it has little to say about the question
of what leads to conditions that allow for elections to be held in the first place,
and held on a regular basis.

In fact, the real-life examples cited earlier in this chapter point to a real
tension inherent in democracy's central mechanism of collective decision-
making, resulting from the intentional inequality in outcomes elections produce
by turning some voters into winners and others into losers at election time.
Because '[d]emocracy is a system in which parties lose elections' (Przeworski
1991: 10), it produces conflict that, in turn, requires peaceful resolution for
the political system to endure. What is more, this conflict is based on numeric

---

[2] Though it should be added that, on occasion, electoral democracy is undermined by the
winners rather than the losers, especially in situations where the current winners anticipate becoming losers. In historical perspective, however, the odds of democracy being undermined by the
losers is much higher than the odds of it being undermined by the winners (Przeworski 2001).

TABLE 1.1. *The incidence of majority rule in contemporary democracies (percent of votes cast)*

Of all governments formed, 1950–95[a]	
Popular majority governments	47.1
Popular minority governments	52.9
Of all first post-election governments formed, 1950–95[b]	
Popular majority governments	43.8
Popular minority governments	56.2
Of all first post-election governments formed, 1970–95[c]	
Popular majority governments	43.0
Popular minority governments	57.0

[a] $N = 456$.
[b] $N = 265$.
[c] $N = 158$.

Notes: This excludes caretaker, transition, and nonpartisan governments.

Source: Michael D. McDonald and Silvia M. Mendes. Data on twenty-one democracies, 1950–95. Binghamton, NY: Department of Political Science, Binghamton University.

inequalities in the distribution of winners and losers in the population as a whole that are little known and seldom stated. While democracy is, for example, commonly conceived as involving elements of majority rule (Dahl 2002), a look at democratic practices around the world reveals several facts that stand in contrast to this assumption. To summarize briefly, it turns out that democracies on the whole are only infrequently ruled by popular majorities; this implies that the share of citizens who did not vote for the incumbent government commonly outnumbers the share of citizens who did.

Some figures may help make the point more forcefully: of all governments formed in the twenty-one most stable contemporary democracies around the world between 1950 and 1995, only around 45 percent were actually elected by popular majorities; that is, in fewer than half of all elections held did the parties that formed the government after the election obtain more than 50 percent of the vote (Table 1.1).[3] This number shrinks even further when we take into account the level of turnout in each country and calculate the percentage of the vote the government received based on the number of eligible voters (Table 1.2). Based on this calculation, the actual number of times that a majority of eligible voters elected a majority government turns out to be even lower

---

[3] Governments are defined as the party or parties controlling the executive branch. The list of countries includes Australia, Austria, Belgium, Canada, Denmark, Finland, France, Germany, Iceland, Ireland, Italy, Luxembourg, Netherlands, New Zealand, Norway, Portugal, Spain, Sweden, Switzerland, United Kingdom, and United States. When the presidential systems of France and the United States are excluded, the figures change only marginally.

TABLE 1.2. *The incidence of majority rule in contemporary democracies (percent of eligible voters)*

Of all governments formed, 1950–95[a]	
Popular majority governments	20.8
Popular minority governments	79.2
Of all first post-election governments formed, 1950–95[b]	
Popular majority governments	18.9
Popular minority governments	81.1
Of all first post-election governments formed, 1970–95[c]	
Popular majority governments	13.9
Popular minority governments	86.1

[a] $N = 456$.
[b] $N = 265$.
[c] $N = 158$.

Notes: This excludes caretaker, transition, and nonpartisan governments.

Source: Michael D. McDonald and Silvia M. Mendes. Data on twenty-one democracies, 1950–95. Binghamton, NY: Department of Political Science, Binghamton University.

at about 20 percent when all governments in office since 1950 are considered, and as low as 14 percent when only governments formed as a result of an election since 1970 are included. This means, simply, that plurality rule, and not uncommonly minority rule, are the norm in contemporary democracies (see also Strom 1984). This also means that, at the level of individual citizens, being on the losing side is a more common occurrence than being among the winners.

Ultimately, this suggests that democracy can be viewed as a system of government by changing minorities. If this is a proper characterization, then, in the end, what the losers think about such a system is crucial to its maintenance. This does not, of course, mean that losers have to be happy with a political system whose levers of power are pushed by those they did not support. But at the very least they have to accept defeat for the system to continue. What makes democracy work and persist, then, is not so much the success of the winners but the restraint of the losers. Losers must accept both a distasteful outcome and the process that produced it. Given the obvious importance of whether and how losers do restrain themselves, it is surprising how poorly understood their behavior and attitudes are.

Outline of the Book

In studying losers' restraint, we proceed, first, by developing a model of losers' consent, which posits that losers' motivations to be disenchanted with the political system are significantly affected by their own characteristics as well as the political context they find themselves in. We then take stock of the behavioral and attitudinal consequences of losing. Our first broad look at the topic is to examine what we label the 'winner–loser gap': that is, the difference in opinions and attitudes between winners and losers at the individual level. We return to the winner–loser gap at several points in this volume, examining differences across a range of attitudes and behaviors and across a range of countries. A direct comparison of the effects of winner and loser status across different kinds of attitudes or behaviors toward government allows us to establish whether the winner–loser effect is of similar magnitude for different kinds of attitudes and behaviors or whether some are more strongly affected by political majority and minority status than others. At the moment, this is an open empirical question, given that much of the existing research on the majority–minority effect has focused on explaining a relatively narrow set of attitudes toward performance of the political regime such as satisfaction with the way democracy works (e.g. Fuchs, Guidorossi, and Svensson 1995; Anderson and Guillory 1997) or confidence and trust in political institutions (e.g. Gabriel 1989; Listhaug 1995; Norris 1999; Anderson and LoTempio 2002; Bowler and Donovan 2002).

As part of this 'mapping' of the winner–loser gap, our goal also is to go beyond David Easton's (1965) distinction between diffuse and specific support for the political system by defining democratic legitimacy in various different ways, and by examining political behaviors of various kinds. For example, as part of this investigation, we seek to establish whether an individual's status as a supporter of the government or opposition affects her evaluations of the fairness of the electoral process and her confidence that individual political action can have an impact on the political process. Losing an election and being in the minority means that one's political preferences were outvoted or at least failed to translate into political power. Because of this, it is plausible to postulate that the winner–loser distinction affects people's sense of whether they have a say in the political system and whether the political system is responsive to their needs. If losing reduces citizens' efficacy, then losers may become less willing to pay attention to or participate in regular political events, and they may withdraw from the political process altogether (exit). Alternatively, they may become politicized and willing to engage in protest behavior and nontraditional or even socially less acceptable forms of protest (voice).

As part of this initial investigation, the following chapter examines the impact of the winner–loser variable as an individual-level factor that shapes political legitimacy by examining the short and long-term dynamics of losers' consent. Specifically, we examine what happens to voters right before and right after an election has been held and different camps of winners and losers are produced. Moreover, we scrutinize the long-run trajectories of winners and losers' attitudes toward the political system. Only if the winner–loser gap changes following a change in government and only if it is sustained over time are we on solid footing in arguing that our focus on losers has both theoretical and empirical merit.

Next, we focus on the individual-level attitudes that may exacerbate or attenuate the negative effect that being on the losing side may have on beliefs about the legitimacy of the political system. Specifically, we concentrate on ideology and partisan attachment as factors that could frustrate some losers more than others or make some losers feel more sanguine about the political process. From this individual-level analysis we move to consider the linkage between losing and political context. Although there is a growing, cumulative body of evidence demonstrating that those in the majority have more positive attitudes toward politics, these results are open to qualification, extension and possibly challenge on at least two fronts: because the rise of democratic systems and the experience of regular elections is a recent phenomenon in many countries of Eastern Europe and Latin America, much of the theorizing and most of the empirical studies about system support in democracies have occurred with western systems and experiences in mind. This means that scholars have examined explanations of system support mostly on the basis of theories generated about, and data collected in, the democracies of Western Europe and North America—that is, a particular and possibly biased sample of contemporary democracies. This means that it is important to examine systematically differences across mature and newly emerging democracies in the extent to which losing matters for system support. Because having experience with democracy is likely to accustom citizens to the idea that sometimes losses happen, we may see fiercer reactions to losing among new and emerging democracies.

From here we move to consider the impact of political institutions on how losers perceive the functioning of the political system. While political institutions may be the object of citizen trust, they also have a causal impact on citizen attitudes and behaviors. How, then, do institutions matter such that institutional design can help losers accept their loss? To answer this question, we investigate the institutional features that may relieve or exacerbate some of the negative impact of losing on citizens' attitudes and behaviors. We can see this in the way in which institutions shape responses to wins and losses. Different institutions shape how much people lose: specifically, some institutions limit the possible downside and hence limit the likely losses. We focus on two features of the democratic process that are particularly relevant in the experience of loss: first, the impact of electoral mechanisms that bring about winning and losing in the first place; second, the effect of policy-making institutions on losers' consent—that is, the mechanisms of how power is exercised once winners and losers have been determined.

We then turn our spotlight exclusively on losers and consider whether and how citizens learn to lose as well as the factors—individual and societal— that help people to accept losing: some might be simple—such as having had a history of winning in the not too distant past. This suggests a central role for expectations. If citizens expect to keep losing—as ethnic minorities do in many US states, for example—then this might well generate long-term and deep-rooted disaffection from politics (Guinier 1998). It may be that, over time, the cumulative impact of losing generates deeper dissatisfaction with the political system. Overall declines in the levels of trust in government, for example, may be driven by the mounting dissatisfaction of an excluded and passionate minority. In looking just at losers we find that losing is experienced differently and engenders predictably more negative responses in different contexts.

Our results show, for example, that losers are more positive in established democracies than in non-established democracies. Moreover, losers' evaluations are more positive in countries with more proportional electoral rules. Also, we find that supporters of losing parties that have never been in government are the most critical of representative democracy, and supporters of the major losing party that formed the government prior to the election feel most positive. Consistent with our findings reported in our chapter on old and new democracies, we find that differences between types of losing parties are more pronounced in less developed countries. In addition, the better educated losers are more satisfied with the functioning of democracy, more positive about the fairness of the election in less developed democracies, and more sanguine about responsiveness in more developed countries.

Finally, we consider the behavioral responses of losers. Specifically, we investigate the question of whether losing means that citizens will either try to change the rules of the game or will stop playing the game altogether. Drawing on examples from democracies around the globe, we observe that voters on the losing side of a political contest are willing to consider quite sweeping changes and do so in pretty much the same terms as elites who consider rule changes in terms of partisan self-interest.

One Final Note

Winning and losing, as well as the relationships of political majorities and minorities that result from them, have time and again drawn the attention of political commentators going back to the ancient political philosophers and, more recently, liberal thinkers like Locke and Mill. Similarly, the framers of the American Constitution were expressly concerned with the possibility of tyranny by the majority (Dahl 1971) or, to put it another way, the consequences of absolute winning. Modern political theorists have recognized the explanatory power of winning and losing as organizing concepts for understanding political life as well, and much of current political science scholarship can be organized around the theme of understanding human conflict over the power to rule and thus, conflict between (potential and real) winners and losers (cf. Riker 1983; Shepsle 2003).

In this book, we seek to make a contribution to this body of knowledge by making one simple point that we believe to be fundamental to the study of politics: namely, that the consent of political losers is essential to the maintenance of any political system. And because this is so, the study of what motivates losers to accept their loss is fundamental to understanding what makes political systems function the way they do. In fact, on the face of it, it is surprising that political systems achieve any semblance of stability and predictability, given the strong incentives losers have to deny the winners their right to rule. What makes losers give in and even affirm their allegiance to the political system is the question that drives the investigation we undertake in this book.

To understand the contours and structure of losers' consent and subsequently to answer the question of why losers consent, we focus on people—voters— who, when they experience defeat at the ballot box, react to this loss in various ways. To understand their reactions, we rely on a wealth of data collected across the contemporary democracies in the form of public opinion surveys administered in countries as different as the United States, Japan, and Ukraine. We examine what we will call the 'winner–loser gap' in attitudes toward the political system, and we trace the dynamics of what happens to losers' reactions over the course of time before and after elections, over the course of electoral cycles, and over long periods of historical time. We also probe the influence of individual motivations to perceive loss in particular ways and ask whether some people take losing an election particularly hard, while others are more sanguine about their loss. As importantly, we examine the contexts in which losing is experienced—be they institutional or historical in nature. In the end, we paint a picture of losers' consent that views losers as repeat players in the political game, and whose experience of loss is shaped by who they are as individuals as well as the environment in which loss is given meaning. This means that, ultimately, there is wide variation in how people express their reaction to being on the losing side in politics, both across individuals and across countries, and that losers' consent is best understood when we try to understand both people and the political environment in which they live.

We also paint a picture of democratic legitimacy in which losers are the crucial players in the democratic game. Only when losers overcome their negative experiences and consent to being governed by those they disagree with does democracy endure and flourish. Winning is easy, we would argue. But, to quote that keen observer of human emotion and behavior, Vince Lombardi, once more: 'It does not matter how many times you get knocked down, but how many times you get up.'

PART I

THE WINNER–LOSER GAP

2

Political Legitimacy and the Winner–Loser Gap

Although political scientists have recognized the importance of election outcomes for how people feel about the democratic political process for some time, few have examined the effect of elections on people's attitudes about government in much detail. This chapter sets out on this exploration in earnest by examining the underpinnings of what we call the 'winner–loser gap' in democratic legitimacy from several perspectives. First, it discusses how social scientists have approached the study of political legitimacy over the years as well as the major findings that have emerged from their efforts. Second, it explains the underlying premises for the winner–loser gap gleaned from different corners of the social sciences. Finally, we develop a model of losers' consent that forms the theoretical core of our empirical investigation.

FIRST THINGS FIRST: THE CONCEPT OF MASS POLITICAL SUPPORT

Because the relationship between citizens and their government is fundamental to the study of democratic politics, concern with citizen attitudes about democratic institutions is nothing new in research on the politics of contemporary democracies (Dalton 2004). Viewed from historical as well as practical vantage points, the importance of understanding how citizens relate to their governments and the political system more generally can hardly be overstated. After all, the second half of the twentieth century witnessed a substantial rise in the number of democracies around the globe, and today's world is populated by more democracies than it has been at any time during human history. This historic increase in opportunities for citizens to influence decision-making in their countries has also meant that understanding what drives citizens' views of the body politic has become more important today than ever before.

At the same time that the number of democracies around the world increased significantly during the so-called third wave of democratization, already-established democracies faced considerable challenges initiated and sustained by citizen claims on government (Huntington 1974). During the restless 1960s and 1970s, for example, the established democracies of the West had to contend with significant upheaval resulting from the rise of social movements produced by shifts in political values as well as economic problems resulting from the oil-shocks of the 1970s (Dalton 2004). Similarly, in the aftermath of the cold war, economic problems, global competition, and the absence of a common and easily defined enemy have produced increased pressures for the established democratic systems of the West to foster transparency, accountability, and greater sensitivity to citizen input. Not surprisingly perhaps, among the side effects of such pressures has been a trend toward lower levels of citizen satisfaction with the performance of democratic government in a number of contemporary democracies (Kaase 1995, 1999; Kaase and Newton 1995; Dalton 2004).

The end of the cold war also has produced considerable challenges for the newly established democracies of Central and Eastern Europe and Latin America where the path of democratic transition and consolidation in many cases has been anything but smooth. As a result, after much initial enthusiasm for democratic governance in the 1980s and early 1990s, problems with economic transitions, the construction of civil society, and the implementation of political reforms have led to disillusionment with politics among many citizens of newly emerging democratic systems (Mishler and Rose 1996; see also Stokes 1996; Lagos 1997). On a practical level, in such an environment of lower citizen trust in democratic governance globally, research into the classic question of what drives public (dis)satisfaction with the democratic process and support for democratic political institutions in recent years has become ever more critical for our understanding of how and how well contemporary democracies function.

The starting point for most studies of what drives political support or legitimacy is the classic work by David Easton who argues that the legitimacy of democracies is affected by the extent to which citizens trust government to do what is right most of the time (Easton 1965, 1975). Citizens' political support (or lack thereof) can take the form of attitudes or behaviors, and it constitutes an input into the political system. Elites consequently produce outputs (policy decisions and implementations), which feed back into citizens' evaluations of, and inputs into, the system.

Easton distinguishes between diffuse and specific support, where diffuse support is taken to be a long-standing predisposition: 'it refers to evaluations of what an object is or represents—the general meaning it has for a person—not of what it does' (Easton 1965: 273). Diffuse support consists of 'a reservoir of favorable attitudes or good will that helps members to accept or tolerate outputs to which they are opposed or the effects of which they see as damaging to their interests' (Easton 1965: 124–5). In contrast, specific support derives from a citizen's evaluation of system outputs; it is performance-based and short term. According to Easton, a political system relies on reserves of diffuse support to tide it over during periods of inferior short-term performance.

Lack of specific support can—in the long run—carry over to more general feelings of dissatisfaction with the political system. Along similar lines, scholars have argued that although specific support is necessary for the maintenance of a government (or administration) in power, diffuse support is needed to uphold a political system as a form of government (Dalton 2002).

While Easton's theorizing was critical for developing ways to think about system support, researchers have commonly pointed out that Easton's two categories do not exhaust the possible varieties of political support (Thompson 1970; Lambert et al. 1986; Weatherford 1987, 1992; Klingemann 1999). Furthermore, on a practical level, the difficulties of separately measuring diffuse and specific support are enormous: separate indicators of the two are generally found to be highly correlated (Löwenberg 1971; Kaase 1988). Easton's distinction between diffuse and specific support thus has mainly been successful at the conceptual level, but not in the world of empirical social research (Küchler 1991). Given the state of the debate about the conceptualization and measurement of the kind of attitude to be explained in this book,[1] we rely on a straightforward but also very general definition of political support, also variously referred to as political trust or political legitimacy, as put forward by Gamson (1968). Political support is the belief that the political system (or some part of it) will generally produce 'good' outcomes (cf. Hetherington 2004). Because political support may have many different objects and a variety of components, we will rely on a variety of measures, dealing with the various dimensions of legitimacy, throughout our analyses.

WHAT DRIVES POLITICAL LEGITIMACY, OR: HOW WE GOT HERE

Over the years, students of political legitimacy have examined a wide variety of factors that may influence what people think about their political system. However, as M. Stephen Weatherford pointed out more than a decade ago, the study of support for democratic institutions can fairly straightforwardly be divided into research taking 'a macro-perspective emphasizing formal system properties, and a micro-view emphasizing citizens' attitudes and actions' (Weatherford 1992: 149). The former commonly has been concerned with the appropriate set-up of democratic institutions that would allow for accountability, responsiveness, and representation, which, in turn, would lead to higher levels of support for the political system (Lipset 1960; Pitkin 1967; Huntington 1968; Dahl 1971; Lijphart 1984). In related fashion, students of democracies as systems have maintained that any set of governmental institutions has to generate outputs that meet citizens' real or anticipated demands (Easton 1965).

[1] A discussion of the merits of this debate is beyond the scope of this chapter. See Weatherford (1992) and Hetherington (2004) for good summaries.

In contrast, studies taking more of a micro-view have examined the individual-level determinants that underlie citizens' attitudes towards, and participation in, a democratic political system (Lipset 1960; Almond and Verba 1963; Barnes et al. 1979; Jennings et al. 1990). Below, we will examine both perspectives in detail.

Individual-Level Theories of Legitimacy Beliefs

What and how citizens think about the political system, and why they think about it the way they do, is frequently analyzed at the levels of individuals and with the help of concepts that are focused on individual characteristics and experiences. Specifically, a large number of studies have examined the effects of citizens' sociodemographic characteristics as well as their political attitudes and involvement on levels of support for the political system. Generally speaking, this cumulative body of research has found that those who are more involved in the political system—both psychologically and in terms of their levels of participation—or who have a greater stake in its maintenance also tend to express the highest levels of support (Finkel 1985; Anderson and Guillory 1997).

At the level of individual citizens, such involvement or stake has been measured with the help of variables such as income and education, as well as age, gender, and race, which tend to be viewed as indicators of an individual's social and economic status or political resources. In *The Civic Culture*, for instance, Almond and Verba (1963) reported that respondents with higher levels of education, income, and work skills were more likely to express pride in their country's political institutions. In addition to these proxy variables for involvement or status, measures of actual attention to or involvement in politics have been found to be related to political support (Almond and Verba 1963; Weatherford 1991). Citizens who understand and participate in the process take a more supportive view of it (Ginsberg and Weisberg 1978; Joslyn 1998). Simplifying greatly, the research on the demographic and attitudinal correlates of system support has established that those with greater interest, investment, and involvement in the existing political system are more supportive of it.[2]

Viewed more broadly, these findings share a common tenet: they explain support for the system as a function of factors measured at the level of individuals. Citizens are found to be more supportive of, or less distrustful toward, political institutions because of who they are, what they do, and what they

---

[2] Some researchers have found that the positive effect of education on political support is less consistent than portrayed by Almond and Verba, for example. Thus, Listhaug and Wiberg (1995) have found, for example, that the effects of education on support for 'order' institutions (church, armed forces, police) are frequently negative while the relationship with support for parliament are mostly positive. In addition, there is a new politics argument that high levels of education can in fact lead to critical attitudes and political dissatisfaction (Dalton 2004).

believe. As such, these literatures traditionally have focused primarily on the correlates of democratic legitimacy with an eye toward characteristics of individuals that are relatively stable, and they revolve around the notion that involved citizens and those with a greater stake in the status quo (such as individuals of higher social status) like the system they are involved with or that which bestows higher status on them.

Political Institutions and Legitimacy

Those who study political legitimacy with an eye toward system properties or, to use Weatherford's distinction once again, those who study legitimacy from a macro-perspective, follow in the footsteps of rich literatures that emphasize the importance of formal and informal political and social structures for understanding political life. Put very simply, social scientists of different persuasions working on different problems have long maintained that institutions and political structures matter because they 'provide the framework within which human beings interact . . .' (North 1981: 201). Constitutional rules, for example, are the most fundamental constraints on political behavior and attitudes because they determine the range of political choices available to citizens. Although citizens' attitudes may drive politics to some extent, the nature of political institutions at least partially determines how and what people think about politics. Politics and political contexts vary widely across individual countries and types of political systems. As a result, party systems, political events, and power relationships, to name just a few examples, differ across countries and are themselves occasionally subject to change over time. Given that institutional structures and political contexts vary across democratic systems, it is reasonable to conjecture that what and how people think about politics is affected by political institutions and varies across contexts as well.

As a consequence, students of comparative politics have routinely assumed that political institutions and people's political behavior and attitudes are connected. To mention some of the most prominent examples of research in this vein, students of electoral systems and their consequences have long maintained that citizens' choices in the electoral arena are conditioned by the political context and electoral rules (Duverger 1954). A plethora of studies have found there are systematic differences in election outcomes (number of parties, success of certain kinds of candidates, electoral volatility, etc.) as a result of different electoral rules (see, for example, Rae 1967; Riker 1976; Daalder and Mair 1983; Pedersen 1983; Lijphart 1984, 1994; Bartolini and Mair 1990). And there is ample evidence in related areas to suggest that individuals are constrained actors within particular, and variable, political environments.

Despite a considerable body of literature that demonstrates the effects of institutions on political behavior and attitudes, an individual's political environment has been incorporated explicitly into explanations of system support less frequently. Instead, much of the research on political legitimacy that takes a more macro-focused view has been concerned with the outputs generated by the political system and how these affect citizens' attitudes toward the political system. In particular, this research has examined the impact of economic performance as a performance indicator that shapes the reputation of political institutions. In contrast, the question of how *political* performance affects system support has received much more limited attention by social scientists.

This is not to say that facets of political systems and system support have not been studied in tandem. In fact, the few studies that do exist are important because they show that political performance and the functioning of formal political institutions matters for how people view the political system. Miller and Listhaug (1990, 1999), for example, have found that opportunities to express discontent and positive perceptions of procedural and outcome fairness are related to positive attitudes about government. Similarly, studies have shown that more proportional electoral systems are associated with higher levels of regime support (Anderson 1998). Aside from institutional elements such as opportunities for dissent, it appears that government stability matters for how people view the political system. Specifically, people in systems with more durable governments and governments that are less corrupt are more supportive of the existing political arrangements (Harmel and Robertson 1986; Anderson and Tverdova 2003). Finally, studies of system support in new democracies have pointed to the importance of political performance as determinants of system support more generally (Mishler and Rose 1997, 2001).

Although these findings lend support to the notion that explanations of system support need to take institutions and the performance of political systems into account, scholars have not ventured very far down this path of inquiry. Below, we seek to build on such studies and add to our understanding of the effects of political performance on political support by investigating whether and how a critical macro-political mechanism—elections—influences people's attitudes toward the existing political order. Because election outcomes link macro-politics and micro-experiences, they are a prime and easily identifiable institutional factor that structures the way in which citizens of a particular system respond to it.

A MODEL OF LOSERS' CONSENT: THE ROLE OF ELECTIONS

One of the institutional features that make democracies as political systems distinctive is that they regularly hold elections. It should therefore not be surprising that the literature on political involvement and legitimacy would suggest that elections can enhance legitimacy through the participation of voters in the electoral process. On the positive side (normatively speaking), elections are not only a way for citizens to influence government, but also a way for governments to enhance citizens' attachment to the system. Participatory political theorists in fact view participation as a crucial element in raising people's consciousness and developing a democratic citizenry (Pateman 1970; Thompson 1970). In contrast, some have argued that elections can serve to tie citizens to the political system and enhance government control (Ginsberg 1982). Without making a judgment about the normative interpretation of the effect of elections on people's attitudes, we know from a number of empirical studies that people's feelings about government become more positive as a result of participating in elections (Clarke and Acock 1989; Clarke and Kornberg 1992). Simply put, participation breeds happiness, and happiness with the system, in turn, is liable to breed participation (Finkel 1985, 1987).

Because elections and, by implication, political parties and the party systems they form, are viewed by many political commentators as so central to the democratic process, a number of researchers also have examined the influence of the electoral process on system support in greater detail. Among the best known attitudinal constructs and behaviors related to electoral processes that are assumed to affect system support have been partisanship and political involvement (Dalton 2002, 2004; Holmberg 2003). Thus, citizens with strong party ties are more likely to support their political systems than are weak partisans or non-identifiers (Dennis 1966; Miller and Listhaug 1990).

In studying losers' consent there are thus two broad avenues of inquiry to consider. The first concerns citizens and their reaction to loss. The second concerns the role institutions play in mediating the sense of loss. Below, we describe a model of election outcomes and democratic legitimacy, which suggests that losers' incentives to deny the outcome and develop low levels of support for the political system is significantly affected by a country's political context as well as their own attitudes. As a consequence, both citizens and institutions have a role in blunting the rougher edge of losing.

Citizens

That citizens may react badly to losing at election time should not be surprising because the creation of winners and losers at election time necessarily generates ambivalent attitudes towards authorities on the part of the losers (Kaase and Newton 1995: 60). Where and how these ambivalent attitudes originate, however, has not been discussed in much detail to date. As it turns out, three theoretical perspectives, focusing respectively on utility maximization, emotional responses, and cognitive consistency, generate insights about the consequences of election outcomes for people's views of government. For expository purposes, we label these phenomena, which are at the heart of why winners and losers differ in their evaluations of the political system, the utilitarian response, the affective response, and the cognitive consistency response.

First, the winner–loser gap is expected to have its roots in the expected benefits that winning and losing bestow on citizens. Viewed from a utilitarian perspective, behavioral economists and game theorists have long known that winning and losing as well as people's desire to avoid losing and experience winning provide significant conceptual and empirical leverage for understanding human behavior (Tversky and Kahneman 1992). The underlying assumption is simple: people prefer winning to losing (Thaler 1994; Kahneman, Wakker, and Sarin 1997). While recent research on loss aversion and risk acceptance has documented that people do not weight losing and winning equally (Tversky and Kahneman 1992; Thaler 1994), it also assumes that winning is preferred to losing; to use economic terminology, the experienced (and expected) utility of winning should be higher than that of losing (Kahneman 1994).[3] If this is true, then winning should lead to higher levels of positive attitudes toward government than losing.

What is more, the preference for winning over losing creates important incentives for citizens to act in particular ways. Specifically, loss motivates losers to bring about change in the political system—either by changing the issue agenda, issue positions, or the rules of the game. As Riker noted

In the study of politics and public policy we devote most of our attention to the analysis and interpretation of the platforms and policies of the winners of political disputes, elections, wars, and so forth. And this is quite proper because the preferences of the winners are the values that are authoritatively allocated. That is, the tastes of the winners are the actual content of social decisions and thus the content of the immediately subsequent present time. Conversely, we ignore the policies and platforms of the losers because these are the junk heap of history, the might-have-beens that never were. But we should not, I think, entirely overlook the losers and their goals for the losers provide the values of the future. The dynamics of politics is in the hands of the losers. It is they who decide when and how and whether to fight on. Winners have won and do not immediately need to change things. But losers have nothing and gain nothing unless they continue to try to bring about new political situations. This provides the motivation for change. (Riker 1983: 62)

Riker's argument, we hasten to add, is one of the rare times that losers have been subject to explicit analytical treatment and marks an even rarer attempt to theorize about loss. Among his many other contributions, Riker puts losers front and center in his analysis of what he labels heresthetics. His work on manipulation, for example, begins with the phrase 'For a person who expects to lose on some decision the fundamental heresthetic device is to divide the majority . . .' (Riker 1986: 1). For Riker, losers will be motivated to find a way to split the present majority and develop the precondition for a new majority to form. Riker's book has several examples of the ways in which politicians such as Abraham Lincoln changed issues in anticipation of loss (see also Shepsle

---

[3] Some social psychologists working in the area of behavioral decision-making have found that behavior consistent with strict utility maximization assumptions cannot always be documented. See, for example, Thaler (1994), and several studies by Kahneman and his colleagues.

2003). Along similar lines, Boix's (1999) study of electoral system change argues that moves to proportional representation are frequently motivated by parties anticipating unusually large electoral losses were they not to make the change.

Aside from utilitarian motivations, there are also more general psychological mechanisms that can be expected to be at work when considering people's reactions to election outcomes. Specifically, winning and losing are likely to generate affective (or emotional) responses, such that losing leads to anger and disillusion while winning makes people more euphoric. While scholars have not systematically addressed the issue of emotion (or affect) in the context of research on political support, Holmberg (1999) notes a 'home-team' effect akin to what people experience when rooting for their preferred football team, such that voting for the winning party or candidate induces individuals to feel positive about the election outcome and the system that produced it, while voting for the losers is likely to make people feel gloomy. In a somewhat related vein, others have found that being opposed to the government, especially when the government is further removed ideologically from voters and produces inferior economic outcomes, increases voters' anxiety (MacKuen, Neuman, and Marcus 2000).

Emotional and physical effects of victory and defeat have been documented in other areas of psychology as well (Neilson 2000). For example, emotions similar to feelings of victory and defeat are documented in the literature on the psychology of motivations (Atkinson 1957; McClelland 1987). Atkinson identifies an achievement motive that involves a drive to succeed and an avoidance motive that captures a fear of failure. Although motivational psychologists define success and failure more broadly than we define victory and defeat, these findings suggest that individuals are motivated to take actions to increase their chances of success or avoid chances of failure.

Thus, studies have found that winning in a competitive sport produces a variety of pleasant emotions and losing produces strong unpleasant ones (Wilson and Kerr 1999), and researchers have found that participation in games of chance produces positive mood changes from winning and negative mood changes from losing (McCaul, Gladue, and Joppa 1992). Wilson and Kerr's (1999) study of Dutch rugby players reports, for example, lower postgame scores for anger and sullenness and higher postgame scores for relaxation for winning compared to losing players. Similarly, in a study of table tennis players, McAuley, Russell, and Gross (1983) found a similar pattern of pleasant and unpleasant moods associated with game outcome. Postgame losers in table tennis were more angry and depressed than winners, and winners were more grateful and proud than losers. Finally, Booth et al. (1989) and McCaul, Gladue, and Joppa (1992), found that males have higher testosterone levels after winning than after losing. Taken together, this line of research strongly indicates that winning and losing can produce predictable emotional responses. In general, winning produces a range of pleasant emotional out-comes and reductions in arousal and stress, while losing produces the reverse (Brown and Dutton 1995).

Aside from emotions, winning and losing are likely to influence people's cognitions as well. Specifically, voting for the losing party or candidate can be expected to lead to more negative evaluations of the political system based on mechanisms rooted in cognitive processes of dissonance avoidance. Psycho-logical studies suggest that this effect may, in part, be grounded in people's well-documented motivation to maintain consistency in their beliefs and attitudes (Festinger 1957, 1964; Abelson and Rosenberg 1958; McGuire 1968).

Theories of behavioral and cognitive consistency are based on the principle that people are motivated to maintain consistency in their beliefs and attitudes (Rosenberg 1956; Festinger 1957; Abelson and Rosenberg 1958; Abelson 1968; McGuire 1968). Although a number of variations on the consistency theme have been proposed over the years, the central elements are essentially identical. Specifically, people frequently experience inconsistencies among their cognitions (beliefs, attitudes, and values) or their cognitions and beha-vior. Such inconsistencies (also called cognitive dissonance) foster psycho-logical discomfort, and people seek to reduce them by restoring consistency. They can do this by changing either their attitudes or their behavior (Festinger 1957).

People's drive for cognitive consistency is well documented in a variety of contexts. In fact, the notion of cognitive consistency is a central element of social psychological theories (Funder and Colvin 1991; Beggan, James, and Allison 1993). While most theories that link attitudes and behaviors assume that attitudes lead to actions, cognitive consistency theory posits that behaviors can cause attitudes. This has been found to be particularly true when a behavior cannot easily be undone (Harvey and Mills 1971). For instance, if people experience dissonance after making a choice, they can reduce their discomfort by valuing the chosen alternative more highly or by denigrating the option they passed over (Brehm 1956).

There is support for cognitive consistency theories and theories derived from them in the context of political behavior (Granberg 1993). For instance, research shows that people resolve inconsistent attitudes toward candidates, parties, and policies by placing them closer to themselves in the ideological spectrum than they really are. Moreover, voting for the winning (losing) party has been shown to make voters more optimistic (pessimistic) about the coun-try's economic situation and to evaluate past economic performance more negatively (positively) (Anderson, Mendes, and Tverdova 2004). Similarly, people often are overconfident in their evaluations of their preferred can-didate's chances of winning (see, for example, Freeman and Sears 1965; Cigler and Getter 1977; Brent and Granberg 1982; Granberg and Brent 1983;

Krosnick 1990; Blais and Turgeon 2004). More importantly for our purposes, cognitive consistency theory has been tested and validated in a number of studies of post-election attitudes. For example, voters very often experience post-election dissonance (Frenkel and Doob 1976; Regan and Kilduff 1988). Regardless of whether they voted for a winning candidate or a loser, for example, people will report more esteem and confidence in the candidate they chose and they will devalue the alternative. Once the outcome is known, however, voters who cast a ballot for a loser tend to see that candidate as more similar to the winner in an effort to justify their choice. Alternatively, these same voters have been found to develop more favorable attitudes toward the winner and less favorable ones toward the loser, even if they voted for the losing candidate (Brehm 1956, 1962; Stricker 1964; Cigler and Getter 1977; Joslyn 1998).

Despite its robustness, this classic theory has not been used to predict people's evaluations of the political system. In the context of voting and democratic legitimacy, we hypothesize that vote choice and attitudes toward the system are the respective action and attitude for which people will seek consistency. Of the two, the vote choice is not altered as easily as the attitude about how the political system is performing or whether government can be trusted—after all, voting happens only every few years, whereas attitudes can be updated at any time. We, therefore, expect voters to adjust their legitimacy beliefs rather than to wait for the next opportunity to change their behavior.[4] Following Rosenberg's (1956) assertion that people who hold a positive attitude towards an object associate it with a belief that it will provide a desired outcome, we argue that election losers should develop systematically more negative attitudes toward the political system than the winners and those who voted for the winning parties will evaluate the political system significantly more positively than those who did not.

Taken together, then, insights generated in a number of contexts and from both economic and psychological vantage points share important understandings of how election outcomes in the form of winning and losing may affect people's responses. They all suggest that winning and losing are fundamental to understanding how people see the political system—that is, that winning and losing are mental constructs people use to understand the political environment (Erber and Lau 1990). And winning and losing, once experienced, are expected to affect subsequent attitudes. Thus, by definition, any political experience such as winning and losing is different and separable from, as well as exogenous to, an attitude. Taken together, this means that the experience

---

[4] This does not mean that consistent people do not change their behavior. They change their behavior as situations change without violating their internal consistency (Funder and Colvin 1991).

of winning and losing must be seen as conceptually and empirically distinct from, as well as causally prior to, attitudes about the political system.

Although this means that the experience is likely to affect several closely related attitudes such as general feelings of goodwill toward the government, we would like to emphasize the importance of viewing experience as an explanation of political trust as theoretically different from a general like or dislike of the government (Morrell 1999). What is more, unlike stable traits political scientists have commonly relied on for understanding political behavior (such as citizens' demographic characteristics or presumably stable political attitudes such as ideology), the lens of winning and losing is a uniquely political phenomenon that can be variable over time for any one individual because different elections produce different results (and different sets of winners and losers).

All else equal, the approaches reviewed above expect those who belong to the political minority to have more negative attitudes toward both the process of government and the outcomes it produces than those in the majority. Because democracy is about winning and losing within the context of set rules adhered to by those participating in political contests, people who voted for a governing party should also be more likely to believe that the government is responsive to their needs, to be satisfied with the government's performance, to feel like they have some impact on the political process, and to be supportive of the way the system works. Put differently, then, because the political system is a less friendly place for those supporting an opposition party, people in the political minority should be more negative about its workings.

In our model, the likelihood of losing resulting in gracious acceptance or violent protest is in part a function of individuals' attitudes and prior experiences. For example, a highly attached partisan may take a loss particularly hard and consider it much more negatively than someone who was relatively indifferent about the contenders for government office. More generally, we believe that there are attitudes—such as strength of partisan attachment—that color and modify the extent to which electoral losses translate into negative evaluations of the political system's legitimacy or, ultimately, rejection of the system altogether.

Aside from such attitudes and expectations, we also argue that electoral experience matters. That is, we contend that democratic regimes are likely to be more seriously threatened if citizens are not used to losing. This may be particularly pertinent in newer democracies, where citizens have not necessarily learned to lose or have yet to learn that both winning and losing are part of the democratic process. Moreover, the idea of learning to lose provides some specific content to the term 'civil society', a term more often used than given concrete definition. Thus, an important lesson to teach citizens in new democracies is not to react too adversely to losses early in the transition—that is, not to react with either extreme 'voice' (violence and rebellion) or 'exit' (complete apathy or withdrawal) from the political system.

Even in more established democracies, however, the attitudes both of losers and towards losing remain of critical importance to an understanding of how democracy and democratic institutions are sustained. In the US presidential election of 2000, for example, the central worry for commentators concerned with democratic legitimacy was not that Gore won more votes than Bush, since the mechanism of the Electoral College made the comparison of national vote totals pointless. Rather, the real worry was whether Bush had actually won the state of Florida. Accusations of vote rigging or a Supreme Court decision tinged by partisan politics spoke to the basic legitimacy of the process in a long-established democracy (Gibson, Caldeira, and Spence 2003; Nicholson and Howard 2003). At this time, we can only speculate how much more worrisome such allegations and charges are likely to be in less well-established democracies.

Institutions

To date, political institutions form a core concern of the literature on losing in two ways. First and following on from the discussion so far, attitudes towards institutions are shaped in important ways by losing. Second, institutions themselves shape the responses of winners and losers. Thus, aside from the characteristics that may mediate the impact of losing on individual voters, we argue that institutions can help shape electoral loss.

As we mentioned above, one of the underlying ideas to research on democratic legitimacy is that being given an opportunity to win an election—as a candidate or supporter—will generate support for the system. Yet, as we mentioned above, simply being allowed to play in the game may not be sufficient to keep citizens happy, given that, when the game is over, individuals who belong to the political majority (the winners) are more likely to be satisfied with the political system than are those in the minority (the losers). Losers can become disaffected with the current institutional processes and may push for changes in the basic institutions of democratic governance (Bowler and Donovan 2000). Such a conceptualization clearly owes much to Riker's insight about loss and losing preparing the ground for new proposals and, hence, new winners. Ultimately, too many and too discontented a set of losers provides a precondition for institutional change (Bowler, Donovan, and Karp 2002).

Saying that institutions can shape the extent of the loss felt by voters means that the extent to which citizen attitudes toward democratic institutions, and by implication the potential for protest or unrest among the losers, is mediated by a country's particular political context. Long-standing and institutionally defined differences both across and within political systems are therefore likely to mediate citizen support for the system. Simply put, '[w]inning and losing mean different things in different systems' (Anderson and Guillory 1997: 68). Translated into the area of political legitimacy, we expect individuals who belong to the political minority to have more negative attitudes toward government than those in the majority if institutions are designed such that losses have particularly weighty consequences. Thus, aside from people's attitudes and experience, institutions mediate the extent to which losses are felt and expressed.

For example, different democratic systems determine the extent to which the winners may do what they want and what rights the losers have to prevent unfettered majority rule in particular ways. That is, democracies are structured differently to allow for different relationships between majorities and minorities. Arend Lijphart has sought to classify democratic designs by characterizing differences across systems in terms of the conceptual map of the majoritarian–consensual continuum (Lijphart 1999), and Bingham Powell refers to it as the proportional versus majoritarian divide (Powell 2000). Regardless of the terminology we employ, it is clear that some societies have designed political systems that allow the majority to implement its preferred policies largely unchallenged whereas others have created systems that allow for significant and regular input on the part of the minority. As this example suggests, political systems are designed to afford differential opportunities for winners and losers of democratic competition to be represented in the political arena and to implement their preferred policies independently or together.

We think of formal institutions in two basic ways: first, institutions determine the rules of the game and how much of a say citizens have in selecting the new government—that is, to specify the process by which losers are created—but second, and as importantly, they also determine how power is exercised. Thus, institutions are about processes as well as outcomes (Tyler 1990, 1999).

The idea that institutions shape the experience of winning and losing has important consequences for institutional design. As Powell's (2000) work shows, the averaging out of policy positions by coalition governments necessarily means that the median policy position of coalition governments is closer to the position of the median voter than is the case under majoritarian systems (but see also McDonald, Mendes, and Budge 2004). Hence, institutional reforms that allow minorities more access to the political process may well raise overall levels of citizen satisfaction with government (Anderson and Guillory 1997: 79; Lijphart 1999; Norris 1999). To investigate whether this and related conjectures are accurate, we propose a model, where the impact of the election outcome on winners' and losers' attitudes and behaviors is constrained by attitudes and institutional arrangements. More generally speaking, this model explicitly links mass behavior to institutions in a way that goes beyond most treatments of the two to date. Specifically, instead of examining the direct effects of institutional variables, as is commonly done in research

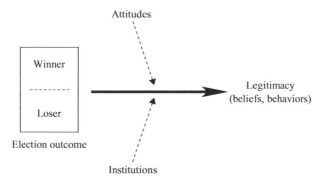

FIGURE 2.1. The production of democratic legitimacy among election winners and losers

on electoral turnout, for example, we connect institutions and models of mass behavior in an interactive—that is, contingent—way. While it is the institutions that create winners and losers, they also condition the effect of winning and losing on democratic legitimacy (Figure 2.1). Thus, institutions both produce conflict and mediate it at the same time. As a result, a lot of the public's attitudes are endogenous to institutions, which means that we can show both the mechanism of institutional effects on mass behavior and the consequences of how this behavior is channeled.

To recap, all else equal, we expect those who belong to the political minority to have more negative attitudes toward both the process of government and the outcomes it produces than those in the majority. And this gap in favorable attitudes should be of varying size across countries—because of differences in political institutions and context—and across individuals—because of differences in motivations to view losses as particularly negative outcomes.

While the more utilitarian 'winner effect' and the more psychological (affective) home team and (cognitive) consistency effects all point to the expectation that winners and losers differ in their responses to the political system, these findings and theories are silent on the issue of whether this gap should be greater with regard to some dimensions and whether this effect is ephemeral or persistent. This raises important issues with regard to the usefulness of the winner–loser distinction for understanding the micro-foundations of democratic legitimacy and for the generalizability of the winner–loser distinction across space and time. Specifically, we would argue that the utility of the winner–loser gap for understanding people's attitudes toward government depends on several conditions: first, the winner–loser gap should be observable across different countries. The smaller and the more particular the set of countries where it holds, the more limited its usefulness may be said to be. Second, the gap should be observable with regard to different kinds of responses people may have when experiencing winning and losing. Again, if the gap exists only with regard to certain kinds of attitudes toward the political system, its usefulness could be circumscribed. Third, for the winner–loser gap to explain different kinds of responses to the political system and to do so consistently, the effect of losing on attitudes toward government ideally should not be short-lived or fleeting.[5] In the next two chapters, we confront these conditions with data.

---

[5] Theoretically, there should be no difference before an election because it is the election that generates winners and losers and hence produces the effect we propose. However, with the exception of first elections in a country or first-time voters, every pre-election period follows on an earlier post-election period. As a result, if winning and losing are a construct people use to understand the political environment, it should be observable, albeit perhaps not to the same degree, in both pre- and post-election environments.

3

The Winner–Loser Gap: Contours
and Boundaries

This chapter starts our empirical investigation by mapping the contours of the
legitimacy gap between political losers and winners. Following the model
we laid out in Chapter 2, we begin our analysis by looking at the direct
effect of winning and losing on legitimacy beliefs and behaviors—that is,
the overall differences in winners' and losers' consent without consideration
to institutional or individual-level factors that may mediate the link between
election outcome and legitimacy. Based on the premise that losers are more
likely to be dissatisfied with the status quo and push for changes in existing
institutional arrangements, we examine the patterns of differences in attitudes
toward government and politics among winners and losers across established
and newly emerging democracies—countries that differ considerably with
regard to their historical trajectories, political institutions, and cultural attributes. Moreover, we investigate the differences in winners' and losers' attitudes
with regard to different kinds of attitudes toward government, ranging from
political efficacy to evaluations of the performance of the political system as
a whole.

CONNECTING THEORY AND EVIDENCE: MEASURING
WINNERS AND LOSERS

Before we explore the winner–loser gap in greater detail, however, it is important to deal with an issue of measurement—in particular, the question of how
we can best identify electoral losers (and winners). Theoretically speaking,
winning and losing really are about a person's sense of allegiance to those
in or out of power. And because, in our model, allegiance and election outcomes are connected, winning and losing are tied up with a person's vote
choice. That is, to examine the effects of winning and losing on people's civic
attitudes requires that we match the outcomes of elections and government
formation with mass surveys that measure people's vote choices based on who

is currently in power. Such a procedure allows us to identify citizens' status as part of the electoral majority or minority.[1]

Respondents can be classified as belonging to the political majority or minority with the help of a survey question that asks which party the individual voted for in the last national election. Alternatively, we can rely on a question that asks respondents which party they would vote for if an election were held at the time of the survey. These responses are then combined with information about the party or parties that controlled the executive branch of government of the respondents' country at the time the survey was conducted. If the respondent's reported vote choice matches the party or parties not currently in power— that is, if the person was among those who voted or would vote for parties not in government—she or he is scored as a member of the minority (loser). Those whose vote choice matches parties in power are categorized as being in the majority (winner).

Two issues that are important in this context: one pertains to operationalization—that is, the translation of the concept (loser/winner) into an appropriate measure; the second has to do with the issue of accuracy (measurement). The simple question is this: do we best categorize voters as winners or losers based on who they say they voted for in the past or who they intend to vote for at the time of the survey? As it turns out, both ways of categorizing voters' allegiances have advantages and disadvantages, and these extend to both operationalization and measurement.

With regard to translating the concept of 'losing' into a good measure, basing the categorization of voters on a so-called recall question implies that it is the actual choice people made at some point in the recent past and admit to that defines winners and losers. In this way, the measure explicitly connects a respondent's past behavior (vote choice) with the attitudes of interest (legitimacy beliefs). This, therefore, very directly and perhaps most appropriately measures the concept of 'loser'. In contrast, basing the categorization of winners and losers on vote intention lacks the behavioral report. This is problematic insofar as we have strong theoretical reasons to assume that it is the actual behavior rather than the behavioral intention that influences support for the political system. Thus, basing the loser-variable on a vote recall question

---

[1] Naturally, this definition of winners and losers does not exhaust the possible universe of the terms' meanings. For example, we could think of winning and losing as being about supporting the party or parties that hold a majority or plurality of seats in parliament or that gained the largest share of the vote in the most recent election. Alternatively, we can conceive of winning as being about winning a higher proportion of the popular vote than in the previous election or making it into a governing coalition despite heavy losses in the election. Beyond these simple examples, there are a number of other ways of conceptualizing winners and losers, many of which may well hold important implications for how voters behave. However, for the purposes of this book, we have decided to focus on one particular aspect of winning and losing—namely, being in or out of government—and are happy to leave it to future research to disentangle the meaning and import of other definitions.

is preferable to basing it on a vote intention question if we are interested in capturing the effect of actual voting behavior on legitimacy beliefs.

However, when it comes to measurement, the vote recall question is not without problems because of the potential problem of biased recall and over reports favoring the victorious party (cf. Wright 1993). Simply put, people are more likely to say that they voted for the winner than is really the case—perhaps because of cognitive dissonance, bad memory, or outright misrepresentation. Regardless of the reason, this means that basing the loser measure on a vote recall question may not be optimal. In this case, basing it on a vote intention question may be as good as basing it on a reported (past) vote item.

Unfortunately, the vast majority of available surveys that include questions about respondents' vote choice as well as questions about their beliefs in government include only one of the two vote choice questions. This means that, for simple reasons of data availability, we are variably forced to rely on either past vote or vote intention to capture winners and losers. Fortunately, as it turns out, however, there is, empirically speaking, relatively little difference between the two measures. To demonstrate that these two measures overlap quite significantly requires a survey that contains measures of both vote intention and vote recall. As mentioned before, such surveys are rare; fortunately, there is a set of surveys collected as part of the Eurobarometer surveys that furnish the necessary information.

Table 3.1 displays the percentages of voters indicating support for winning and losing parties (in and out of government parties) both in terms of who they report having voted for in the last national election as well as who they would vote for if an election were held tomorrow. The table also displays the correlation coefficient, indicating the extent to which the two choices (retrospective and prospective) are correlated. These data show quite clearly that the vast majority of voters reports voting for the same parties prospectively and retrospectively. Roughly 93 percent of respondents report voting for the same party in the last election that they would vote for in the next election; the correlation coefficient between these two choices overall is a more than respectable 0.86. While there is some variation across countries—with almost 100 percent (97.9) of German voters' choices matching prospectively and retrospectively and about 90 percent (88.0) of Irish voters' choices matching— the overall pattern is quite strong. Put simply, then, assuming that there is some degree of measurement error inherent in *any* measure of vote choice, there seems to be little difference between classifying winners and losers on the basis of vote recall (past vote) or vote intention (future vote).

THE WINNER–LOSER GAP AND DIMENSIONS OF POLITICAL SUPPORT

Earlier, we mentioned Easton's (1965, 1975) distinction between diffuse and specific support. While the distinction's usefulness has been limited by the

TABLE 3.1. *Correspondence of prospective and retrospective reports of vote choice for winning and losing parties*

	Percent consistent[a]	Correlation coefficient[b]
France	88.4	0.75
Belgium	94.8	0.90
Netherlands	89.6	0.78
Italy	94.2	0.88
Luxembourg	95.5	0.90
Denmark	94.4	0.89
Ireland	88.0	0.77
United Kingdom	90.8	0.78
Greece	90.7	0.82
Spain	92.2	0.82
Portugal	93.4	0.87
Germany	97.9	0.96
Norway	94.1	0.76
Total	92.9	0.86

[a] Percent consistent between retrospective and prospective vote choice.

[b] Correlation coefficient between retrospective and prospective vote choice.

Source: Data are from Eurobarometer 42, November/December 1994.

fact that separate indicators of diffuse and specific support tend to be highly correlated (Anderson 2002), it remains an interesting and important way to think about different dimensions of legitimacy. The fact that these dimensions tend to be correlated is not entirely surprising, given Easton's theorizing that specific support and diffuse support are liable to be connected in the long run, such that an erosion of specific support is likely to drain the reservoir of diffuse support; conversely, with time, persistently high levels of specific support may well help fill the reservoir of goodwill toward the political system.

Following on Easton's seminal contributions, an important research program in political science has sought to categorize different dimensions (and indicators) of support for the political system along a continuous dimension from more specific to more general, or diffuse, support (Klingemann 1999; Norris 1999). A number of conceptualizations have been offered to capture this distinction (Westle 1989; Fuchs 1993). In such classification schemes, specific support usually pertains to particular actors or institutional elements in the political system while general support tends to refer to the system as a whole. For example, Norris (1999) lists the following categories, ranging from specific to general: political actors, political institutions, regime performance, regime principles, and political community.

We do not seek to resolve the problems arising from operationalizing Easton's distinction nor do we subscribe to any particular way of framing differences between diffuse and specific support (see Weatherford 1992 for an overview). Instead, our goal, for present purposes, is to examine as many different facets of legitimacy beliefs as we can and as many as seems helpful for establishing the dimensions and boundary conditions for the winner–loser effect we hypothesize. For understanding the winner–loser gap, it seems important to distinguish between aspects of legitimacy geared toward the *principles* of democratic governance versus the *performance* of specific institutional actors or particular processes of governance. For example, if we are concerned about the state and stability of democracy in a country, losers' consent to democratic norms or regime principles is likely to be more crucial than losers' support for specific actors or institutional elements.

Since much of the original research on the majority–minority or winner–loser effect focused on explaining attitudes toward performance of the political regime—such as satisfaction with the way democracy works (e.g. Fuchs, Guidorossi, and Svensson 1995; Anderson and Guillory 1997; Yoshinaka 2002) or confidence and trust in political institutions (e.g. Anderson and LoTempio 2002; Norris 1999)—we examine the impact of losing and winning on various dimensions of support to assess if the mechanism generalizes to all dimensions in the political support hierarchy (Norris 1999). If the impact is soft, we may find that only specific dimensions of support are affected; if the impact is hard, we expect to find that support for democratic principles are influenced as well. At this point in our investigation, we consider it an open question whether we should expect the differences in attitudes between winners and losers to be smaller or larger across the dimensions of political support. The bottom line is this: for the winner–loser effect to have theoretical leverage, it has to demonstrate empirical purchase; that is, it has to be observable with regard to fundamental attitudes toward political institutions, actors, and processes.

While we are not able to cover the whole range of political support measures from the vast research on political legitimacy to validate the existence of the majority–minority distinction, we nevertheless examine a number of different measures of political system support, including attitudes toward the electoral process, people's sense of whether government is responsive, satisfaction with the performance of the political regime, attitudes toward engaging in unconventional participation or protest, and support for democratic principles in our investigation of legitimacy. Such an investigation allows us to generalize beyond the particular indicators used previously and make more general statements about system support in global perspective. It also allows us to develop a sense of the quantity, range, and magnitude of the majority–minority effect on attitudes toward government.

DIFFERENT ATTITUDINAL DIMENSIONS AND THE
WINNER–LOSER GAP

People's levels of support for political institutions, agreement with democratic principles, or willingness to engage in political protest tell us different things about the legitimacy of a regime or the potential for change brought on by citizens with the incentive to modify the status quo. While support for the regime focuses on the institutions of government as the object, support for the principles of democratic governance is a more abstract and fundamental way of thinking about the political system. In contrast to both of these, the propensity to protest indicates a willingness and tolerance for going beyond established forms of participation. Regardless of citizens' attitudes toward specific institutions or democracy as a system, people's predisposition to participate in high-cost political activities is indicative of the level of potential for change inherent among different groups in the electorate.

Depending on the effect of political loser and winner status on these variables, different conclusions can be drawn regarding the legitimacy and stability of political institutions. When citizens are disenchanted with specific institutional actors or rules, they may push for reform, but they may not question the existence of democratic self-government. However, citizens who disapprove of democratic principles may question the reason for submitting to the state's coercive powers altogether. Alternatively, losing or being in the minority may well lead to both a lower level of support for existing institutions and a lowered level of support for democracy writ large. As a consequence, there is the potential that losing elections leads to a sense of disillusion with politics and a decrease in confidence that (democratic) political participation makes a difference. That is, losers may simply tune out politics. Using Hirschman's (1970) terminology, losing and especially sustained losing may well lead to exit from the body politic. If this is the case, political institutions are unlikely to be challenged, but they also would be consistently valued differently by those who have power and those who do not. In contrast, if being in the minority leads to less positive attitudes toward government but does not affect people's sense that democracy is flawed, then the political system may be more likely to be challenged by an efficacious minority and may well be challenged in unconventional ways (voice). Which of these scenarios—that is, whether losing leads to exit, voice, or both—is most plausible is an empirical question we take up below.

Attitudes Toward the Fairness and Efficacy of Elections

Given that democratic elections produce winners and losers in the first place, we turn first to how citizens view elections as a mechanism of electoral democracy. Specifically, we examine their evaluation of the fairness of the most recent election as well as their sense that elections matter. In particular, we suspect that losers are more likely to take a critical view of a process that did not favor them. People's evaluations of the fairness of elections were tapped by the following question:

In some countries, people believe their elections are conducted fairly. In other countries, people believe that their elections are conducted unfairly. Thinking of the last election in (country), where would you place it on this scale of one to five, where one means that the last election was conducted fairly and five means that the election was conducted unfairly?

Citizens' evaluations of whether elections matter were measured by employing the following survey item:

Some people say that no matter who people vote for, it won't make any difference to what happens. Others say that who people vote for can make a difference to what happens. Using the scale on this card (where one means that voting won't make a difference to what happens and five means that voting can make a difference), where would you place yourself?[2]

We then recoded these two variables to form a five-category scale, ranging from −1 for the most negative response to +1, indicating the most favorable response. Winners and losers were coded on the basis of a recall question that asked respondents which parties they voted for. If respondents voted for a governing party, they were coded as winners; otherwise, they were categorized as losers. Table 3.2 presents the mean scores of responses observed among winners and losers in each country for both dimensions of support for electoral democracy. It also shows the gap between the responses of the winners and those of the losers (the winner–loser gap).

Speaking generally, both winners and losers expressed very positive assessments of the most recent election's fairness. And as expected, winners' judgments are very positive when it comes to evaluations of the fairness of the electoral process, and they tend to be more positive than the losers'. An overwhelming majority of winners believe that the election was conducted fairly. Only in a few instances do we see a negative verdict as winners expressed some doubts about the fairness of the election in Mexico and Japan, for example. In fact, Japanese winners (and losers) had the most negative evaluations on this dimension.

Losers basically agreed with winners about the fairness of the most recent election. Everywhere, except in Japan, a strong majority said that the election had been conducted fairly. This is a striking indicator of consent. That being said, losers tend to be slightly less sanguine about electoral democracy

---

[2] The question about the fairness of the electoral process was not asked in Australia and Belgium. The number of cases is therefore slightly reduced with respect to this dimension of support.

TABLE 3.2. *Winners' and losers' evaluation of electoral democracy*

	Fairness of election			Vote can make a difference		
	Winners	Losers	Gap	Winners	Losers	Gap
Australia				−0.53	−0.38	−0.15
Belgium				−0.27	−0.26	−0.01
Canada	0.63	0.47	0.16	−0.36	−0.29	−0.07
Czech Republic	0.78	0.47	0.31	−0.69	−0.43	−0.26
Denmark	0.93	0.89	0.04	−0.55	−0.55	0
Germany	0.85	0.80	0.05	−0.51	−0.50	−0.01
Iceland	0.71	0.61	0.10	−0.66	−0.54	−0.12
Japan	0.26	0.05	0.21	−0.05	−0.11	0.06
Mexico	0.31	0.31	0	−0.60	−0.58	−0.02
Netherlands	0.84	0.77	0.07	−0.49	−0.38	−0.11
New Zealand	0.60	0.58	0.02	−0.55	−0.49	−0.06
Norway	0.90	0.85	0.05	−0.49	−0.57	0.08
Poland	0.55	0.51	0.04	−0.54	−0.42	−0.12
Portugal	0.73	0.60	0.13	−0.41	−0.38	−0.03
Slovenia	0.52	0.53	−0.01	−0.58	−0.51	−0.07
Spain (1996)	0.53	0.62	−0.09	−0.49	−0.54	0.05
Spain (2000)	0.72	0.50	0.22	−0.58	−0.52	−0.06
Sweden	0.83	0.78	0.05	−0.54	−0.49	−0.05
Switzerland	0.83	0.83	0	−0.53	−0.50	−0.03
United Kingdom	0.67	0.67	0	−0.46	−0.37	−0.09
Total	0.69	0.64	0.05	−0.49	−0.45	−0.04

Notes: Entries are means; variables range between −1 and +1.

Source: Comparative Study of Electoral Systems (CSES) surveys, 1996–2000.

than winners. The gap between the two groups is small but consistent across the board. A real exception to this pattern is in the Czech Republic, where the winner–loser gap is most pronounced as winners are much more likely to say that the election was conducted fairly, while losers tend to be much more doubtful. The most striking exception to the general rule that winners are more positive than losers is the 1996 Spanish election, where losers' judgments turn out to be more positive. In part this exception can be explained by voters' expectations: prior to the 1996 context, polls had predicted a landslide victory for the conservative Partido Popular (PP) and a crushing defeat for the incumbent Socialists. While the PP did indeed emerge victorious, the Socialists did much better than expected. The outgoing Socialist Prime Minister Felipe Gonzalez was even quoted as saying that 'Never has defeat been so sweet nor victory so sour' (*The Observer*, March 10, 1996). And perhaps predictably, the opposite, and more typical, pattern emerges in the subsequent 2000 election.

When it comes to the question of differences between winners and losers on the question of whether the vote matters, a contrasting pattern emerges. First, people's views are much more negative. The great majority of winners and losers believe that the vote does not make much of a difference. Second, the winner/loser gap is reversed. In six of the twenty cases, there is no real difference between winners and losers, in only three cases are winners more likely to say that voting matters, and in the majority of cases (eleven) losers actually are more likely to say that voting makes a difference. Thus, this may well be an indication that people do not expect too much from elections. And, if anything, losers are more likely than winners to believe in the efficacy of the ballot for determining the direction of the country. This 'reverse loser–winner gap' is particularly large in Australia and the Czech Republic.

Taken together, then, the results shown in Table 3.2 suggest that being a political loser leads to slightly less positive evaluations of the fairness of the electoral process, but it does not seem to diminish people's sense that elections matter. In fact, the results suggest that losers are slightly more inclined to believe that who they vote for matters for what happens in the future. Overall, the pattern of results suggests that winners are more likely (than losers) to believe that the process that made them winners in the first place is fair, though few losers really question the legitimacy of the election. Finally, few voters are convinced that elections matter but, perhaps surprisingly, skepticism about the import of elections is somewhat weaker among losers.

Attitudes about the Performance of the Political System

Turning next to attitudes toward the political system, we examine two dimensions of losers' assessments of the political regime: first, we examine people's evaluations of whether they think the political system works well—also known as support for the performance of the political regime (cf. Klingemann 1999; Norris 1999). The survey item asked respondents whether they thought the political system (democracy) worked well in their country. This measure does not capture citizen attitudes toward democracy as an ideal; instead, it focuses on people's responses to the actual process of democratic governance and their attitudes toward a country's 'constitutional reality' (Fuchs, Guidorossi, and Svensson 1995: 328). Using Easton's categories, this indicator has been widely used in studies of system legitimacy and has been identified as a measure of support for the performance of the political regime (cf. Klingemann 1999; Norris 1999; Linde and Ekman 2003). Satisfaction with democracy was measured by the standard question: 'On the whole, are you satisfied, fairly satisfied, not very satisfied, or not at all satisfied with the way democracy works in (country)?'.

Second, we also examine people's sense of the political system's responsiveness—also sometimes referred to as external efficacy. Political efficacy is 'the feeling that individual political action does have, or can have, an impact upon the political process, ... the feeling that political and social change is possible, and that the individual citizen can play a part in bringing about this change' (Campbell, Gurin, and Miller 1954: 187). To have a sense of influence on the political process, an individual has to believe that she or he has the means to affect the process (internal efficacy). Moreover, citizens have to believe that the political process must be open and responsive to such influences (external efficacy) (Lane 1959; Balch 1974). It is the latter we focus on here.

Three survey items were used to form an index designed to measure people's sense of the responsiveness of the political system. The first has to do with the capacity of elected representatives to understand the concerns of ordinary voters: 'Some people say that members of Parliament know what ordinary people think. Others say that members of Parliament don't know much about what ordinary people think. Using the (one to five) scale, where would you place yourself?'. The second concerns the willingness of parties to respond to voters' concerns: 'Some people say that political parties in (country) care what ordinary people think. Others say that political parties in (country) don't care what ordinary people think. Using the (one to five) scale, where would you place yourself?'. The third question ascertains the system's perceived responsiveness: 'Some people say it makes a difference who is in power. Others say that it does not make a difference who is in power. Using the (one to five) scale, where would you place yourself?'. These three questions are combined to form a responsiveness index.

As before, the dimensions of support are measured on a scale where -1 represents the most negative evaluation and $+1$ represents the most positive evaluation. We then calculated the mean scores for respondents in the winner and loser categories and calculated the gap between winners and losers. Figure 3.1 shows the winner–loser gap for satisfaction with democracy; Figure 3.2 displays the winner–loser gap with regard to people's sense of external efficacy.

First off, the overall results for all countries combined show that system performance evaluations and responsiveness assessments were quite positive.

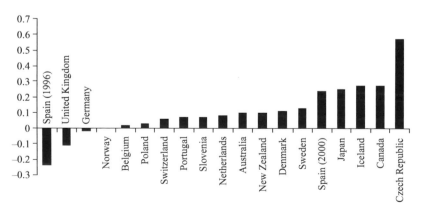

FIGURE 3.1. Winner–loser gap in satisfaction with democracy

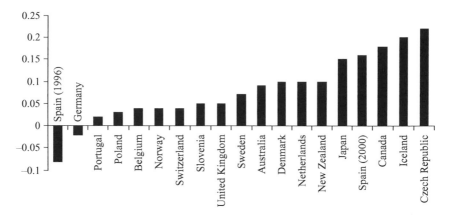

FIGURE 3.2. Winner–loser gap in evaluations of system responsiveness

Moreover, overall winners have more positive attitudes toward the performance of the political regime than losers (democracy satisfaction: 0.27 [winners] versus 0.22 [losers]; external efficacy: 0.16 [winners] versus 0.10 [losers] [all countries]). And while the size of the gap is usually not very large, it does appear in fifteen of nineteen cases with regard to the satisfaction with democracy question and in seventeen of the nineteen cases with regard to people's sense that the political system is responsive. A real exception to the moderate size of the winner–loser gap overall is the striking gap in the Czech Republic, where winners are much more likely to say that democracy is working well, while losers tend to be much more doubtful. In addition, the gap between winners and losers is also relatively large in Canada, Iceland, Spain (2000), and Japan.

Taken together, then, the results shown in Figures 3.1 and 3.2 suggest that being a political loser leads to more negative evaluations of the political system's performance and the fairness of the electoral process, and it diminishes people's confidence in their ability to influence the political process in the same way that it reduces their faith in the political system. Overall, we find the expected gap in democracy satisfaction in fifteen of nineteen cases, and in evaluations of system responsiveness in seventeen of nineteen cases included in these data. The countries that exhibit the most significant gaps in the direction of decreasing faith in the political system efficacy are the Czech Republic, Canada, Iceland, Japan, and Spain (2000). However, it is also worth noting that Spain (1996) appears to be the only real outlier, as losers are consistently more positive on the different dimensions of support than winners in this election (as mentioned earlier).

Thus, while the data show that there is a gap in attitudes toward government between citizens who are in the majority and those who are in the minority such that losers have more negative attitudes about the functioning of government, this diminished faith in the fairness of elections and the performance of the political regime does not imply that losers are more likely to believe that their vote does not matter—if anything, they are more likely to express their faith in the efficacy of elections for determining the directions of things in the country.

The Winner–Loser Gap and Support for Democracy as a Form of Government

Moving to the top of the political support hierarchy, we examine the winner–loser gap in support for democratic principles. To do so, we rely on data from the 1999 European Values Survey, which includes nearly all countries in Europe—East and West—and which has unique coverage in terms of the political support items included in the survey. Specifically, support for democratic principles is a composite measure of eight items that include general support for democracy, rejection of alternatives to democracy (strong leader, army, experts), and rejection of criticisms of democracy (see the Appendix for details about questions). We created an index for support of principles by summing the values for the dichotomized items (1: positive; 0: negative). The index has a maximum value of 8 and a minimum value of 0; winners and losers are measured on the basis of a vote intention measure (for more details on the variables, see the Appendix to this book).

Figure 3.3 shows the winner–loser gap in support for democratic principles across all those European countries included in the survey that were considered

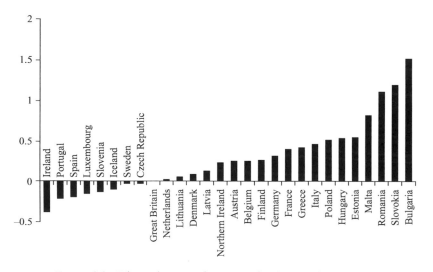

Figure 3.3. Winner–loser gap in support for democratic principles

'free'—that is, democratic—at the time of the survey. First off, the graph shows a winner–loser gap in the expected direction in the majority of countries—all in all, in nineteen of the twenty-eight countries. And these gaps are quite considerable in some of the countries, in particular in new democracies such as Bulgaria, Slovakia, and Romania, but also in established democratic countries such as Italy, Greece, France, and Germany. Then there is a group of countries without much of a gap either way (Great Britain, the Czech Republic, and Sweden), as well as some countries where the gap is actually reversed (Ireland, Portugal, Spain, Luxembourg, Slovenia, and Iceland), though the gap is not particularly large there.

Overall, we see that winners express higher levels of support for democratic principles than losers although exceptions clearly do exist. A quick eyeballing across the types of democracies suggests that the differences between winners and losers are larger in new democracies than in the mature democratic systems, an issue that we will come back to in later chapters.

Is There a Winner–Loser Gap in Attitudes Toward Protest?

Following Riker's assumption mentioned in Chapter 1, we also seek to establish whether and how an individual's status as a member of the political majority or minority affects the potential for political change. Specifically, we examine whether losing heightens the potential for protest behavior presumably because of frustration with the electoral process that has not favored their preferences. Losing an election and being in the minority means that one's political preferences were outvoted. Thus, it is plausible to postulate that the winner–loser distinction affects people's beliefs in the efficacy of conventional political participation.

In some ways, the willingness to play the game of electoral democracy to gain the upper hand presupposes an acceptance of the chance of losing. Riker assumes, in other words, that losers are willing to keep playing the game for the foreseeable future. Once they are willing to lose, a large part of the battle of institutionalizing electoral democracy has been won since it marks an internalization of the possibility of losing. This, we would argue, may be reasonable to assume in a system like the United States or Great Britain, but that it is a strong assumption to make, especially in countries that have significant political cleavages or little experience with democracy as a system for resolving conflicts.

But even if one accepts the possibility of loss right from the outset, losing does not necessarily result in passivity or graceful acceptance. The door remains open for protests, perhaps violent ones, against both the result and the regime. This is likely to be especially the case in an electoral contest involving highly emotional issues and contests where competing sides are easily delineated. Even less violent reactions open up the possibility of widespread apathy and resignation, which also run counter to our understanding of how citizens should behave in a democracy and what makes for a healthy democracy.

The results so far suggest that losing systematically affects people's view of the performance and responsiveness of the political system as well as feelings toward democratic principles but does not consistently diminish their confidence that the vote matters. In fact, electoral loss may well serve to raise people's cognitive involvement and confidence in their ability to influence the political process. How, then, does losing affect people's propensity to engage in political protest?

We measure protest potential with the help of a battery of questions collected as part of the International Social Surveys Project surveys that tap into people's predisposition to engage in protest activities, also occasionally referred to as unconventional or uninstitutionalized political action. Respondents were asked whether they either would engage in certain protest activities or think they should be allowed. Although the question wording differs slightly between items, we expected them to tap into the same underlying dimension—a predisposition to engage in political protest. The first two questions ask directly whether people would perform certain political acts, whereas the second set of questions asks people whether they think certain acts should be allowed. Because it is likely that some respondents feel more comfortable telling an interviewer that a particular act of protest should be allowed rather than divulging that they personally would perform such an action, both items are designed to help tap into the predisposition to protest.[3] Figure 3.4 shows the winner–loser gap in people's scores on this scale, with winner–loser status measured with the help of a vote recall question.

As the results indicate, election losers are more prone to exhibit the potential to protest. Our results show that loser status significantly affects the potential for protest in at least nine of the fourteen countries examined here. Thus, the evidence points to voice rather than exit when it comes to the participatory consequences of election losses. There are two countries where losers and winners are indistinguishable with regard to their propensity to engage in protest—Norway and Slovenia—and there are three countries—Ireland, Sweden, and Italy—where losers appear less likely to protest than winners. Overall, however, the evidence consistently points to losers expressing greater discontent with the status quo. By and large, losing breeds protest potential in the sample of countries we investigate here.

---

[3] To ensure that this was indeed the case, we performed factor analyses and reliability tests. Results of factor analyses showed that, in fact, the questions tap into the same underlying dimension, with all items loading highly on a single dimension. Moreover, reliability tests showed that these items were highly correlated with one another (Cronbach's alpha: 0.82), allowing us to form a single consistent and reliable scale based on the factor analyses, which ranges from -1 to $+1$.

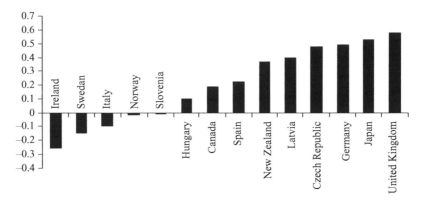

FIGURE 3.4. Winner–loser gap in protest potential

SUMMARIZING THE RESULTS SO FAR

The connections among political processes, such as elections, and citizen attitudes toward democracy are a subject of particular relevance to contemporary debates about democratic performance. It involves the question of the extent to which citizen attitudes toward democratic reality, and by implication the potential for protest, unrest, or even a collapse of the political system are affected by the consequences of the most routine of democratic mechanisms. Democracies are designed to produce winners and losers on election day, and subsequently, majorities and minorities to govern the country. Such inequality is part of what makes a country a democracy. At the same time, this necessary democratic mechanism produces tensions that have consequences for how citizens view the political system.

Our initial investigation of potential differences between election winners and losers shows that, in most countries, being in the political majority generally translates into more positive attitudes toward government, while losers have more negative attitudes toward the political system. We find that there usually is a gap in winners' and losers' sense of whether elections are fair, their evaluations of the performance of the political system as well as feelings about whether government is responsive. Moreover, losing elections appears to diminish people's support for democratic principles overall, and losers exhibit a heightened propensity to engage in political protest.

Depending on one's perspective, these findings can be taken to be good news or bad news. They are good news for our investigation because they confirm the existence of the winner–loser gap with regard to people's attitudes toward the political system in a variety of countries and with regard to different dimensions of legitimacy. Moreover, they provide corroborative evidence that the effect exists in countries as different as the Czech Republic, Great Britain, or Japan.

The findings are bad news were we to insist that the winner–loser distinction provides empirical and conceptual leverage for every kind of attitude toward politics and unfailingly across all countries. Clearly, the results show that this is not the case.

Naturally, the results reported in this chapter are the first step toward understanding the contours and dynamics of losers' consent and are intended as more of a validity check than clinching evidence. Moreover, on the surface, they raise as many questions as they answer. While these results consistently point in the direction of a winner–loser gap, the majority–minority effect is not of uniform magnitude across countries, nor does it affect all attitudes toward government equally. Specifically, while the data show that losers are consistently less enthusiastic about various aspects of democratic governance, they do not necessarily think that elections are not worth having, as is evidenced by the attitudes toward the efficacy of the vote. And while we find that there is a significant and consistent winner–loser gap in the Czech Republic, for example, we find weaker and sometimes contradictory effects in countries such as Ireland, Portugal, or Sweden. Moreover, countries with large winner–loser gaps on some dimensions of legitimacy do not necessarily have such gaps with regard to other dimensions.

At this point, it is unclear why these differences exist, and the reasons for why the expected gap does not appear without fail could be numerous. Our model outlined in Chapter 2 would suggest that likely reasons have to do with differences across political contexts and individual predispositions that may be more common in some countries than others. To be sure, our results suggest that we need to examine the cross-national differences in the size of the winner–loser effect, given that the majority–minority distinction matters more powerfully in some countries than others.

Moreover, why the winner–loser gap appears more sizable with regard to some facets of legitimacy than others in the same country is a question worth pondering. For the moment, we speculate that it is entirely possible that these latter differences are the result of the timing of surveys and the political conditions of the moment in the countries under consideration. Evidence for this view is apparent in the case of Spain and Britain, for example. While, in the Spanish case, the expected gap emerges with regard to indicators of electoral fairness, system responsiveness, and democracy satisfaction in 2000, there is no gap or even the reverse gap (with losers expressing more positive views than winners) in 1996. Similarly, in Britain, we see a sizable and expected gap in protest potential between winners and losers, as well as a moderately large gap in system responsiveness, losers appear no more negative than winners in 1997 when it comes to questions of electoral fairness or support for democratic principles.

It may be more than just coincidence, however, that both of these countries (Spain in 1996; Britain in 1997) saw the defeat of long-term incumbents on the left (Spain) and right (Britain). In these cases, the political dynamics of the day and the recent changes in electoral fortunes may well have created a context where the expected winner–loser gap is less likely to appear. More generally, these apparent anomalies point to the potential importance of investigating in more detail the dynamics of losers' consent before and after elections as well as during the course of the electoral cycle. Specifically, while we know from previous research that political support can be volatile, only trend-based analyses can help us put our finger on what happens to the attitudes of those in the majority and minority over time. Specifically, it would be important to examine what happens to long-term winners and losers, such as the supporters of the Spanish Conservative and British Labour parties during the 1980s and 1990s, for example. Both countries saw the dominance of one political party throughout the decade, thus turning a significant portion of the electorate into a perennial minority. Do those who are in the minority (majority) for prolonged periods of time become significantly unhappier (happier) with the political system as their chances of becoming part of the majority are repeatedly frustrated (successful)? We examine this and related questions in the next chapter.

4

The Dynamics of Losers' Consent: Persistence and Change in the Winner–Loser Gap

As we mentioned in the previous chapter, for the winner–loser gap to explain different kinds of responses to the political system and do so consistently, the effect of losing on attitudes toward government normally should not be short lived or fleeting. That is, we should expect to see winners and losers exhibit differences after an election as well as throughout the electoral cycle. In this chapter, we examine whether this gap is ephemeral or relatively stable; toward this end we also investigate the trajectories of attitudes toward government over time in a number of select countries, which afford us the opportunity to examine trends in some detail. Before turning to our analysis of the data, however, we discuss our understanding of the dynamics that can and do underlie the winner–loser gap.

TIME AND LOSERS' CONSENT

At the outset, we conceive of the dynamics of the winner–loser gap and what happens to how losers view the political process over time from three perspectives: short term, medium term, and long term. In the short term, we are particularly concerned with the issue of what happens to losers' consent immediately after an election. For the electoral outcome to matter, it must affect losers' consent when there is a switch in government. That is, in situations where one party (or group of parties) loses power and another gains it, citizens should be noticeably affected such that the new winners develop more positive and losers more negative attitudes about the political system. What is more, we also would expect the winner–loser gap to switch sides as well. Those who supported an incumbent government that lost an election should go from more positive attitudes toward the system to less positive ones. Conversely, those who, by virtue of the election outcome, were turned from losers into winners should become more positive in their attitudes, and possibly more positive than the former winners.

Aside from such a short-term 'switch' in losers' consent, we can also conceive of the dynamics of losers' attitudes as a medium-term phenomenon. For one, the winner–loser gap should not simply be fleeting—that is, be the

TABLE 4.1. *Expectations regarding the dynamics of losers' consent*

	Winners	Losers
Short term	Increase between pre- and post-election period	Decrease between pre- and post-election period
Medium term	High	Low
Long term	Loyalty	Exit or voice

product of momentarily unhappy losers whose post-election misery diminishes with time. Simply put, while there may be fluctuations in citizens' happiness with the political system during the course of the electoral cycle because of short-term performance issues, scandals, and the like, there also should be a sustained gap in the attitudes of the winners and losers. If this is the case, it is reasonable to presume that being (or not being) in the driver's seat constitutes a fundamental lens through which citizens view the political process.

Finally, a third way of conceiving of the dynamics of winners' and losers' happiness with the political system is over the long run—that is, beyond a single electoral cycle. Specifically, we ask what happens to losers' consent when citizens experience losing more than once. Being in the minority for prolonged periods of time could conceivably provoke two reactions: first, losing repeatedly could lead to disillusionment with the political regime and to citizens 'dropping out'—that is, voters who continue to lose may well become more disenchanted with politics but also less interested and less likely to participate in it. To use Hirschmann's terminology mentioned earlier: losers may exit politics altogether. Second, and alternatively, losing continually may lead to the exact opposite effect; namely, it may frustrate citizens such that they will become ever more politicized and involved in the process with the aim of bringing about change in a system that appears stacked against them—that is, losers may make their voice heard (cf. Table 4.1).

TRACING THE DYNAMICS OF LOSERS' CONSENT

An examination of the dynamics of losers' consent requires repeated measurements of people's attitudes toward government over relatively short as well as relatively long periods of time. Unfortunately, there are few data sources that fulfill these conditions. Moreover, an analysis of the long-term dynamics of losers' consent requires repeated measures from countries where voters have experienced electoral losses over a number of elections as well as countries where voters experienced a change in government. Fortunately, for present purposes, the Eurobarometer surveys conducted by the European Commission in the member states of the European Union since the 1970s furnish data that allow us to test our conjectures regarding the dynamics of losers' consent in the short run and over the long term. More specifically, three of the countries that are part of the Eurobarometer series have experienced periods of relatively long rule by a party or coalition as well as significant changes in government: Britain, Germany, and Spain. With one exception, we will therefore focus on these countries for the remainder of this chapter.

To measure people's attitudes toward the political system, we relied on the item used to gauge people's satisfaction with the outcomes produced by the political system: 'On the whole, are you very satisfied, fairly satisfied, not very satisfied, or not at all satisfied with the way democracy works in your country?' This question has the advantage of having been asked regularly as part of the Eurobarometer surveys, and it has been classified as measuring people's evaluations of the political regime (cf. Klingemann 1999). Classifying citizens as winners and losers requires that we measure their political allegiances to parties in and out of power. As mentioned in the previous chapter, ideally, we would do so by relying on vote recall questions (Who did you vote for?) and categorizing voters as either winners or losers. This strategy is not entirely unproblematic, in part because of biases in recall (cf. Wright 1993), but in large measure in our case because of the shortage in the number of times that a vote recall question was asked in the Eurobarometer. We therefore rely primarily on vote intention to measure winners and losers, though we employ vote recall measures whenever possible.[1]

THE PRE- TO POST-ELECTION SWITCH

One of the conditions for the winner–loser gap is that an election should bring about a switch in the views of the political system among former and newly minted losers and winners. By newly minted we mean that, when there is a complete changeover in government, pre-election losers become post-election winners and pre-election winners become post-election losers. As a result, changes in government change the lens through which voters who voted for the winners and losers view the political system. With this switch in voters' status as members of the governing majority or the opposition, we expect to see a switch in how voters evaluate the political system.

We examine Britain, Germany, and Spain in detail. Among the countries for which we have longitudinal data, these are also the best cases for tracing the short, medium, and long-run dynamics of system support because all three experienced the necessary conditions for the purposes of our analysis: they all had changes in governing parties, they experienced prolonged periods of single-party (or coalition government) rule, and they vary considerably in their political histories and institutional and contextual conditions. In the

---

[1] Perhaps unsurprisingly, in light of the consistency of vote choice reported in the last chapter, it turns out to make little difference whether vote intention or vote recall is used to categorize winners and losers.

British case, the 1979 election brought about a change from a Labour to a Tory government, which lasted for some eighteen years until the 1997 election produced the reverse outcome. In Germany, 1982/83 brought, first, the fall of the Social Democratic/Free Democratic (SPD–FDP) coalition that had been in power since 1972 and the election of the new Christian Democratic-led coalition under Helmut Kohl. Sixteen years later, in 1998, Germany's government changed hands once again from the CDU/CSU-FDP coalition to a coalition of the Social Democrats (SPD) and the Greens. Finally, Spain's 1996 election brought a real sea change in Spanish politics and the first significant change in government since 1982, when the Socialists who had taken power under Felipe Gonzalez were defeated by the Conservatives under Prime Minister Aznar.

To examine the pre- and post-election attitudes of voters who went from being losers to being winners and vice versa as the result of an election, we calculated the percentage within each camp who expressed satisfaction with the functioning of democracy before and after the election.[2] Table 4.2 shows the results for the five elections in the three countries.

The table provides several important pieces of information. First, it shows the percentages of winners and losers who express satisfaction with the performance of the political system. Specifically, it shows levels of satisfaction among voters in all three countries who were among the previous-election losers-turned-post-election-winners and the previous-election winners-turned-post-election-losers. Moreover, the table shows the pre- and post-election winner–loser gap in satisfaction with democracy, as well as the change in satisfaction for each group of voters from the pre-election to the post-election period. We calculated levels of satisfaction by combining the groups of respondents who indicated that they were very or fairly satisfied with the working of democracy in their country.

Looking, first, at the winner–loser gap before the election, the results show that the winners were in all cases more satisfied with the political system's performance and in most instances significantly so. For example, 66.9 percent of Britain's pre-1979 (i.e. 1974) election winners—supporters of the Labour Party—expressed satisfaction with democracy, while 60.9 percent of the opposition—supporters of the Conservative Party—expressed similar views, thus creating a 6 percent gap in satisfaction between previous-election winners and losers. This, however, changed markedly after the election of the new Tory government under Margaret Thatcher. After the election, 72 percent of the new (1979 election) winners—supporters of the Conservative Party—expressed satisfaction with the performance of the political system, while only 46.6 percent of the post-election losers (Labourites) indicated the same.

---

[2] That is, we compare party supporters' evaluations of the political system as measured in surveys preceding and following the election. While the Eurobarometer surveys are not election surveys, the lag is as short as a month but no longer than five.

TABLE 4.2. *Pre- and post-election evaluations of the political system in Britain (percent satisfied with the political system's performance)*

Election	Before election	After election	Change
Britain 1979			
Pre-election winner/			
post-election loser (Labour)	66.9	46.6	−20.3
Pre-election loser/			
post-election winner (Tories)	60.9	72.3	+11.3
Gap	+6.0	−25.7	
Britain 1997			
Pre-election winner/			
post-election loser (Tories)	78.6	72.5	−6.1
Pre-election loser/			
post-election winner (Labour)	44.0	76.8	+22.8
Gap	+34.6	−4.3	
Germany 1983			
Pre-election winner/			
post-election loser (SPD)	80.8	70.2	−10.6
Pre-election loser/			
post-election winner (CDU/CSU)	67.4	88.8	+21.4
Gap	+13.4	−18.6	
Germany 1998			
Pre-election winner/			
post-election loser (CDU/CSU-FDP)	64.8	79.6	+14.8
Pre-election loser/			
post-election winner (SPD-Greens)	47.1	75.6	+28.5
Gap	+17.7	+4.0	
Spain 1996			
Pre-election winner/			
post-election loser (PSOE)	90.7	92.3	+1.6
Pre-election loser/			
post-election winner (PP)	58.6	95.7	+37.1
Gap	+32.1	−3.4	

As a result, the 6 percentage point pre-election gap in satisfaction between Labour supporters and Tories turned into a 25.7 percentage point gap in favor of the Tories.

A similar dynamic is at work in the 1997 election, when the Tories, after eighteen years in office, lost power to Labour. While there was a substantial gap in democracy satisfaction in favor of the previous-election majority of about 35 percentage points (Tories: 78.6 percent; Labour: 44.0 percent), the gap was not only reduced but reversed after the election (Tories: 72.5 percent; Labour: 76.8 percent), producing a 4.3 percentage points gap in satisfaction with democracy in favor of Labour supporters and an almost 40 percentage points overall shift in the winner–loser gap pre- and post-election.

In the German case, the 1983 and 1998 elections produced an overall swing in the winner–loser gap of 32 and 13.7 percentage points, respectively. In 1983, 80.8 percent of pre-election winners (Social Democrats) expressed satisfaction with democracy, while only 67.4 percent of pre-election losers (Christian Democrats) did, creating an overall gap of 13.4 percentage points. After the election was over and the Social Democrats had lost, only 70.2 percent of their supporters expressed satisfaction with democracy, while 88.8 percent of the victorious Christian Democrats did, thus producing an 18.6 percentage point gap in favor of the new majority.

In the Spanish case, a remarkable 90.7 percent of previous-election winners expressed satisfaction with the way democracy works, while only about 60 percent of pre-election losers said the same. Yet, after the election, this gap was reversed, if only slightly so, in favor of the new winners, the supporters of the conservative Partido Popular (PP).

While there were differences in the levels of satisfaction across countries and within countries before different elections, this general pattern holds for all cases with one small exception, namely the 1998 German election, where post-election losers in 1998 were slightly more satisfied than post-election winners. The German results for 1983 are also worth evaluating with some caution, given that the old Social-Democratic government had already been out of office for a few months by the time the election was held as a result of Germany's constructive vote of no confidence.[3]

Overall, however, the positive gap we find in all pre-election cases and the negative gap we find in four of the five post-election cases indicates that previous-election winners evaluated the political system more positively than previous-election losers, and so did post-election winners relative to post-election losers.

The results also show whether and how much pre-election-winners-turned-post-election-losers and pre-election-losers-turned-post-election-winners changed in their evaluation of the political system. The last column of Table 4.2 calculates the pre- to post-election change in satisfaction levels for the two groups. Using the 1979 British election as an example, we find that satisfaction among Labour supporters dropped precipitously in the aftermath of the election. Specifically, while 66.9 percent of Labour supporters proclaimed satisfaction with the political system prior to the contest, only 46.6 percent said so afterwards. Conversely, while 60.9 percent of the eventual winners (Conservatives) expressed satisfaction with the system before the election, this percentage increased to 72.3 percent after the contest. Thus, while Labour

---

[3] However, because Germany's political situation was so fluid at the time and because the Social Democrats had been in power since 1969, it would be reasonable to think of that particular election as having had two 'incumbent' parties—that is, the outgoing SPD and the newly installed incumbents who called the election, the CDU/CSU.

supporters experienced a 20.3 percentage point drop in satisfaction, satisfaction levels among Conservative voters rose by 11.3 percentage points.

The data tell a similar story of increase (in the case of new winners) and decline (new losers) for the other cases, though the pattern is not uniform. In Germany's 1983 election, post-election losers' satisfaction declined by 10.6 percentage points, while post-election winners' satisfaction jumped by 21.4 percentage points. In Spain's 1996 election, satisfaction levels of post-election losers stayed roughly the same, while post-election winners' satisfaction jumped by a remarkable 37.1 percentage points. The only slight exception to the pattern of significantly less satisfied post-election losers, again, is the 1998 German election, which showed an increase in satisfaction levels among both winners and losers. However, although the election appears to have boosted satisfaction levels among both groups, the increase in satisfaction was twice that among the post-election winners (28.6 points) than the post-election losers (14.8 points).

Thus, different countries, with different political parties, during different elections and political periods show a switch in how people evaluate the political system, depending on the outcome of an election. Thus, in situations where one government loses power and is replaced by another, the winner–loser gap alternates as well. Those who supported an incumbent government that lost an election go from more positive attitudes toward the system to less positive ones. Conversely, those who were turned from previous-election losers into post-election winners become more positive in their attitudes and almost always more positive than the former winners.

LOSERS' CONSENT OVER THE COURSE OF THE ELECTORAL CYCLE

These calculations discussed above provide evidence of the switch that an election outcome brings about in how winners and losers view the political system. One question that has not been answered so far, however, is whether the switch, once it occurs, is sustained over time and whether it occurs regardless of who is in power—that is, irrespective of the ideological composition of the government or who leads it. There is some evidence that this is indeed the case. In a study of system support in Western Europe, Huseby (1999) combined responses from eight West European countries and examined the winner–loser gap for the 1975–94 period (Figure 4.1). She finds that, overall, supporters of the government are significantly more positive in their evaluations of the political system's performance than opposition supporters.

While this evidence is suggestive, we sought to examine our question in greater detail with the help of Eurobarometer data for Britain and Germany from the mid-1970s to the mid-1990s and for Spain from the mid-1980s to the mid-1990s—that is, time periods for which we have available both the political

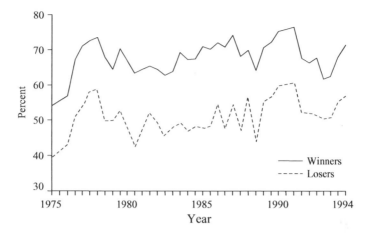

FIGURE 4.1. Levels of satisfaction with democracy among winners and losers 1975–94 (in percent)

Note: The countries are France, Belgium, Netherlands, Germany, Italy, Denmark, Ireland, UK.

allegiance variables as well as regularly repeated readings of the satisfaction with democracy measure.[4]

Specifically, we calculated the levels of satisfaction among winners and losers for each country over time.[5] This means that we tracked levels of satisfaction among the two groups of voters over the course of two decades in the case of Britain and Germany and one decade in the case of Spain. Several aspects of this analysis deserve highlighting. For one, this time period covers four elections and parts or all of five electoral cycles in the British case, where elections were held in 1979, 1983, 1987, and 1992. In the German case, the data span five electoral cycles and six elections (1976, 1980, 1983, 1987, 1990, and 1994). In both of these countries, voters also experienced a change in power, with the election of the Tory government in Britain in 1979, and the election of the Christian Democratic–Liberal coalition under Helmut Kohl in Germany in 1983. In the Spanish case, our data unfortunately do not contain a change in government, but they do cover three elections (1986, 1989, and 1993) as well as parts of all of three electoral cycles.

All three graphs, shown in Figures 4.2, 4.3, and 4.4, tell a similar story. While there is variation across countries and over time in voters' levels of

[4] We suspended these trend analyses in 1995 because the Eurobarometer discontinued asking the question about democracy satisfaction for several years.

[5] The Eurobarometer surveys are calculated twice yearly. When variables were unavailable to calculate winner and loser satisfaction levels for a survey, we interpolated satisfaction levels from two adjacent surveys. This is the case for three surveys in each country's time series.

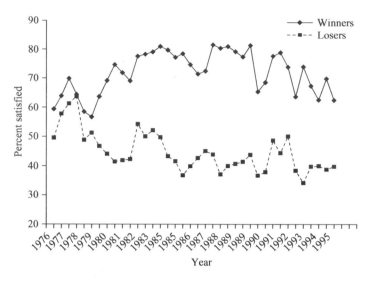

FIGURE 4.2. Evaluations of the political system in Britain, 1976–95

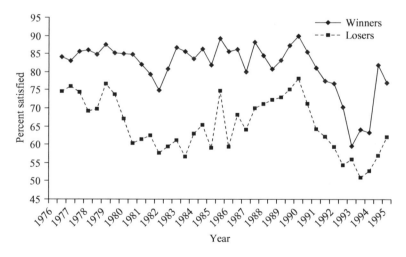

FIGURE 4.3. Evaluations of the political system in Germany, 1976–95

satisfaction with their political system, it also is very clear that the winner–loser gap is sustained over long periods of time. Moreover, and as importantly, while the size of the winner–loser gap varies over time, it is virtually never the case that losers are more satisfied with the political system than winners. It is important to note that the gap exists, therefore, regardless of who is in power,

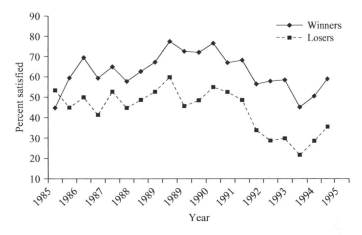

FIGURE 4.4. Evaluations of the political system in Spain, 1985–95

and it is a phenomenon that is sustained beyond the immediate post-election period. Put another way, instead of being the mark of temporary disappointment with the election outcome, it appears to be a lasting aspect of how voters view the political system's performance. Losing breeds lower levels of content not just immediately after an election; and discontent remains over the course of the electoral cycle.

Looking at the results in a bit more detail, we find that the winner–loser gap is particularly sizable in Britain and rather substantial after the 1979 election (Figure 4.2). That is, while the gap is relatively small in the mid- to late-1970s, it achieves its highest reading during the mid- to late-1980s, after which it declines somewhat. Overall, however, we find that British losers are significantly less satisfied than British winners. On average, well over 70 percent of British winners express satisfaction with the workings of democracy, while around forty-five percent of the losers do so. This result is consistent with findings from a cross-national study, which shows that the winner–loser gap is particularly pronounced in more majoritarian political systems like Great Britain's (Anderson and Guillory 1997).

The results for the German case reveal a very similar picture to that found in Britain, with about 81 percent of German winners on average expressing a positive evaluation of the way democracy works and about 65 percent of losers doing so. There is, however, an interesting difference to the British case that is quite obviously related to an exogenous shock in the form of German unification. The winner–loser gap is fairly steady throughout much of the 1970s and 1980s (Figure 4.3). Right before German unification (1989–90), however, both winners and losers become more satisfied with the political system. In large part, we speculate that these developments were the result of the euphoria surrounding German unification (and maybe Germany's success in the soccer World Cup!). After unification was successfully achieved and the post-unification hangover set in, however, both winners' and losers' evaluations of the political system became much less positive, though the gap between winners and losers remained throughout.

Spain, finally, saw a winner–loser gap between 1985 and 1995 that was quite steady and similar in size to the one observed in Germany (Figure 4.4). On average, about 63 percent of Spanish winners expressed satisfaction with the political system, while only about 44 percent of the losers said so. Beyond this, we see a bit of a decline in overall satisfaction levels among both winners and losers during the early 1990s, a period of particular economic difficulty in Spain. Overall, though, the winner–loser gap is consistent and persistent throughout.

The fact that the winner–loser gap appears so dependably supports our general contention. In fact, it is even more remarkable because evaluations of the political system's performance are not usually expected to be completely steady. Thus, temporary developments in a nation's political or economic life may lead one to expect possible and sudden shifts that may have the potential to invert the winner–loser gap. Yet, this does not seem to be the case. Moreover, it is important to point out that the countries experienced multiple elections during the period examined here and that both Britain and Germany saw a change in power during this time. Yet, again, and consistent with the results we reported earlier in this chapter, a change in government does not erase the winner–loser gap, nor do periods of election campaigns seem to alter the basic difference in how winners and losers evaluate the political system. The final question for this chapter then becomes whether losing over long periods of time leads to a deterioration in losers' consent.

THE EFFECT OF REPEATED LOSING

Does losing repeatedly affect losers' consent? If so, how? Examining these questions requires data on citizens' beliefs that include cases where supporters of one or several parties have lost elections time and again over a relatively long period of time. While such occurrences of persistent loss are relatively rare across democratic systems, there are some well-known cases of one-party dominant regimes, such as Japan or Sweden during much of the post-Second World War period (Pempel 1990). In the context of our study, we examine the British, German, and Spanish cases, all of which had long periods of single-party (or coalition) rule. Specifically, from 1979 to 1997—for some eighteen years—Britain was ruled by the Conservative Party, first under Prime Minister Margaret Thatcher and subsequently under John Major. This period spanned five elections, the first four of which were lost by those who were not supporters of the Conservative Party. Germany, similarly, saw about sixteen years of rule by the Christian Democratic/Liberal coalition led by Chancellor Helmut Kohl from late 1982 until 1998. As in Britain, this period spanned five elections (1983, 1987, 1990, 1994, and 1998), with only one defeat (the last election) for the incumbents. Spain, finally, saw over thirteen years of rule by the Socialists during the 1982–96 period, during the course of which the country held five elections as well (1982, 1986, 1989, 1993, and 1996); the Socialists were eventually defeated in 1996.

Our working hypothesis is that repeated losing corrodes support—that is, it has the effect of producing ever more negative feelings on the part of losers, as their chances of being in the majority are repeatedly frustrated. To test this idea, we conducted analyses at the aggregate and the individual level. We track the trajectories of losers' consent over time and we calculate whether the direction of change is consistently in one direction (whether there is a downward trend), and whether this change over time is statistically significant.

Figure 4.5 shows the trajectory of losers' satisfaction with the political system in Britain between 1979 and 1995. While there is significant variability in satisfaction levels within any few years, there does appear to be a downward trend in satisfaction levels as time wore on. Calculations show that, on average, each year brought with it a 0.25 percentage point drop in democracy satisfaction levels among losers. That is, satisfaction levels among the losers were slightly below 50 percent in 1979 but dropped to below 40 percent by the middle 1990s. Another way to look at the numbers would be to say that satisfaction declined from 45–50 percent at the beginning of the period examined here to about 35–40 percent later on. While this may not seem like a substantial

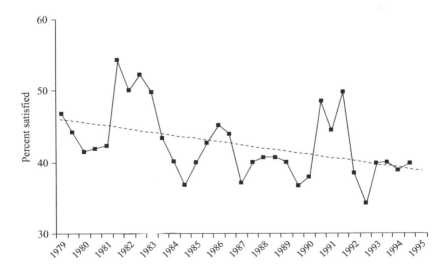

FIGURE 4.5. Democracy satisfaction among losers: Britain, 1979–95

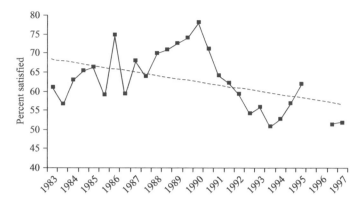

FIGURE 4.6. Democracy satisfaction among losers: Germany, 1983–97

trend, the cumulative effect of this drop is noteworthy. Simply losing time and again and staying a loser makes citizens less allegiant to the political system. Needless to say, this is hardly good news for system legitimacy.

The German case tells a similar story, though one that was interrupted by the euphoria of unification. Losers' consent actually increased between 1983 and 1990 (the time of unification), after which it declined precipitously (Figure 4.6). More importantly, however, despite the massively positive shock of unification, which brought on high levels of goodwill toward the political system and the political community, the overall trend in losers' satisfaction with regime performance is downward. Our calculations show that each passing year meant a concomitant 0.37 percentage point decrease in levels of satisfaction with democracy in Germany. Thus, while losers' satisfaction levels were as high as the low to mid-70 percent range in the middle to late 1980s, they dropped to slightly above 50 percent a few years after unification. Moreover, we should note that our data only include responses from the former West Germany in order to make the percentages (populations) comparable over the entire time period. When East Germans are included in the post-1990 calculations as well, the decline in satisfaction levels, unsurprisingly, is even more pronounced. (To estimate more precisely whether the overall trend was the result of a growing disillusion with unification, below, we will more formally account for this possibility in a regression analysis.)

An inspection of the Spanish results shows that the general downward trend in system performance evaluations experienced by perennial losers is a general phenomenon (Figure 4.7). There too, losers' satisfaction levels declined over time. In fact, if anything, the decline observed in the Spanish case is more conspicuous than that in the other two countries because it was larger in magnitude and occurred over a shorter period of time. While losers' satisfaction was relatively stable during the mid- to late-1980s, it dropped from about

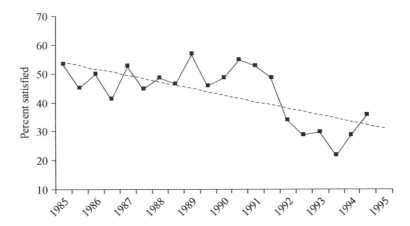

FIGURE 4.7. Democracy satisfaction among losers: Spain, 1985–95

50 percent in the late-1980s to about 30 percent by the mid-1990s. Thus, as in Britain and Germany, losers' happiness with the way the political system worked declined after losses began to accumulate in Spain as well.

When we examine the three countries' trajectories with an eye toward satisfaction levels at the time of elections as well as similarities with regard to the overall trends, two things stand out: first, it appears that losers' satisfaction increases prior to an election—that is, in the run-up to an opportunity to wrest power from the current incumbent. For example, losers' evaluations in Britain become more positive in the two years prior to balloting from 1981 to 1983, 1985 to 1987, and 1990 to 1992 (cf. Figure 4.2). Similar dynamics are at work in other countries.

Second, we find that there is a difference between first and second election losses on one hand and subsequent ones on the other. Specifically, we find that losers' consent is relatively stable or even increases between the first and second election loss—this is the case in both Britain and Germany, where we have data to observe this change—but then a significant decline after the first opportunity to win back power was frustrated. Thus, the decline, when it occurs, is less noticeable earlier in the period of losing and much more pronounced later on. While this suggests that losing starts taking a toll on legitimacy after the second election defeat in a row, this finding is consistent with the general idea that losing repeatedly frustrates voters to an ever greater degree.

To calculate whether there was, indeed, a downward trend that was statistically significant, we performed two sets of analyses. First, we regressed levels of losers' satisfaction in each country on a simple time variable (coded 1 for the first survey, 2 for the second, and so on) with the help of aggregated

TABLE 4.3. *Long-term trends in losers' satisfaction with democracy in Britain, Germany, and Spain*

Country	Individual level	Aggregate level		
Britain (1979–95)	−0.01***	−0.50**		
	(0.001)	(0.17)		
	$N = 15,575$	$N = 32$		
Germany (1983–95)	−0.01***	−0.57[a]	−0.69*[b]	
	(0.002)	(0.39)	(0.33)	
	$N = 11,753$	$N = 27$	$N = 27$	
Spain (1985–95)	−0.05***	−2.40***		
	(0.004)	(0.57)		
	$N = 7,168$	$N = 22$		

***$p < 0.001$.
**$p < 0.01$.
*$p < 0.05$.

Notes: Entries are unstandardized ordinary least squares regression coefficients for 'year' variable. Standard errors in parentheses. Two-tailed tests of statistical significance are given:
[a] significant at the 0.07 level, one tailed;
[b] when model includes variable for German unification.

Source: Eurobarometer Cumulative File, ICPSR No. 3384.

time series data; second, we regressed losers' consent at the individual level on a time variable as well.[6] Both sets of results are shown in Table 4.3.

The estimations of trends in the data reveal a consistent pattern: persistent losing leads to drops in positive evaluations of the political system that are statistically and substantively significant. Regardless of whether we analyze individual or aggregate level data, the coefficients for the year of the survey variable are negative, indicating that later years saw more negative evaluations. Moreover, with one small exception, these coefficients are statistically significant. The one exception is the German case, where the aggregate level analysis fails to achieve statistical significance at conventional levels. However, when we include a variable for the period surrounding unification (with a dummy variable to account for surveys taken in late 1989, all of 1990, and early 1991), the German coefficient for the trend variable becomes statistically significant as well. Substantively speaking, the results show that the drop was more notable in Spain; in both the individual-level and aggregate-level analyses, the Spanish coefficients were larger than those found in Germany and Britain. We speculate that this may well be due to the fact that Spain is a less established

---

[6] Instead of numbering the surveys, an alternative would be to measure the number of months party supporters have been losers. Unsurprisingly, both strategies yield essentially identical inferences.

democracy—a question we will take up more systematically in comparisons of old and new democracies in Chapter 6. Moreover, the coefficients were of similar magnitude in the latter two countries.

LOSERS' CONSENT OVER THREE DECADES

Finally, we examine the dynamics of losers' consent over a long stretch of time, where losers experienced varying periods of winning and losing. To do so, we make use of the rich series of American National Election Studies (NES) to trace the dynamics of losers' consent in the United States in presidential election years between 1964 and 2000. First, this allows us to demonstrate if losers in recent years were more distrusting than losers of previous decades. Republicans at the mass and elite level in the United States were visibly hostile to President Clinton, for example, due to his low popular vote total, opposition to some of his policies, and also due to his 'cultural' and 'lifestyle' positions (admissions of drug use and adultery, tolerance of homosexuality in the military, etc.). The lack of Republican consent with Clinton's presidency culminated in the impeachment by the congressional Republican party in 1997. Does this mean, however, that a Republican voter who supported Bob Dole in 1996 was more distrusting of the government than, say, a Democratic voter who supported Gore in 2000, or a Republican supporting their party's loser in 1976 (Ford)? Second, the 2000 election—where a Democrat won the popular vote for President but nonetheless lost the election—may have been such a dramatic loss that it created significantly more serious erosion in trust in the government among Democrats than occurred in previous Democratic defeats.

Third, examining the relationship between losing and trust across time may tell us something about why mass distrust of government has increased over time. If losing in the electoral arena is one of the determinants of distrust in government, what happens if there are more losers over time? Trends in US elections—both in terms of voter turnout and electoral results—suggest that a smaller proportion of citizens now vote for whoever wins the presidency or whoever controls the Congress. Has this change in the electorate's composition changed the nature of the effect losing has on attitudes toward government?

We use cross-sectional NES data from 1964 to 2000 to estimate trust in government as a function of support for the losing party. Specifically, we test how support for losing candidates is associated with distrust by estimating a simple model of trust for each presidential election year the NES sampled during this period. Our dependent variable here is measured with the NES question, 'generally speaking, can the [federal] government, that is, the government in Washington DC, be trusted to do the right thing'. Response categories range from 1 to 4, with 1 being 'none of the time' and 4 being 'a lot'. Trust is estimated with a simple model that controls for the respondent's age, gender, race (black), education, union status, and unemployment.

The effect of being a loser in the electoral arena is coded as a dummy variable, where 1 means that the respondent voted for a party different from the president's party; and 0 means that the respondent voted for the president's party. To separate out voters for major contenders from supporters of minor party candidates, we estimated two models: in one, losers were all voters for the major party competitor to the eventual winner; in the other, all voters for losing candidates were included in the losing category. Thus, in one model, a Democratic voter in 1972 was coded as a loser, while a Republican voter in 1964 was coded as a loser. In the other, all those who did not vote for Nixon in 1972 or Johnson in 1964 were coded as losers. By using the same basic model for all contests conducted between 1964 and 2000, this method allows us to isolate a coefficient that reflects the magnitude of the relationship between political trust and being an electoral loser.

Table 4.4 reports two series of coefficients for each presidential election year from 1964 to 2000. Each column reports OLS regression coefficients for the effect on trust of voting for a party not in control of the White House, controlling for other social and demographic traits. The first column lists the effect for a model where all major party losers were coded as losers, while the second column reports the effect for all losers.[7]

Several things are illustrated by these data. First, losers are not always the least trusting citizens. For example, in 1976, Republican voters are coded as losers, while, in 2000, Democrats are. In both of these years, losers are significantly more trusting than other citizens. However, in each of these elections, surveys were conducted immediately after (or during) the election and campaign. At the same time, the NES data do show a pattern where the effect of losing on distrust is consistent when losers vote for a party that has not controlled the White House for at least one election cycle (Republican voters in 1964 and 1996; Democrats in 1972, 1984, and 1988). This pattern might reflect delayed effects of losing on trust, and/or the fact that surveys conducted at the election are not timed well for detecting such effects. Incidentally, this delayed response is consistent with the findings reported for the European countries; namely that a marked decline in losers' consent sets in subsequent to the second, rather than the first, electoral loss.

Second, the effect on trust of losing in the 2000 contest—that is, the effect of not having voted for G. W. Bush—is not particularly remarkable. In fact, Gore voters were still modestly more trusting of government at the time of the 2000 election, just as G. H. W. Bush voters were in 1992. Viewed from this perspective, the 2000 election is not exceptional. Gore voters surveyed by

---

[7] This analysis implicitly assumes that only the White House matters or that it matters more than winning in the US Congress, for example. There is evidence to support this view—specifically, that US voters react to winning and losing the presidency but not winning and losing either chamber of the US Congress (cf. Anderson and LoTempio 2002).

TABLE 4.4. *The impact of voting for losing US presidential candidates on trust in government, 1964–2000*

	Voted for major party loser	Voted for major or minor party losers
1964	−0.33*	−0.33*
1968	0.15*	0.04
1972	−0.24*	−0.25*
1976	0.10*	0.11*
1980	0.12*	0.07
1984	−0.16*	−0.14*
1988	−0.19*	−0.21*
1992	0.01	−0.04
1996	−0.20*	−0.20*
2000	0.11*	0.10*

*$p < 0.05$ (one-tailed).

Notes: Dependent variable is trust in the federal government, predicted with age, sex, race (a dummy for black), education, labor union member, personally unemployed, and a dummy for non-voters. Losers are coded as those who voted for the losing presidential candidate of major party (first column), or any losing presidential candidate (second column).

Source: American National Election Studies series. The dependent variable ranges from 1 (distrusting) to 4 (trusting).

NES after the Supreme Court awarded Florida's Electoral College votes (and the presidency) to G. W. Bush, however, did have significantly colder feelings (measured in thermometer scores) than Gore voters interviewed prior to the decision (Bowler and Donovan 2003*a*, *b*).

Third, Table 4.4 illustrates that the effect of winning on trust has been fairly invariant across time—with 2000 being no particular exception. Despite a three decade long trend toward greater distrust of government, the relationship between losing and trust shows no clear pattern over this period. The reason for this lack of any clear trend may lie in the relatively frequent alternation that has occurred in American politics, in part produced by term-limits on presidential terms, in part simply the result of two strong and nationally competitive political party organizations. Divided government, which allows one party to control the executive while another controls the legislature, may also be a factor. Overall, then, these results for the United States are consistent with our findings both on the relative stability of the winner–loser gap between elections as well as the impact of long-term losing on political support. They also hold out the possibility that one of the reasons for the remarkable stability of the American political system lies in the unvarying magnitude of losers' restraint.

DISCUSSION

In this chapter, we traced the dynamics of losers' and winners' attitudes about the political system along three dimensions: immediately after an election, over the course of electoral cycles, and over long periods of time. Our results show that winning and losing, once it occurs, has immediate but also lasting effects. When elections reshuffle the cards of the political game, the new losers—that is, those who were used to being the winners—become less content with the political system. Conversely, the new winners who were used to being the losers are elated and become significantly more positive about a political system that smiled on them this time around. Yet, these effects, while possibly tinged with euphoria immediately after the election, persist over the course of an electoral cycle and beyond as losers remain consistently less satisfied than winners between elections. That is, losing has negative effects for system legitimacy, and this effect is stubborn. Finally, we show that repeated losing serves to increasingly undermine losers' attitudes toward the political system— while losing once does not immediately serve to undercut losers' attitudes toward government, losing twice starts a process that leads to a gradual erosion of support for a system that consistently fails to make them winners.

Implicitly, these results suggest that long periods without alternation in power lead to progressively less positive views about the political system among the losers. We would speculate that a lack of alternation therefore may well produce a breeding ground for significant change in the political system. While doubtlessly not as severe as rebellion or civil strife, Japan's political crisis that brought about a significant change in the country's party system and expressed desire for political reform in the early 1990s may serve as an example that even apparently mature democracies with political cultures that value stability possess the inherent potential for significant upheaval when losers, instead of tuning out, ask for the political system to address their grievances.

Our findings regarding the long-term trends of losers' consent touches upon a research program that has sought to document and explain the apparent long-run downturn in citizens' trust in political institutions across the developed democracies (Dalton 2004). This research tells a story about changing citizen expectations. According to this view, people are more committed to democracy than ever, but also have high expectations of democratic institutions that are frequently and perhaps necessarily disappointed because democratic government is imperfect. Our findings suggest that, perhaps, one source of the decline in trust that has been documented may be a lack of alternation. When governments fail to turn over, losers may start dropping out, leading to lower turnout and trust over time.

But even in the short run, the relative stability of the winner–loser gap we observe during the course of electoral cycles regardless of who is in power has obvious implications for democratic governance. Unhappy (or at least, relatively unhappy) voters are unlikely to be as cooperative as happy ones when it comes to viewing policy outcomes or supporting government policies. Thus, governments time and again face a sizable and comparatively less happy segment of voters who are liable to view their actions through the lens of losing.

Finally, the results we present in this chapter indicate that winning and losing are both short-term and long-term based phenomena. In the short run, losers feel bad about a system that did not favor them in the most recent election. In the medium term, the initial disappointment gives way to viewing the political system in ways that are consistent with the initial disappointment and the reality of being out of power.

So far, then, we have shown that there is a winner–loser gap that exists across countries, is observable with regard to different dimensions of legitimacy, and persists over time. Our next step, then, is to move from the question of whether there is a gap to the question of why it may vary both across countries and across different individuals. The next chapter, therefore, focuses on the latter by examining the factors particular to individual voters that can create differences in the extent to which losing distresses voters.

PART II

UNDERSTANDING DIFFERENCES IN LOSERS' CONSENT

5

Individual Differences in Losers' Consent

In previous chapters, we showed that there tends to be a gap in winners' and losers' attitudes and that this gap persists over time. Yet, it is also clear that this gap does not exist unfailingly. And there may be good reasons for this. As our model presented in Chapter 2 argues, the strength of the effect of losing on system support is likely to be a function of a variety of factors, including the political contexts in which losing and winning are experienced, as well as individuals' predispositions and motivations to view losses and wins in a particular light.

Before turning to cross-national differences, in this chapter we focus on individual-level differences in how winners and losers come to develop attitudes toward government. While winning and losing are experienced by individuals and create a lens through which citizens view politics, in this chapter we examine whether different political predispositions voters bring to the table matter for how they view the system. That is, we suspect that not all losers are created equal when it comes to the translation of loss into legitimacy beliefs, and we examine what makes some winners and losers more likely to have strong reactions to being in the majority and minority, and what makes others less likely to exhibit much of a reaction to the election outcome.

In the model we outlined in Chapter 2, the likelihood that losing produces gracious acceptance or violent protest was said to be in part a function of individuals' attitudes and prior experiences. That is, the model posits that citizens cope with loss differently, and that there are therefore differences in voters' predisposition to view loss as being devastating or normal business. In this chapter, we focus on two key differences among individuals that may help shape losers' consent: ideology and attachment to political parties. Specifically, we examine whether those outside the political mainstream and those very closely attached to their political party may take a loss particularly hard and consider it much more negatively than voters who are relatively indifferent about the contenders for government office and who are closer to the political center.

INDIVIDUAL PREDISPOSITIONS AND LOSERS' CONSENT

At the most basic level, we expect that individuals' political predispositions affect how the experience of winning and losing translates into varying degrees of support for the political system. In particular, we argue that individuals may carry predispositions that can serve to amplify or mute the positive effects of winning and the negative effects of losing on citizens' consent. Below, we focus on partisanship and ideology as two prominent examples of such predispositions. Both are said to be formed early in life and have been shown to be quite stable during people's lifetimes. This means that they are unlikely to be strongly, if at all, affected by short-term political events and also constitute lenses through which individuals view the political world around them. Regardless of the specific hypotheses about how each of these predispositions may work to affect legitimacy beliefs—which we will discuss in greater detail below—we start our investigation by suggesting that beliefs either mute or amplify the effects of winning and losing on attitudes toward government. Figure 5.1 depicts this proposed interaction effect.

According to this conceptualization, a muting attitude reduces the level of positive attitudes toward the system among the winners as well as the level of negative attitudes among the losers. Conversely, an amplifying predisposition will enhance winners' positive beliefs about the system and enhance losers' already negative attitudes even further. In the context of our theoretical model shown in Chapter 2, this interactive effect suggests that the negative influence of losing is muted when individuals are predisposed to have faith in the system and amplified when their predispositions aggravate the already unpleasant experience of losing an election and finding oneself in the opposition (Figure 5.2).

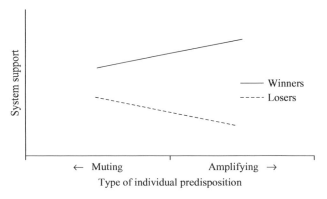

FIGURE 5.1. Interactive effects of winner–loser status and individual predisposition on system support

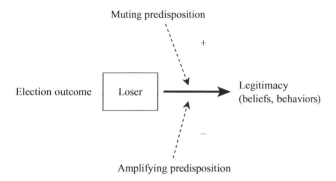

FIGURE 5.2. The mediating role of individual predispositions on legitimacy beliefs among losers

PARTY IDENTIFICATION AS A LINK BETWEEN LOSING AND CONSENT

The notion that party identification, also variously referred to as partisanship or partisan attachment, can serve to mediate the impact of winning and losing on legitimacy beliefs appears straightforward at first sight. After all, winning and losing should matter more to people who feel a strong bond with the party they support. As a result, we would expect strongly partisan winners to rejoice more and strongly partisan losers to be more dejected after an election, and this should translate into varying levels of support for a system that produced the welcome or unwelcome outcome. Put simply, then, partisanship should be an amplifying predisposition. Whether this is a reasonable conjecture and one that is supported by the data, however, is a topic we address below.

Partisanship is a concept that has a long and distinguished tradition in research on political behavior (Green, Palmquist, and Schickler 2002). It generally refers to an individual's affective or emotional attachment to a political party, which, according to the Michigan school of thought, has its origins in early socialization experiences (Campbell et al. 1960). In contrast, researchers taking a rational choice perspective view such an attachment as more of an instrumental attitude and a cognitive short-cut that represents a running tally of retrospective assessments of party performance (Fiorina 1981). Either way, both perspectives consider partisan identification as an attitude that disposes the individual both to dependably vote for a particular political party in different elections and to interpret new political information in ways that are consistent with the party's interests and policy stances (Zaller 1992). A short perusal of the literature on partisanship reveals that a large body of scholarship on attitude formation recognizes that citizens are prone to adopt the issue positions and political orientations of the political party and candidate they support (Campbell et al. 1960; Brody and Page 1972; Jackson 1975;

Markus and Converse 1979; Franklin and Jackson 1983; Jacoby 1988). Consistent with this, we view partisanship as a lens through which individuals view the political world around them.

However, partisans clearly are not created equal when considered from the perspective of winners and losers. After an election has been held, one set of partisans had their choice confirmed by the electorate as a whole, while the choice of the other set was repudiated. To those strongly attached to their political party, such a confirmation or repudiation may well be especially consequential. However, exactly how this is expected to work is not entirely clear. On one hand, we would expect strong partisans to be more likely to delight in their victory and be more frustrated in their defeat relative to those who are relatively less attached to the parties that competed in the contest. In a way, strength of partisanship thus would be a measure of how intensely voters experience winning and losing, and we would expect the winner–loser gap to be particularly pronounced among strong partisan identifiers. If this is the case, partisanship should amplify, not mute, the impact of the election outcome on attitudes toward the system.

On the other hand, however, this expectation is open to challenge, based on what we know about the role of partisanship in the formation of support for the political system, and based on what we know about how people seek to avoid cognitive dissonance. Regarding the former, in a democratic political system populated with parties that accept the existing political order, individuals with party attachments should have higher levels of support for the idea that the political process matters and is worth paying attention to than non-identifiers. Partisans care about their party and possibly by implication, the political process. Unsurprisingly, therefore, research consistently has found that attachments to political parties are a major factor in the formation of public support for the political order in which they are embedded. People who identify strongly with a party tend to be much more supportive of the idea that the political system functions properly than people without strong party attachment (Dennis 1966; Miller and Listhaug 1990; Holmberg 2003).

This relationship has been assumed to be of direct relevance to the health of, and the outlook for, a democratic political system (Dalton 2002; Torcal, Gunther, and Montero 2002; Holmberg 2003). Specifically, it has been speculated that the oft-noted decline in party identification may well lead to declining levels of support for party-based democracy (Dalton 2002). Viewed from this perspective and based on the existing evidence, then, we would speculate that partisanship may actually serve to mute the impact of losing because strong partisans accept the process to a greater extent than unattached voters do. In this case, it should not matter so much for political legitimacy whether an individual is among the losers of an election, but the fact that this person is strongly attached to a political party. Partisanship as a system-affirming attitude, therefore, should breed content with the system and, as a result, mute the impact of the election outcome on losers' consent. Thus partisan winners should be happier with the system, but partisan losers might also be happier when compared with non-partisan ones (Paskeviciute and Anderson 2004).

This is consistent with research on cognitive dissonance, which has found that voters very often experience post-election dissonance and will try to reduce it by forming consistent beliefs (Frenkel and Doob 1976; Regan and Kilduff 1988). For example, people usually will report more esteem and confidence in the candidate they choose and they will devalue the alternative. Once the outcome is known, however, voters who cast a ballot for a loser tend to see that candidate as more similar to the winner in an effort to justify their choice of candidate. Alternatively, these same voters have been found to develop more favorable attitudes toward the winner and less favorable ones toward the loser, even if they voted for the losing candidate (Brehm 1956, 1962; Stricker 1964; Joslyn 1998). This latter stream of research would imply that strongly partisan losers will be more likely to report that they value the process they just voluntarily participated in. If this is the case, we should not expect to find significant differences between strongly versus weakly partisan winners and losers' evaluations of the political system. Instead, the major difference should be observed between those with an allegiance to a political party and those without, rather than between strongly attached winners and losers.

PARTISAN ATTACHMENT AND EVALUATIONS OF THE POLITICAL SYSTEM

To examine the differences in winners' and losers' levels of contentment with the functioning of the political system, we first take a look at how winners and losers who are strongly attached to the political party they voted for in the election differ in their evaluations of the political system from those who say they are only somewhat or not at all attached to the party they supported. For this reason and given the evidence about the winner–loser gap presented in the previous chapter, the analysis in this chapter focuses on satisfaction with democracy as the dependent variable.

If partisan attachment makes voters more likely to have a strong reaction to the election outcome, then we would expect winners who are close to the party they supported to be most positive about the political system and losers who are close to their party to express the most negative evaluation of the political system. Alternatively, if being a partisan means having higher levels of allegiance to the existing political order, then we would expect the usual winner–loser gap, but also strongly partisan winners and losers to be more positive in their evaluations of the system than unattached winners and losers.

To examine which of these scenarios was supported by the data, we relied on surveys from the Comparative Study of Electoral Systems surveys used earlier in this book to calculate the mean levels of satisfaction (on a 1–4 scale) for election winners and losers in fifteen countries, split also by whether they indicated that they were very close to their political party or not very close.[1] In the total sample, 19.1 percent of respondents (including nonvoters) indicated that they were very close to their party; 5.8 percent of the total sample were very close to a political party and also electoral winners; 5.2 percent said they were very close and also fell into the category of electoral losers. Winners and losers were categorized on the basis of a vote recall question and we included those respondents who indicated that they did not have any party attachment in the category of not very close. Table 5.1 shows the results for the countries for which the necessary variables were available.

The results show that, if anything, the expected effect of partisanship as an amplifier exists for winners but not for losers. Overall, in ten of the fifteen countries included here, winners who are close to their political party are also the most supportive of the political system; thus, winners with strong allegiances to the political party of their choice are particularly happy with the way the political system works in countries as different as Australia, Canada, the Czech Republic, Denmark, Iceland, Japan, Portugal, Spain, Sweden, and Switzerland. This constitutes two-thirds of the cases analyzed here.

In contrast, the evidence is somewhat less supportive of partisanship as an amplifier effect for losers. While unattached losers exhibit the lowest levels of satisfaction with the performance of the system in only a small number of countries (Australia, Denmark, Iceland, and Spain), strongly partisan losers were particularly dejected and evaluated the political system particularly negatively in seven countries. We found such an effect in Canada, the Czech Republic, Japan, Poland, Portugal, Sweden, and Switzerland.

Overall, the pattern of results is in the direction of an amplifying effect of partisanship, but this effect is not universal. While unattached winners exhibit the most positive attitudes toward the political system in some countries (Poland), attached losers do in others (Germany, the Netherlands, and Norway). And although there are more instances of happy winners than of happy losers, and despite the fact that, overall, attached winners are happiest and attached losers are least happy, there also is significant cross-national variation in these results.

Taken together, then, we find that partisan losers expressed the most negative, and partisan winners simultaneously the most positive, opinions about the political system in six of the fifteen cases: Canada, the Czech Republic, Japan,

---

[1] The question wording for the partisanship measure consists of a series of questions as follows: 1. 'Do you usually think of yourself as close to any particular party?' If yes to question 1, 'Which party is that? Do you feel very close to this party, somewhat close, or not very close?' If no to question 1, 'Do you feel yourself a little closer to one of the political parties than the others? Which party is that?' The approach followed here—that is, focusing on strong identifiers—is useful because the biggest problem concerning the measuring of partisan attachment concerns those who say they are partisan but add that they are not strongly partisan (Blais et al. 2001: 14).

TABLE 5.1. *Satisfaction with democracy among strong and weak partisans*

Country	Loser–Winner	Not close	Close to party
Australia	Winner	3.15	**3.23**
	Loser	*2.98*	3.06
Canada	Winner	3.12	**3.43**
	Loser	*2.71*	*2.71*
Czech Republic	Winner	2.89	**3.18**
	Loser	2.28	*1.79*
Denmark	Winner	3.20	**3.38**
	Loser	*3.16*	3.22
Germany	Winner	*2.71*	2.72
	Loser	2.74	**2.84**
Iceland	Winner	3.07	**3.24**
	Loser	*2.77*	2.78
Japan	Winner	2.84	**3.00**
	Loser	2.63	*2.11*
Netherlands	Winner	3.09	*2.94*
	Loser	3.01	**3.18**
Norway	Winner	3.19	*3.13*
	Loser	3.19	**3.22**
Poland	Winner	**2.78**	2.70
	Loser	2.66	*2.61*
Portugal	Winner	2.54	**2.55**
	Loser	2.48	*2.40*
Spain	Winner	2.98	**3.24**
	Loser	*2.84*	2.94
Sweden	Winner	2.85	**2.98**
	Loser	2.76	*2.55*
Switzerland	Winner	2.86	**2.91**
	Loser	2.86	*2.78*
United Kingdom	Winner	*2.83*	2.89
	Loser	**3.03**	2.97
Total	Winner	2.91	**2.97**
	Loser	2.86	*2.81*

Notes: Highest values are shown in bold; lowest values are shown in bold and italics.
Dependent variable ranges from 1 (dissatisfaction) to 4 (satisfaction).

Source: Comparative Study of Electoral Systems (CSES) surveys (1996–2000).

Portugal, Sweden, and Switzerland. Thus, while the 'partisanship as amplifier effect' does exist, it exists neither uniformly nor simultaneously for both winners and losers in most countries. In contrast, there are also four cases (Australia, Denmark, Iceland, and Spain) where unattached losers display the lowest levels of satisfaction with democracy, thus suggesting that strong partisanship mutes the impact of losing on losers' consent in these countries. Thus, the evidence suggests that strong attachments to political parties can, but do not necessarily, lead to greater joy about the functioning of the political system among the winners or more disappointment with it among the losers.

To help fix these effects with greater accuracy, we conducted multivariate estimations of democracy satisfaction that controlled for a host of factors that, when accounted for, may produce crisper effects for the mediating influence of partisanship on legitimacy. Specifically, we controlled for demographic variables such as age, education, and income, but also an important political variable, voting participation, in order to separate out nonvoters and voters. Moreover, to test the idea that partisanship may have either an amplifying or muting effect—that is, that strongly partisan winners would be most positive about the political system and strongly partisan losers either most negative (amplifying) or more positive than unattached losers (muting), we created two dummy variables that captured these two populations; the reference category includes nonpartisan winners and losers. The coefficients for these two dummy variables are shown in Table 5.2.

TABLE 5.2. *The effects of partisan winner–loser status on evaluations of political system performance*

Country	Strongly partisan winner	Strongly partisan loser
Australia	0.068	−0.009
Canada	0.561***	−0.195*
Czech Republic	0.594***	−0.779***
Denmark	0.215**	0.049
Germany	−0.035	0.052
Iceland	0.301***	−0.095
Japan	0.179[a]	−0.639***
Netherlands	−0.138	0.149
Norway	0.036	0.067
Poland	0.019	−0.150
Portugal	0.028	−0.027
Sweden	0.234*	−0.232**
Switzerland	0.059	−0.074
Spain	0.327***	−0.089
United Kingdom	−0.005	−0.030
Pooled sample	0.067**	−0.068**

***$p < 0.001$.
**$p < 0.01$.
*$p < 0.05$.
[a] $p < 0.05$, one-tailed.

Notes: Unstandardized OLS regression coefficients. Coding of extreme winner (loser) status: extreme winners (losers) = 1; others = 0; reference category is non-extreme winners and losers. Based on multivariate estimation models controlling for age, education, gender, income, and voting participation. Dependent variable ranges from 1 (dissatisfaction) to 4 (satisfaction).

Source: Comparative Study of Electoral Systems (1996–2000).

The coefficients shown in Table 5.2 tell a story that is similar to that told by the simple averages. We find that strongly partisan winners expressed significantly more positive evaluations of the political system in six of the fifteen countries (Canada, the Czech Republic, Denmark, Iceland, Sweden, and Spain). Thus, *when significant*, the results for strongly partisan winners points to winners being more positive. That is, when strength of partisanship matters among winners, it amplifies the impact of the election outcome.

Similarly, strongly partisan losers express the most negative opinions about the working of democracy in four countries (Canada, the Czech Republic, Japan, and Sweden). Thus, considering significant winner and loser effects together, of the fifteen cases, eight showed no discernible differences among partisan winners, partisan losers, and nonpartisans, and there were three (Canada, the Czech Republic, and Sweden) where partisanship amplified the impact of both winning and losing on attitudes toward the system. Among the remaining four, winners were most positive but losers not most negative in three countries (Denmark, Iceland, and Spain), and losers were most negative but winners not most positive in one country (Japan; though the winner coefficient is statistically significant using a one-tailed test). Thus, when we consider the evidence from the perspective of the muting hypothesis, we find that there was no case where the observed pattern supports the notion that partisanship helps buffer the effect of losing.

On balance, then, the evidence points in two directions: first, the (perhaps heroic or naïve) expectation that election outcomes would unfailingly translate into particularly high or low levels of joy or sorrow with the political system, for partisan winners and losers, is supported only in a minority of cases. More often than not, such unambiguous differences do not emerge. At the same time, however, *when they do exist*, they point in the direction of strongly partisan winners being most positive and strongly partisan losers being most negative about the workings of the system, thus providing consistent but also restricted support for the amplifying hypothesis.[2]

As should be clear from our analyses in Chapter 4, however, it is worth pointing out that in two of our cases analyzed here (Germany and the United Kingdom), the elections preceding our surveys marked the end of long periods

---

[2] Given the debate over the applicability of the concept of partisanship to countries outside the United States (Budge, Crewe, and Farlie 1976; Richardson 1991; Clarke, Stewart, and Whiteley 1997; Schickler and Green 1997; Sanders and Brynin 1999; Blais et al. 2001; Green, Palmquist, and Schickler 2002), we conducted additional analyses in order to validate the findings for strength of partisan attachment. Specifically, we relied on a battery of questions included in the CSES surveys that asked respondents to indicate, on a 0–10 scale, for each political party in the country whether they liked or disliked that party. Using the same analytical strategy employed for partisan attachment, we found that disliking political parties other than one's own tends to deepen losers' negative views of the political system, while it does not elevate winners' views. Conversely, we found that strong attachment to one's political party heightens evaluations of the political system among the winners but does not necessarily depress them among losers.

of incumbent rule. Perhaps not coincidentally, these are also cases that did not exhibit any significant pattern. As mentioned before, in such cases the high levels of support for the political system among the old winners—that is, the new losers—may not have quite worn off, and particularly high levels of support among the new winners—that is, the old losers—may not yet have become entrenched.

To provide further tests of the mediating impact of partisanship, we examined data from the United States—that is, the country where the concept has experienced the greatest degree of empirical support and examination. Specifically, we were able to draw on the American National Election Studies (NES) series of surveys conducted every two years from 1964 to 2002. We coded citizens who did not have the same political allegiance as the President's party as losers for 'on-year' and 'off-year' surveys. Thus, our 'losing' variable reflects not being aligned with the party controlling the White House. We also examined how strength of partisanship influenced the impact of loss by dividing respondents into a category of weakly attached or unattached partisans on one hand and a category of strongly attached partisans on the other.

We subsequently estimated multivariate ordinary least squares models of trust in government that control for the respondent's age, gender, race (black), education, union status, unemployment, and voting participation. The dependent variable is measured with the NES question, 'generally speaking, can the [federal] government, that is, the government in Washington DC, be trusted to do the right thing'. Response categories range from 1 to 4, with 1 being 'none of the time' and 4 being 'a lot of the time'. Table 5.3 shows the results.

Several things are illustrated by these data. First, the effect of losing (and, by extension, the inverse effect of winning) is most pronounced among strong partisans. Although losers from the overall sample (column 1) are generally less likely to trust the government, this effect is greatest among the strong partisans. This makes sense if we consider that partisans have the keenest interest in politics and are more informed, and, thus, are most likely to have specific concerns about election outcomes.

Second, losers are not always the least trusting citizens—at least not in the short term. The data suggest that former losers, who may have been more distrusting while out of power, quickly change their perception of government once their party controls the White House. For example, in 1968, Democratic identifiers are coded as losers for having lost the presidential election that year—yet their party had controlled the executive and legislature from 1960 to 1968. Immediately after the 1968 election, they remained more trusting than other citizens. After just two years out of power (in terms of control of the presidency), however, strongly partisan Democrats became significantly less trusting of government. Likewise, Republican identifiers were more trusting of government in 1992 after their party had controlled the White House for twelve straight years. However, after two years of the Clinton presidency, they were significantly less likely to trust the government. Thus, the results for the

TABLE 5.3. *The effects of partisan loser status on trust in government in the United States, 1964–2000*

Year	Partisans coded as losers	All respondents	Weak party ID and independents	Strong party identifiers only
1964	R	−0.13*	−0.08*	−0.23*
1966	R	−0.23*	−0.13*	−0.50*
1968	D	0.13*	0.09*	0.21*
1970	D	−0.04	0.01	−0.20*
1972	D	−0.12*	−0.11*	−0.14
1974	D	0.04	0.01	0.08
1976	R	0.11*	0.08*	0.22*
1978	R	−0.10*	−0.07*	−0.21*
1980	D	0.10*	0.08*	0.14*
1982	D	−0.06*	−0.06*	−0.08*
1984	D	−0.09*	−0.09*	−0.11*
1986	D	−0.12*	−0.09*	−0.25*
1988	D	−0.11*	−0.05	−0.29*
1990	D	−0.06*	−0.03	−0.17*
1992	R	0.07*	0.11*	−0.03
1994	R	−0.06*	−0.01	−0.23*
1996	R	−0.13*	−0.07*	−0.28*
1998	R	−0.09*	−0.08*	−0.14*
2000	D	0.09*	0.09*	0.10*
2002	D	−0.12*	−0.09*	−0.20*
Average		−0.05	−0.02	−0.12

$*p < 0.05$.

Notes: Cell entries are OLS regression coefficients. Dependent variable is trust in the federal government, predicted with age, sex, race (a dummy for black), education, labor union member, personally unemployed, and a dummy for non-voters. Losers are defined in terms of identification with the major party opposite of that controlling the presidency.

Source: American National Election Studies series. Dependent variable ranges from 1 (distrusting) to 4 (trusting).

US case confirm the notion that strongly partisan losers are more likely to express negative views of the government than others.

Finally, this analysis gives us another perspective on the effects of the acrimonious 2000 US presidential election, and suggests that the long-term effects of losing for that election fit the historical pattern displayed in Table 5.3. Democrats had controlled the White House from 1992 to 2000, and strong Democratic identifiers were more trusting than others at the time of the 2000 NES survey. By 2002, after two years of the G. W. Bush presidency, they were significantly less trusting of government. The magnitude of the effect of being a loser by 2002, moreover, was consistent with two other years where strong partisans had seen their parties out of power for two years (1994 for Republicans, and 1970 for Democrats). We hasten to add, however, that it is plausible to conjecture that the impact of losing measured in 2002, which suggests that the 2000 election did not produce unusually large effects among losers when viewed from historical perspective, could be due to an opinion rally associated with the September 11, 2001 attacks and the October 21, 2002 Congressional authorization for the US war on Iraq.

Overall, our results regarding partisanship can be summarized as follows: when partisanship matters at the individual level, it amplifies the impact of winning and losing. At the same time, partisanship alone is not likely to be the sole explanation for individual differences in the impact winning and losing may have on people's views of the political system.

IDEOLOGY AND LEGITIMACY

Aside from partisanship, we believe that ideology may be another important individual-level variable that can serve to modify the extent to which losers develop negative attitudes and winners develop positive ones. A number of scholars have argued that individuals with attitudes that tend toward the extremes have stronger motivations to develop an interest in politics, to express their views, and to participate in the political process more generally. This expectation is based on the idea that extremists, or what some have referred to as hardcore opinion holders, may be more committed to their views and more willing to promote them.

Among others, this idea has its origins in Noelle-Neumann's work on the spiral of silence and the argument that the hardcore are 'not prepared to conform, to change their opinions, or even be silent in the face of public opinion' (Noelle-Neumann 1974: 48). More importantly for our purposes, such individuals are unlikely to be satisfied with the status quo and likely to derive utility from bringing about political change and mobilizing for it. Conversely, people may locate themselves in the political mainstream precisely because they are not much involved in politics, either psychologically or physically: instead, they simply accept the dominant position without giving it much consideration. As a result, the very lack of interest in political affairs that leads to the acceptance of the mainstream position in society may also be responsible for individuals' low engagement in politics.

A common way to think about how we can locate people in relation to the prevailing political climate is with the help of the median voter. A country's political discourse and its underlying political space are commonly defined by a simplifying language—often referred to in terms of ideology—that facilitates political communication and competition. More specifically, ideology is usefully summarized as a left–right ideological dimension, which also is commonly considered a summary of voters' positions across a range of policies (see e.g. Klingemann 1979).

Left–right placement is a useful indicator of people's location in a country's political space because it measures political orientations at a very general level and in commonly understood and widely accepted terms (Inglehart and Klingemann 1976; Klingemann 1979; Fuchs and Klingemann 1989). As importantly, the left–right ideological dimension is crucial to how voters choose among parties, parties compete for voters, and policy positions are packaged in party platforms (Huber 1989; Gabel and Huber 2000). Simply put, left–right measures the nature of political competition in a political system as well as where an individual locates themself within that space—in particular, whether an individual places themself in the political mainstream, close to the median opinion, or at the extreme as their political convictions become more divergent from those of others in the country.

When it comes to losers' political consent and political action more generally, supporters of the opposition, and in particular those with attitudes further removed from the country's mainstream, have a greater incentive to be psychologically and otherwise engaged in politics. This expectation can be derived from the potential utility of action for bringing about political change. As we have mentioned before, winning and losing matter because the stability and continued functioning of political systems depends on actors' incentives for institutional change. If this is the case, then those outside the political mainstream—that is, those on the political extremes—are more likely to deny consent and try to bring about change or mobilize for it. Following this logic of incentives to bring about change, we would expect losers who are located on the political margins to be even less satisfied with the political system than losers closer to the mainstream.

IDEOLOGICAL EXTREMISM AND EVALUATIONS OF THE POLITICAL SYSTEM

To examine the question of whether ideological extremists who also are losers are the least satisfied with the political system and extremist winners the happiest with the performance of the political system, we followed similar analytical procedures to those undertaken in our examination of the effects of partisan attachment. The only difference is that we coded individuals as falling into the extreme categories if they placed themselves between 0 and 2 on the left and 8 and 10 on the right end of the political continuum (other, more generous or narrow codings yielded similar results). 19.4 percent of respondents (including nonvoters) in the overall sample placed themselves at the extreme ends of the ideological spectrum; 8.1 percent of the respondents were simultaneously electoral winners and ideologically extreme, while 8.5 percent were both extreme and electoral losers. Table 5.4 shows the mean evaluations of ideologically extreme and mainstream winners and losers by country.[3]

---

[3] For reasons of data availability, we were able to analyze responses from twelve countries.

TABLE 5.4. *Satisfaction with democracy among extreme and mainstream ideological voters*

Country	Loser–Winner	Not extreme	Extreme
Australia	Winner	3.12	**3.21**
	Loser	3.03	*2.90*
Belgium	Winner	2.63	2.57
	Loser	**2.64**	*2.40*
Canada	Winner	3.15	**3.28**
	Loser	2.79	*2.70*
Denmark	Winner	**3.25**	3.13
	Loser	3.10	*3.07*
Germany	Winner	2.65	2.66
	Loser	**2.79**	*2.45*
Iceland	Winner	3.04	**3.15**
	Loser	2.77	*2.71*
Netherlands	Winner	**3.07**	3.02
	Loser	*2.96*	2.98
New Zealand	Winner	2.85	**3.04**
	Loser	2.80	*2.78*
Norway	Winner	**3.19**	*3.04*
	Loser	**3.19**	3.17
Sweden	Winner	2.85	**2.93**
	Loser	2.70	*2.77*
Switzerland	Winner	2.86	**2.88**
	Loser	*2.79*	*2.79*
United Kingdom	Winner	2.88	*2.78*
	Loser	3.01	**3.04**
Total	Winner	2.81	**2.91**
	Loser	*2.78*	2.86

Notes: Highest values are shown in bold; lowest values are shown in bold and italics.

Source: Comparative Study of Electoral Systems (CSES) surveys (1996–2000).

Overall, the differences between the four categories are rather moderate. As it turns out, however, with only three exceptions (the Netherlands, Norway, and the United Kingdom), losers with extreme ideological positions were the least enthusiastic group regarding the political system's performance. Moreover, in six of the twelve countries (Australia, Canada, Iceland, New Zealand, Sweden, and Switzerland), ideologically extreme winners were significantly more positive about the way the political system worked than all others. Finally, in these same six cases, extreme winners were happiest and extreme losers simultaneously gloomiest about the system's performance. Perhaps more importantly, there was only one case (the United Kingdom), where extreme losers expressed the most positive evaluation of the political system.

TABLE 5.5. *The effects of extreme winner–loser status on evaluations of political system performance*

Country	Extreme winner	Extreme loser
Australia	0.131*	−0.113
Belgium	−0.049	−0.231***
Canada	0.341**	−0.226***
Denmark	−0.001	−0.107**
Germany	−0.045	−0.249***
Iceland	0.203***	−0.181**
Netherlands	−0.013	−0.001
New Zealand	0.202***	−0.037
Norway	−0.136	−0.030
Sweden	0.182*	−0.005
Switzerland	0.044	−0.081
United Kingdom	−0.086	0.060
Pooled sample	0.018	−0.044**

$*p < 0.05.$
$**p < 0.01.$
$*** p < 0.001.$

Notes: Unstandardized OLS regression coefficients. Coding of extreme winner (loser) status: extreme winners (losers) = 1; others = 0; reference category is non-extreme winners and losers. Based on multivariate estimation models controlling for age, education, gender, income, and voting participation.

Source: Comparative Study of Electoral Systems (1996–2000).

Moreover, in two cases (Belgium and Germany) the mainstream losers actually turned out to express the most positive evaluations of the political system's performance. Noticeably, there also were two cases where the mainstream winners expressed the most positive evaluations of the political system: Denmark and the Netherlands, with a third (Norway) where mainstream winners and losers were roughly equal in their evaluations. This suggests that the political system in these countries is most positively evaluated by those in the political middle who manage to obtain power—largely consistent with stereotypes about the sources of stability in these consensus-driven democracies (Lijphart 1999).

Again, as a check on the robustness of these conclusions, we conducted a series of multivariate analyses of responses to the satisfaction with democracy question that included a number of control variables alongside two dummy terms for ideologically extreme winners and ideologically extreme losers. The coefficients for these two variables are shown in Table 5.5. They reveal that, in five of the twelve cases (Belgium, Canada, Denmark, Germany, and Iceland), extreme losers were significantly more likely to express low levels of support for the performance of the political system than others. Similarly, in five of the twelve (Australia, Canada, Iceland, New Zealand, and Sweden) extreme winners were significantly more likely to have positive evaluations of the political system than others, while there was no difference among the various groups in the Netherlands, Norway, Switzerland, or the United Kingdom. Perhaps more importantly, *when significant*, the relationships between ideologically extreme winner–loser status and attitudes toward the performance of the political system indicate that extreme winners are more positive and extreme loser more negative in their evaluations of the political system than other groups. On balance, then, our findings suggest that ideological extremism, when it mediates the impact of winning and losing on voters' beliefs about the political system, has an amplifying rather than muting effect.

CONCLUSION

In this chapter we set out to examine how voters' political predispositions may help to mediate the impact of winning and losing on attitudes toward government. Specifically, we focused on how two prominent individual-level differences—partisanship and ideology—affect what makes some winners and losers more likely to have strong reactions to being in the majority and minority, and how they make others less likely to translate the experience of winning and losing into positive or negative attitudes about the political system.

At the outset, it is not obvious how partisanship should serve to strengthen or weaken the influence of election outcomes on voters' consent. While partisanship can be a system-affirming and consistency-inducing attitude—thus leading winners and losers who are strongly attached to their political parties to be happier with the political system—it can also be viewed as amplifying the sense of loss experienced among the losers and the sense of triumph among the winners. Similarly, ideological extremism can be viewed as an expression of a prior dissatisfaction with the status quo, thus serving to amplify differences between winners and losers in their reaction to a political system that produced a favorable or unfavorable election outcome. At the same time, not being at the ideological extreme—that is, being in the mainstream—can be viewed as a lack of strong commitment to or cognitive involvement in the political process, thus leading losers who express their indifference by claiming the political middle to find the political system less appealing than others.

Our results suggest a fairly nuanced interpretation of the impact of individual-level differences on whether and how voters' experiences as winners and losers translate into different levels of positive and negative attitudes toward the political system. For one, the mediating effect of political predispositions is not ubiquitous. Thus, individual-level differences in terms of strength of partisanship or ideological extremism do not affect levels of winners' and losers' consent in all circumstances. However, in those cases where we find evidence of these mediating effects, they point to such predispositions acting as amplifiers rather than muting the winner–loser effect.

Specifically, we find that, when influential, strength of partisan attachment colors and modifies the extent to which electoral losses translate into negative evaluations of the political system's legitimacy among winners and losers. For example, winners who are strongly attached to their political party volunteer significantly more positive appraisals of the political system's performance than other winners. However, such effects are not quite as apparent among losers, though they do exist for them as well. This suggests that winners' feelings toward their own party help color their feelings toward the political system, while this is not quite as consistently the case for losers.

When it comes to ideological extremism, we found that it adds to the strain of losing and heightens the pleasure of winning. Thus, ideologues are particularly prone to view the system through the lens of winning and losing. However, as in the case of partisanship, while these effects can be documented, they are not universal. Taken together, then, these findings for partisanship and ideology suggest the following conclusions for understanding the winner–loser gap. First, voters bring political predispositions to the table that heighten the effect of winning and losing. Second, however, because such effects are not ubiquitous and because their substantive impact is moderate, they cannot serve as the sole explanation for the variations in the winner–loser gap in attitudes toward the political system. Given that, in the countries examined here, ideological outliers and strong partisans on average represent fewer than 20 percent of the population, other sources of cross-national variations in the winner–loser gap are worth considering as well. This is a question we turn to in our next chapter.

Winning and Losing in Old and New Democracies

As we argued at the outset, among the most critical aspects of understanding losers' reactions is the impact 'losing' has on political support. And as the previous chapters have demonstrated, those who vote for parties that are in government tend to exhibit higher levels of support for the political system than those who vote for parties that are part of the political opposition. In this chapter, we further explore this relationship by examining whether and how the effect of winning and losing is dependent on a country's political and historical context. Specifically, we compare the impact of losing on consent in old and new democracies.

We ask a simple question: is there any reason that the effect of winning and losing elections might be different in new democracies compared to older ones? As it turns out, several arguments can be raised to answer the question—and they might not all point in the same direction. For example, given that the experience of being among the winners or losers of elections is new in recently established democratic systems, the distinctions between winners and losers hypothesized for the established democracies may not yet exist in these contexts. Alternatively, this distinction may be much more powerful because losers have not yet learned that they will be in a position to become winners next time around. Similarly, losing may mean different things and may be of dissimilar importance, depending on the political cultural context of a nation. Losing and winning may be important in western democracies with individualist cultural values, but it may hold much less importance in collectivist cultures. Given that there are a number of ways to think about the utility of the winner–loser distinction, we investigate whether there is structural equivalence in attitudes among winners and losers in western, more established democracies and newer democratic states as well as in politically and culturally dissimilar ones.

LEARNING TO LOSE: COMPARING LOSERS' CONSENT IN OLD AND NEW DEMOCRACIES

The existing evidence, which shows that electoral losers generally have more negative attitudes toward politics and government, is open to challenge and extension on at least two fronts: first, because the rise of democratic systems and the experience of regular elections is a recent phenomenon in many countries around the globe (e.g. Eastern Europe, Latin America, Africa), much of the theorizing and the vast majority of empirical studies about system support in democracies has occurred with western systems and experiences in mind (for exceptions, see, for example, Finkel, Muller, and Seligson 1989; Seligson 1993; Lopez-Pina, McDonough, and Barnes 1994; Rohrschneider 1999). That is, scholars have examined variations in system support mostly on the basis of theories generated about, and data collected in, the democracies of Western Europe and North America rather than a random sample of contemporary democracies and usually not with an eye toward understanding the political dynamics of nascent democratic systems.

To assess the utility of the loser–winner distinction for explaining differences in attitudes toward government in differentially situated democracies, we therefore analyze people's attitudes toward government in a sample of contemporary democracies that varies on one crucial dimension: the novelty of the democratic political system. Bringing new democracies into the equation is especially important if one wants to give more weight to the idea that it is the political behavior and reactions of losers more than winners that are crucial for an understanding of the state of democracy (Nadeau and Blais 1993). In most stable democracies citizens have become accustomed to the experience of winning and losing as the fortunes of parties shift over time. As a result of this learning process, citizens understand that winning really is the precursor of losing, as parties that win an election tend to lose votes already at the next election (Paldam and Skott 1995; Stevenson 2002). This is consistent with the results presented in Chapter 4, that losing has a more significant impact after the second rather than first loss. In contrast, citizens in new democracies will not have experienced winning and losing—and losers, therefore, may not have learned how to lose gracefully. As a consequence, the experience of losing in new democracies may be less tempered than the comparable experience in mature democracies.

There are two quite different sources that may underlie the stronger feelings of losers in new democracies. The first has to do with the consequences of democracy and elections for structuring and reorienting power relations in a newly democratized society; the second with the novelty of the democratic experience and predictions for the future. In terms of the theoretical model that underlies our analyses, this means that the old versus new democracies distinction we examine in this chapter relates to the two dimensions of mediating factors (individuals and institutions). Viewed from the macro-level, there are cross-national differences produced by variations in political cultures and histories, as well as the novelty of democratic institutions, that may attenuate or intensify the experience of losing. Viewed from the perspective of individual citizens, there are individual-level differences in the sense that losing can be learned when experienced over time and is experienced by different kinds of losers; both of these may modify the way losing is translated into attitudes toward the government (Anderson and Tverdova 2001; see also Rohrschneider 1999).

The most obvious explanation for why we may expect the winner–loser gap to differ across old and new democracies comes from the fact that a sizable chunk of losers in such societies may be drawn from a pool of voters who were guaranteed to be winners in the old, nondemocratic, system. Supporters of the old Communist parties in Central and Eastern Europe come to mind as a group representing this category. For this group, as well as more generally for those who are used to winning, the experience of losing a democratic election may be especially hard, and may lead to a low level of support for all aspects of the political system. We could call this the 'big loser' argument. Somewhat paradoxically, big losers might also be found on the winning side if parties that represent the nondemocratic past form the government in the new democracies. We expect this group to have lower levels of political support than winners who cast their vote for parties that do not represent the nondemocratic past because winning in a democratic system might be viewed as second best only to completely dominating a polity and being guaranteed power.

Another reason for the gap to differ is that elections in new democracies frequently are contests between widely divergent ideologies and struggles over how the country should be run or the system be set up. Maybe more importantly, during the initial phase of transition, elections often set the rules for who has access to power or who gets to change these rules in favor of those currently in power (Boix 1999). Not surprisingly, the aftermath of founding elections frequently brings about efforts to introduce changes in electoral systems that would benefit the current incumbents. Simply put, in a nascent democracy, being the minority and majority can be expected to weigh more heavily because citizens are less sure when and whether that there will be another opportunity to determine who has the power to rule and who does not.

Moreover, in new democracies the outputs produced by different political camps are likely to constitute more divergent visions of the good society than in more established ones. As a result, not being among the majority in a new democracy creates a more acute sense of lacking a stake in the system than in an older democracy. Consequently, we expect that legitimacy beliefs are more strongly affected by allegiance to those in power. In the context of the present study, this would suggest that being in the minority or majority should have a stronger effect in newer democracies relative to mature ones. Based on these considerations, we expect to find an interaction between minority and majority status on one hand and length of democratic experience on the other: the more recent the establishment of democratic institutions, the more powerful the effect of winning and losing should be on beliefs about government.

The second aspect that may underlie the stronger feelings of losers in new democracies compared with old democracies is the process of learning that occurs at the individual level. Given that individuals develop expectations about the political system over time, citizens' beliefs about the predictability of political processes will affect their attitudes toward the system (Evans and Whitefield 1993; Whitefield and Evans 1994; Anderson and O'Connor 2000). Specifically, citizens in established and new democracies undergo distinctly different learning and socialization processes (Mishler and Rose 2002). While pre-adult socialization within a democratic country as well as the habitual behavior of participation in democratic elections predisposes citizens in established democracies to develop positive attitudes toward the political system (Easton 1957; see also Mishler and Rose 2002; Plutzer 2002), citizens in newly established democracies have not undergone such socialization. This means that the break with the authoritarian past forces these citizens to learn democracy from the ground up. Under conditions of uncertainty about the consequences of transition, including the democratic transition, learning democracy may be particularly unpleasant for electoral losers. Only after some time has passed and citizens have gone through an accumulation of experience of transition should we expect losers to be somewhat sanguine about their loss (see also Whitefield and Evans 1994). After some time has passed, this is likely to lead to greater stability: 'Constitutions that are observed and last for a long time are those that reduce the stakes of political battles. Pretenders to office can expect to reach it; losers can expect to come back' (Przeworski 1991: 36).

That is, depending on where citizens are along the learning curve, they may view the role and outcomes of elections in a democratic system very differently. The longer democracy has been the status quo, the higher the individual citizen's subjective probability that there will be another election in the future and the greater the certainty about when that election will be held. Knowing that another election will come to pass makes any one election win or loss comparatively less consequential for citizens of established democracies. The experience of routine elections and the peaceful transfer of power they ensure reinforces for citizens in older democracies that any one election outcome will not fundamentally reorient the relations of power or the outcomes produced by the system.[1] Put simply, losing can be learned.[2] Thus, even for

[1] To be sure, we would expect idiosyncracies in citizens' learning curves at the individual level, depending on their cognitive sophistication or political interest, and because of differences in personal experiences with democracy resulting from generational differences. However, in the aggregate, democratic longevity is assumed to affect all citizens in similar ways because of a reorientation of the country's political culture (Almond and Verba 1963; Dahl 1989).

[2] In addition, there is the possibility that, aside from being the result of learning, democratic values can be spread through processes of diffusion (Rohrschneider 1999). As Rohrschneider's research on the East and West German case shows, however, changes and differences in democratic values having to do with tolerance and pluralism are likely to be the result of institutional learning rather than diffusion.

new democratic losers who vote for parties without links to the old power structure, losing might not be easy when measured against expectations that the democratic revolution created, and negative reactions might be more prevalent than among losers in mature democracies where experiences of shifting political fortunes have accumulated over the years, teaching citizens to lose without blaming the institutions and principles of democracy, or at least be tempered in such reactions.

At the same time, these expectations of a larger winner–loser gap in new relative to old democracies may be offset by expectations generated by differences in cultural orientations or the particulars of the political situation in a country. For example, as we mentioned above, differences in political cultures and values across countries may make winning and losing less consequential, depending on the cultural context. For example, losing and winning may be important in western democracies with individualist cultural values, but it may hold much less import in collectivist cultures. Similarly, new democracies typically undergo periods of orientation and volatility in political parties, party systems, governing coalitions, and structures of government, which often are in a fluid state. This may well serve to reduce citizens' ability to identify who is a winner and who is a loser—that is, the transparency of the new system—as well as the saliency of winning or losing and, as a result, may reduce the difference we can expect between winners and losers. Which perspective carries the day is, in the end, an empirical question which we tackle next.

DIMENSIONS OF LOSERS' CONSENT IN OLD AND NEW DEMOCRACIES

The data for our comparison of winners and losers in old and new democracies come from the 1999 European Values Study, which includes nearly all countries in Europe—East and West—thirty-three in total. This particular set of surveys has unusually broad coverage in terms of the political support items included in the survey and that are relevant to our concerns. Moreover, by relying on this particular set of European countries we are able to control for a variety of factors that might affect responses, such as differences in political cultures, histories, or institutions. As a result, the comparison of old and new European democracies allows us to zoom in on the conceptually critical old–new distinction while controlling for other factors.

This set of countries includes eighteen old democracies and fifteen postcommunist countries. To differentiate among them beyond the simple old–new dichotomy, we classify these thirty-three countries in a fourfold table following criteria set forward in earlier work by Klingemann (1999) and Mishler and Rose (2001). The classification has two dimensions: experiences of regime change in the last twenty years (yes or no), and the democracy rating of the Freedom House index (Freedom House, 2001). This allows us to divide the countries

TABLE 6.1. *Classification of countries by change of regime and levels of freedom*

	Free Freedom House index ≤2.5	Partly free/not free Freedom House index >2.5
No regime change last twenty years	*Stable democracies* France Great Britain West Germany Austria Italy Spain Portugal Netherlands Belgium Denmark Sweden Finland Iceland Ireland Northern Ireland Greece Luxembourg Malta	*Stable nondemocracies*
Regime change	*New democracies* East Germany Estonia Latvia Lithuania Poland Czech Republic Slovakia Hungary Romania Bulgaria Slovenia	*Transitional regimes* Croatia Russia Ukraine Belarus

Notes: The classification is based on Klingemann (1999), Mishler and Rose (2001), and the freedom scores for appropriate years as published by Freedom House (2001).

into two groups: free (index value of 2.5 or lower) and partly free or not free (index value higher than 2.5). In Table 6.1 we show that eighteen countries can be classified as stable democracies, eleven countries as new democracies, and four countries are listed as transitional regimes. Using this classification scheme reveals that none of the countries fall in the category of 'stable non-democracies'.[3] Taken together, then, this means that our group of thirty-three

[3] In the study by Mishler and Rose (2001), which made use of the World Values Survey with global coverage, five countries (India, Mexico, Taiwan, Turkey, and Venezuela) were located in this category. In a slight deviation from Mishler and Rose (2001) we count Spain as a stable democracy—as we do with Portugal and Greece. This follows from applying the criterion of

countries falls into three categories: stable democracies, new democracies, and transitional regimes.

Among the new democratic countries, at the time the survey data were collected Bulgaria (2.3) and Romania (2.2) had relatively low Freedom House scores that bring them close to the cutoff point for the criterion variable of free versus not free. The Freedom House scores for the countries that are classified as transitional regimes were 3.4 for the Ukraine, 4.4 for Croatia, 4.5 for Russia, and 6.6 for Belarus. Looking at the trend for the years after the collection of data (1999), we see a negative development for Russia and Belarus, with only the latter becoming classified by Freedom House as 'not free'. Croatia is the only one of the four countries that moves in a positive direction during this time, passing the threshold to free (a somewhat more detailed description of these classifications is given by Listhaug and Ringdal 2004).

The dependent variable in this study is the gap between winners and losers, with an emphasis on losers, on measures of political support. Winners and losers are coded on the basis of a vote intention question, and the coding of parties into winners and losers is described in Appendix 6A.1. We start by describing these differences for the three groups of countries in Table 6.1. The purpose of this description is twofold. First, we want to find out if the expected gap between winners and losers exists in the first place; and second, to get the first piece of evidence to judge the merits of the hypothesis that the gap is in fact larger in new democracies than in stable democratic systems.

Before we venture too far afield, the hypothesis that winners and losers are different with respect to political support needs to be further qualified according to which aspect of political support we are discussing. Thinking of support for the political system along a continuous dimension from specific to general (diffuse) support, it may be tempting to say that losers' consent is more crucial with regard to regime principles and political community rather than particular actors or institutions if we are concerned about the state of democracy and the political system in a country. In fact, given that democratic principles are almost universally accepted around the globe, including undemocratic countries (cf. Klingemann 1999), it would be particularly important to find that there is a gap in support for democratic principles between winners and losers. At the same time, however, it may be the immediate dissatisfaction of the losers with existing political arrangements, rather than a dislike of democracy per se, that poses the greatest threat to democratic stability. At this point, we consider

a period of twenty years since regime change, but the decision is also in line with the conventional view on the state of democracies in these countries. In Western Europe a question mark could be used for the classification of Northern Ireland. The country is not a completely sovereign state and has at different points been subject to political rule that many would consider nondemocratic in some form or other.

it an open question if the difference between winners and losers is variable across different dimensions of political support.

Support for the Political Regime

We first examine people's attitudes toward the political regime, its institutions, and performance. As a stylized fact, it is true that the new democracies examined here are post-communist countries that switched to some form of democratic government during and after the revolution of 1989 and onwards. At the same time, in some cases, like Hungary and Poland, we could argue that the democratization process started a few years before. Thus, it should not be forgotten that all transitions from dictatorship to democracy have their peculiar characteristics and trajectories, and these paths may in turn also have influences on how winners and losers perceive and evaluate the new political order. While we are aware that our study thus is limited in its ability to generalize to all new democracies, variation within the group of post-communist countries allows us to study if losers' consent is different in different types of post-communist countries.

In a recent study of political support in new, or incomplete, democracies, Mishler and Rose (2001) argue that 'idealist' measures of support for democracy that come from the political culture tradition are of little value in assessing the state of things in the new democracies as citizens have had little time to experience the new forms of government. As an alternative to political culture measures—ones based on support for democracy as an ideal—they propose comparisons with the past: 'While citizens may have little knowledge of democratic principles they have a lifetime experience with undemocratic regimes. At the start of a new regime, the natural tendency is to evaluate the new regime by comparisons with the regime it has replaced' (Mishler and Rose 2001: 306). The idea to measure support in this manner is simple and intuitively meaningful, and will be added to the list of the traditional support variables to see how much this conceptualization contributes beyond what we get from the traditional measures.

We thus begin with the rating of the current regime as compared to the past, based on a question that elicits people's views on the differences between the current political system versus the previous regime on a scale ranging from −9 (previous regime very good and current regime very bad) to +9 (previous regime very bad and current regime very good). We should add that this comparison is qualitatively different in the two major groups of systems. Whereas in post-communist states the comparison is between the current democratic system and the communist system, in stable democracies the comparison is between the system as it is today as compared to ten years ago. In both cases we expect a positive difference in mean responses to this question between winners and losers, and Figure 6.1 demonstrates that this is what we find.

Differences in Losers' Consent

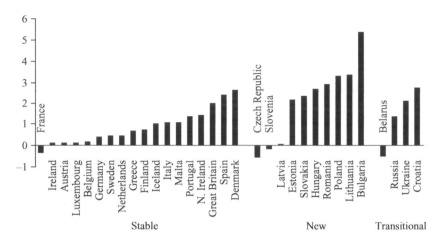

FIGURE 6.1. Winner–loser gap in support for new versus old regime

There are four exceptions to this pattern: France among stable democracies, the Czech Republic and Slovenia among new democracies and Belarus among transitional regimes. Thus, in twenty-nine of the thirty-three countries, winners had more positive evaluations of the current regime. At the same time, however, we find that is considerable variation within the groups in terms of the size of the winner–loser gap.

At this point, it does not make much sense to try to explain the exceptions and variations in too much detail unless we find that the same countries also constitute exceptions on other support items and unless we were to confirm these gaps to be statistically and substantively significant. Suffice it to say that, in those countries where the gap is (unexpectedly) negative, it is also quite small. Thus, overall, it may be safer to say that we see countries where there is a gap and where there seems to be none—for example, among the stable democracies, the gap is small in Ireland, Austria, Luxembourg, and Belgium and sizable in Denmark, Spain, and Great Britain. Similarly, among the new democracies, the winner–loser gap is small in Slovenia and Latvia and very large in Bulgaria, Lithuania, and Poland.

On the key question of whether the gap between winners and losers is larger in new democracies, a quick eyeballing of the graph suggests that the gap is larger in new democracies and transitional regimes than in stable democracies. However, the data in Figure 6.1 are not designed to provide clinching evidence, given that the comparison between new democracies and transitional regimes and stable democracies can be somewhat misleading on this dimension as the frame of comparison is between the current regime and past communism for the former group, and between the current system and the (same) democratic system ten years ago for stable democracies. The results for the remaining

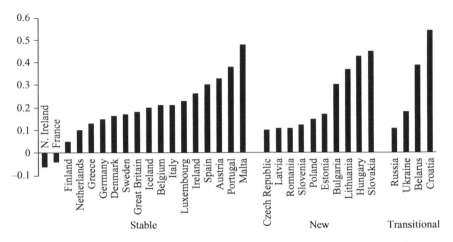

FIGURE 6.2. Winner–loser gap in support for parliament

indicators of political support are more directly comparable as they have the same substantive reference across systems.

Next, we consider support for a critical regime institution—parliament—based on a question asking people to express their level of confidence in parliament on a scale ranging from 1 (none at all) to 4 (a great deal). Given that the scale and reference points for this support question are directly comparable across all countries in the study, we can compare the absolute size of the winner–loser gap across countries and groups of countries. The data reveal that the winner–loser gap is largest in Croatia (Figure 6.2) and especially sizable in countries such as Malta, Slovakia, and Hungary. In contrast the gap is quite small in Finland, the Netherlands, the Czech Republic, Latvia, Romania, and Russia. The results show that the gap in mean responses between winners and losers on support for parliament is positive in all countries except for France and Northern Ireland, which are weakly on the negative side, thus indicating the usefulness of the winner–loser distinction across countries and types of democracies.

Next, we examine the gap in evaluations of regime performance, or confidence in regime processes, as operationalized by a question that measures citizens' satisfaction with how democracy is developing on a scale ranging from 1 (not at all satisfied) to 4 (very satisfied) (for question wording, see the appendix to this book). As in the case of confidence in parliament, the gap is substantial in Malta (Figure 6.3) but also in Bulgaria and Croatia. In contrast, countries such as Denmark, Northern Ireland, the Netherlands, Finland, and Portugal (among the old democracies) and Latvia, Slovenia and Belarus (among the new democracies and transitional regimes) have somewhat small gaps. Yet, overall, the data show that exceptions to the hypothesized pattern

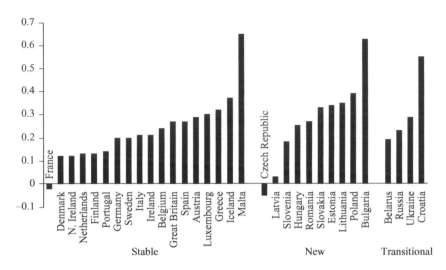

FIGURE 6.3. Winner–loser gap in evaluation of political system

are few and far between. Only France and the Czech Republic are marginally on the negative side (with losers expressing higher levels of satisfaction).

While it is generally not a good strategy to explain away deviating cases with post facto arguments, there may be substantively interesting explanations for some of the deviations. France, where the winner–loser gap is consistently reversed, is obviously a case in point as it is a case of divided government with the left in control in parliament and a popularly elected president from the right (Chirac). For this analysis, we have counted the left as in-parties (winners) based on the argument that the French parliamentary government is now more powerful than the president although it is obvious that *cohabitation* muddles the distinction between winning and losing. Clearly, the data suggest that the president is more powerful than the prime minister in the minds of the voters. Incidentally, such an interpretation is consistent with research on economic voting, which shows that French voters are more likely to hold the President accountable for the state of the economy than the Prime Minister as a representative of the parliamentary majority (cf. Anderson 1995; Lewis-Beck and Nadeau 2000).

So far, then, the evidence quite clearly supports the contention that losers exhibit more negative attitudes toward the political regime, its institutions, and its performance. Whether this gap in consent extends all the way up the political support hierarchy to basic principles of democratic governance is a question we investigate next.

Support for Democratic Principles

Moving to the most general end of the political support dimension, we examine how winning and losing are related to support for democratic principles. Support for democratic principles is a composite measure of eight items that includes general support for democracy, the rejection of alternatives to democracy (strong leader, army, experts), and rejection of criticisms of democracy (see the appendix to this book for details about the survey questions). We created an index for support of democratic principles by summing the values for the dichotomized items (1: positive; 0: negative). This index ranges from a minimum value of 0 to a maximum value of 8.

Figure 6.4, which graphs the winner–loser gap across the countries in our study, shows that losers are less supportive of democratic principles than winners. In fact, the winner–loser gap is particularly large in Bulgaria, Slovakia, and Romania, as well as Malta. At the same time, however, exceptions to this rule are slightly more numerous than for the other, more specific, dimensions of political support investigated above, as the number of countries without much of a gap or even a negative one is larger than before (e.g. stable democracies: Netherlands, Great Britain, Sweden, Iceland, Luxembourg, Spain, Portugal, Ireland; new democracies: Slovenia, the Czech Republic, Lithuania, Latvia; transitional regimes: Croatia, Belarus).

Moreover, a quick inspection of the winner–loser gap across the types of democracies suggests that the differences between winners and losers are larger

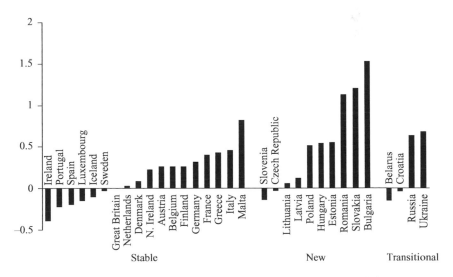

FIGURE 6.4. Winner–loser gap in support for democratic principles

in new democracies than in the mature democratic systems. Thus, overall, an analysis of the winner–loser gap in support for democratic principles shows that this gap does, indeed, exist for this dimension of system support as well; however, it is somewhat less consistent than with regard to other dimensions.

COMPARING LOSERS' CONSENT IN OLD AND NEW DEMOCRACIES

Having demonstrated that losers generally have lower system support than winners, and having hinted that the gap is larger in new than in old democracies, our next step is to be more precise in fixing these effects. We make a first attempt at this by comparing the mean levels of support for winners and losers on the four support variables across the three categories of political systems (Table 6.2). A quick horizontal comparison establishes the finding that support is higher in stable democracies than in new democracies and transitional regimes (for more details, see Listhaug and Aardal 2003).

TABLE 6.2. *Mean levels of political support by type of country and winner/loser status*

	Stable democracies	New democracies	Transitional regimes
Difference of current political system versus previous regimes			
Winners	0.55	0.87	−0.01
	(N = 5,482)	(N = 2,675)	(N = 434)
Losers	−0.41	−0.78	−2.00
	(N = 5,527)	(N = 4,029)	(N = 1,782)
eta coefficients	0.208	0.220	0.218
Confidence in parliament			
Winners	2.55	2.29	2.32
	(N = 5,925)	(N = 2,751)	(N = 450)
Losers	2.33	2.03	1.95
	(N = 5,990)	(N = 4,088)	(N = 1,833)
eta coefficients	0.140	0.164	0.177
Satisfaction with how democracy is developing			
Winners	2.81	2.40	2.16
	(N = 5,796)	(N = 2,755)	(N = 435)
Losers	2.51	2.19	1.76
	(N = 5,855)	(N = 4,128)	(N = 1,799)
eta coefficients	0.181	0.144	0.206
Democratic principles			
Winners	6.40	5.63	5.69
	(N = 4,936)	(N = 2,065)	(N = 293)
Losers	6.26	5.22	5.38
	(N = 5,023)	(N = 2,967)	(N = 1,201)
eta coefficients	0.043	0.113	0.064

Notes: For coding and question wording, see the appendix to this book.

Source: European Values Study (1999).

The results also show that winners are always more positive in their attitudes toward the political system, regardless of the dimension of support and regardless of whether respondents live in a stable democracy, a new democracy, or a country with a transitional regime. Moreover, comparing losers' responses across types of systems, we find that, on every dimension of support, losers in less democratic countries are less enthusiastic about democracy and the democratic political system. Comparing across types of support, the data show that the winner–loser gap is least pronounced when it comes to support for democratic principles. This latter finding is not entirely surprising, as other researchers have found that support for democracy as a form of government tends to be very high and nearly unanimous around the globe, regardless of type of system in place. Yet, here too, we find a gap between winners and losers.

Overall, there seems to be a bifurcation in the patterns of winners' and losers' support between stable democracies on one hand and new democracies and transitional regimes on the other. A comparison of the size of the gap between winners and losers, as indicated by the values of the eta coefficients, shows that the gap is larger in post-communist states than in established democracies. While the pattern is not perfectly consistent in the case of people's satisfaction with regime processes (how democracy is developing), overall the evidence supports the notion that losing is harder in countries with more recent democratic experiences.

Given that a large number of factors have been found to influence political support in previous research, the question becomes whether the differences we have found so far hold up once we control for these potential influences on political support measures. We turn to this analysis in the next section by constructing a proper multivariate individual-level model of support that includes a number of control variables. In addition to the primary analytical variables relating to losing and the interaction between losing and political context, the model includes variables that tap the likely effects of ideology, performance, and demographic factors.[4]

The results are presented in Table 6.3. Please note that the effect for losers in stable democracies is the effect for the dummy variable losers in the model, given that the impact of the interaction term of losers and type of democracy

---

[4] 'Left' is a dummy variable for traditional leftist policy positions on support for state control of the economy and redistribution, and 'right' is a dummy variable indicating support for market policies and freedom from state intervention (see the appendix to this book for survey questions). This means that those with centrist policy positions are in the reference category. The standard hypothesis would be that an individual's ideological location relative to the partisan composition of government—that is, as the policy distance between citizens and government—will determine political support. In the current analysis we investigate the effect of ideology (measured by the two dummy variables) without considerations of the ideological position of government parties and hence simply include them as control variables.

TABLE 6.3. *Multivariate analysis of political support (OLS estimates)*

	Difference of current political system versus previous regime		Confidence in parliament		Satisfaction with how democracy is developing		Democratic principles	
	b	Beta	b	Beta	b	Beta	b	Beta
Constant	−1.477		2.025		2.382		4.948	
New democracies and transitional regimes	0.382	0.063**	−0.182	−0.112**	−0.315	−0.203**	−0.644	−0.179**
Losers	−0.988	−0.163**	−0.195	−0.120**	−0.231	−0.149**	−0.092	−0.026*
Nonvoters	−1.171	−0.129**	−0.428	−0.178**	−0.328	−0.142**	−0.391	−0.070**
Left	−0.636	−0.086**	−0.080	−0.040**	−0.135	−0.071**	−0.323	−0.072**
Right	0.220	0.030**	0.005	0.003	0.063	0.034**	0.045	0.011
Household's income	0.035	0.029**	0.001	0.002	0.006	0.021**	0.057	0.081**
Life satisfaction	0.227	0.179**	0.038	0.112**	0.062	0.191**	0.078	0.099**
Concerned for immediate family	0.083	0.021**	−0.022	−0.027**	−0.005	−0.006	0.045	0.026**
Gender	0.157	0.026**	0.002	0.001	0.009	0.006	0.015	0.004
Education	0.147	0.042**	0.039	0.042**	−0.036	−0.040**	0.290	0.141**
Age	−0.007	−0.039**	0.004	0.081**	−0.001	−0.011	−0.002	−0.022**
Losers * New democracies/ trans. regimes	−0.575	−0.084**	−0.075	−0.041**	−0.045	−0.025*	−0.266	−0.063**
R^2	0.112		0.099		0.191		0.136	
N	18,221		19,096		18,857		15,332	

*$p < 0.05$.
**$p < 0.01$.

Notes: For coding and question wording, see the appendix to this book. Data are weighted.

Source: European Values Study (1999).

is 0 for this group (stable democracies are coded 0). For new democracies and transitional regimes (which are collapsed into one category in the multivariate analysis because the number of transitional regimes is small), the effect is the sum of the effect for losers and the interaction term (since these countries are coded 1).

First off, the results of the multivariate analysis confirms the existence of a winner–loser gap, even when we control for a host of factors thought to influence people's attitudes about democratic governance. The loser variable has a statistically significant influence on all measures of political support. Moreover, and as importantly, the results show that the interaction term is statistically significant and has a negative sign for all support variables. This confirms the bivariate findings reported in Table 6.2: the gap between winners and losers is significantly larger in the new democracies of Central and Eastern Europe relative to the stable democratic regimes of Western and Southern Europe. In fact, the interaction coefficient for the difference variable shows that the negative effect of losing on political support is largest with regard to evaluations of the current versus the old system, somewhat smaller with regard to support for democratic principles, followed by confidence in parliament and satisfaction with democratic performance.

Of the remaining variables in the model we find a consistent negative effect for voting participation, suggesting that nonvoters are less trusting than voters, regardless of winner–loser status. We also find that there is a negative effect of leftist policy positions on support while the effect of a rightist position is mostly positive, but much weaker. In an expanded analysis of these data and patterns, Listhaug and Aardal (2003) show that policy is more polarized in new democracies and transitional regimes than in stable democracies, with the left having lower support levels than the right. This is consistent with the interpretation that policy distance is important. In post-communist countries the leftist policy hegemony is broken and we expect that dissatisfaction on the left will be stronger than in mature democracies where citizens have not experienced equivalent policy dominance. Looking at the other control variables, we find that household income tends to increase support, and life satisfaction has the strongest positive effect on support while the effects of concerns for family are weak or inconsistent. The demographic variables have a weak impact, but we note a positive sizable effect of education on support for democratic principles.

Taken together, then, the analysis of system support in old and new democracies so far indicates that losing clearly has a negative effect on political support in all systems, but that the effect is more pronounced in post-communist countries than in stable democracies in Western Europe. Among the explanations we have offered for this difference was the notion that losers in new democracies have not yet learned to lose—that is, that they simply have not developed the experience necessary for behaving like graceful losers. And the stronger negative effect of losing that we find is consistent with this interpretation. Another explanation we have offered has to do with the types of losers living in post-communist countries. Specifically, we made the case that losing may be hardest for voters of the parties that were in power during the communist system, given that they went from being guaranteed winners to temporary (or not so temporary) losers.

Among this group of losers, these parties now exist in two main varieties: old style communist parties and reformed communists running under a new name (see Appendix 6A.1 for coding of parties). We expect that followers of these parties will have a weaker attachment to the democratic order than those who vote for other parties. More specifically, we expect that voters for old-style communist parties will have the lowest support levels, followed by reformed communists and then other parties. Moreover, because the communists had the benefit of hegemony under the old system, we expect that the differences between winner and losers will be stronger with regard to people's

TABLE 6.4. *Political support by type of party and winning/losing*

	Winners	Losers	Gap
A. *Difference of current political system versus previous regime*			
Old communist parties	−1.89	−3.84	1.95
	(N = 77)	(N = 946)	
Reformed communist parties	−2.10	−1.99	−0.11
	(N = 102)	(N = 1,107)	
Other parties	0.86	−0.47	1.33
	(N = 2,755)	(N = 3,239)	
B. *Confidence in parliament*			
Old communist parties	2.60	1.95	0.65
	(N = 77)	(N = 968)	
Reformed communist parties	2.42	2.00	0.42
	(N = 98)	(N = 1,122)	
Other parties	2.27	1.98	0.29
	(N = 2,853)	(N = 3,320)	
C. *Satisfaction with how democracy is developing*			
Old communist parties	2.44	1.71	0.73
	(N = 66)	(N = 952)	
Reformed communist parties	2.09	2.04	0.05
	(N = 107)	(N = 1,123)	
Other parties	2.35	2.07	0.28
	(N = 2,840)	(N = 3,303)	
D. *Support for democratic principles*			
Old communist parties	4.99	4.18	0.81
	(N = 47)	(N = 542)	
Reformed communist parties	5.42	4.85	0.57
	(N = 77)	(N = 841)	
Other parties	5.61	5.49	0.12
	(N = 2,103)	(N = 2,373)	

Notes: See Appendix 6A.2 for coding of communist parties; for coding and question wording, see the appendix to this book.

Source: European Values Study (1999).

evaluations of the present system relative to the communist past than with regard to evaluations of various aspects of the present system.

To examine the differences in support for the political system between communist winners and losers and supporters for other parties, we calculated mean levels of support for supporters of old communist parties, reformed communist parties, and all other parties for respondents in the post-communist countries only. The findings, laid out in Table 6.4, reveal mixed support for our hypotheses. For comparisons with the past we find a fairly consistent pattern in favor of the hypothesis. When they are among the losers, traditional communists have the most negative views when the present system is compared with the past, followed by the reformed communists and the voters for the other parties. This is also the pattern that we see among winners and losers, but this pattern is most apparent among the losers.

Except for the item measuring confidence in parliament, a similar pattern applies to the rank ordering of support levels among the supporters of different kinds of parties. Looking down the columns, when it comes to evaluations of regime performance (satisfaction with democracy) and support for democratic principles, supporters of old communist parties are the least positive (negative) in their expressions of support when they are among the losers.

Moreover, regardless of type of support item analyzed, when we rank order the various groups by support level we see that losers who support the old communist parties are the least supportive of all groups included in the analysis. In addition, we find that the gap between winners and losers is most pronounced for the supporters of the old communist parties. Clearly, these descriptive statistics suggest that losing is especially hard for the supporters of the parties of the old communist regime.

To assess the effect of party in a more comprehensive fashion, we estimate a set of models that take other relevant explanations into account. To arrive at a more satisfying statistical formulation, we use a model that is close, but not identical, to the model presented in Table 6.3. The model shown in Table 6.5 is estimated only for the set of new democracies and transitional regimes since it makes sense to estimate the effects of communists classified in the relevant categories only for these countries.

The findings provide quite consistent support for the 'big loser' hypothesis— that is, that the supporters of old communist parties take losing particularly hard. And as before, we find that losers express significantly more negative attitudes toward democratic governance. More importantly for the purposes of the big loser hypothesis, however, we find the expected rank order for three of the four support variables, with old communists reporting the lowest levels of support for the democratic system, followed by reformed communists. Using 'other parties' as the reference category, the coefficients for old communists and reformed communists show that old communists are significantly more disaffected than reformed communists, and both groups are significantly more disaffected than the supporters of other parties.

Interestingly, the impact of the party support variables is virtually zero when it comes to confidence in parliament. We speculate that there might be several explanations for this deviating finding. We know from the Russian experience that the communist party there has had considerable influence in the parliament and has used this institution as a base for attacks on the president. This experience—namely, that parliament can serve the interests of the old guard—might lead to a more positive judgment of this institution than of other aspects of the political system. Since Russia is a case where this argument is undoubtedly valid, we performed a separate analysis of the model in Table 6.5 for Russia. We find that Russian voters who support the Communist party have

Differences in Losers' Consent

TABLE 6.5. *Multivariate analysis of political support in former communist regimes (OLS)*

	Difference of current political system versus previous regime		Confidence in parliament		Satisfaction with how democracy is developing		Support for democratic principles	
	b	Beta	b	Beta	b	Beta	b	Beta
Constant	−1.780		2.150		2.046		4.371	
Losers	−1.261	−0.174**	−0.296	−0.184**	−0.265	−0.178**	−0.244	−0.065**
Old communists	−2.696	−0.223**	−0.001	0.000	−0.228	−0.091**	−0.990	−0.145**
Reformed communists	−1.432	−0.133**	0.031	0.013	−0.025	−0.011	−0.380	−0.070**
Nonvoter	−1.873	−0.188**	−0.461	−0.213**	−0.348	−0.172**	−0.417	−0.079**
Left	−0.715	−0.087**	−0.031	−0.017	−0.117	−0.069**	−0.422	−0.096**
Right	0.451	0.048**	−0.014	0.006	0.039	0.020	0.259	0.055**
Household's income	0.025	0.017	−0.002	−0.006	−0.001	−0.004	0.029	0.039**
Life satisfaction	0.222	0.154**	0.029	0.090**	0.058	0.194**	0.041	0.054**
Concerned for immediate family	0.278	0.070**	−0.042	−0.047**	0.004	0.005	0.173	0.087**
Gender	0.217	0.030**	−0.014	−0.009	0.025	0.017	0.006	0.002
Education	0.378	0.084**	−0.033	−0.032**	−0.020	−0.021	0.374	0.155**
Age	−0.004	−0.016	0.003	0.058**	0.000	0.005	−0.005	−0.044**
R^2	0.206		0.060		0.109		0.118	
N	8,208		8,437		8,369		6,145	

*$p < 0.05$.
**$p < 0.01$.

Notes: For coding and question wording, see the appendix to this book. Data are weighted.

Source: European Values Study (1999).

even more confidence in parliament compared to all old communists, with a *b*-coefficient of 0.121 (compared to −0.001 in Table 6.5). While the coefficient fails to achieve conventional levels of statistical significance, it stands out against the negative coefficients for the remaining support variables, which are equal to or stronger than the comparable effects in Table 6.5.

CONCLUSION

In this chapter, we examined the dimensions of losers' consent in old and new democracies. Specifically, we developed the idea that losing has stronger negative effects in new democracies relative to mature democracies since losers have not yet learned to lose in countries where democratic governance is of such recent vintage. Moreover, we investigated how the transition from dictatorship to democracy affects political support with an eye toward support for the new political system among supporters of the hegemonic Communist parties of the past who frequently find themselves in the opposition under the new system. Using data from the 1999 European Values Study we examined how support for the democratic system varies by winners and losers in eighteen old democracies and fifteen post-communist countries. Our results show that, with few exceptions, political losers have lower support levels than winners across all dimensions of political support that we investigate, including beliefs in core principles of democracy. Moreover, we find that the winner–loser gap is more prominent in newly democratized and democratizing states.

The data also indicated that the supporters of the old Communist parties exhibit significantly lower levels of support for the democratic system than voters for other parties, and in particular if they are not in power. This is not unexpected since the followers of these parties are the big losers in the sense that democracy replaced a system where winning was guaranteed. In an amendment to these core results, we found that voters for Communist parties are at least as confident in parliament as the supporters of non-communist parties. We speculate that this may be explained by the fact that Communist parties in some of the new democracies have been able to use parliament as a basis for a continued fight for their cause.

The finding that support for democratic principles was affected by the loser–winner distinction, and particularly so in new democracies, is sobering as it points to inexperienced losers as a particularly weak link in the chain of stable democratic governance. Not only do electoral losers in new democracies express particularly negative attitudes toward regime institutions and processes, they also are least likely to endorse democracy as a good way of governing their societies. Perhaps unsurprisingly, these negative views are exceptionally evident among supporters of the old regime—old, unreformed communist parties. These results point to the need to pay particular attention to this group of disaffected democrats among those concerned with the stability and legitimacy of the new democratic system. Efforts to win over the old-winners-turned-new-losers may be a particularly wise strategy in light of the findings we report in this chapter.

Most generally speaking, the results presented in this chapter speak to the notion that context—that is, broad historical trajectories and experiences that are somewhat path dependent—matters for understanding the way in which winning and losing translate into higher or lower levels of system support. Having experience with the electoral process and the fact that losing is part of the democratic game significantly shapes how voters respond. In the next chapter, we turn to a related set of macro-level factors—political institutions—that, we believe, also contribute to cross-national differences in the patterns of winners' and losers' consent.

APPENDIX 6A.1. *Coding of parties*

Country	Party	In gov?	Ideological index	Left–right self-placement
France	Extrême-gauche	Yes	17.8	2.6
	Parti communiste	Yes	19.4	2.7
	Parti socialiste	Yes	22.6	3.4
	Les Verts	Yes	20.8	4.1
	Autre écologistes	Yes	19.9	4.5
	Union pour la démocratie française	No	25.0	6.5
	Démocratice libérale	No	25.9	6.1
	Rassemblement Pour la Républicue	No	26.2	7.4
	Le Front National de Jean-Marie Le Pen	No	23.4	6.7
	Le Front National de Bruno Mégret	No	24.5	7.8
United Kingdom	Conservative	No	25.9	6.4
	Labour	Yes	22.1	4.5
	Liberal Democrat	No	21.4	4.8
	Social Democrat	No	27.0	5.0
	Plaid Cymru	No	23.7	5.0
	Scottish National Party	No	22.2	4.0
	Referendum Party	No	20.0	4.7
	UK Independence Party	No	24.9	6.0
	Green Party	No	19.8	4.2
Germany	Christian Democratic Union (CDU/CSU)	No	24.7	6.3
	Social Democratic Party (SPD)	Yes	24.2	4.4
	Free Democratic Party (FDP)	No	25.1	5.9
	Alliance '90/Green Party	Yes	23.8	4.2
	Party of Democratic Socialism (PDS)	No	19.7	3.3
	Republikaner	No	22.7	8.5
Austria	Social Democratic Party of Austria (SPÖ)	Yes	25.0	4.7
	Austrian People's Party (ÖVP)	Yes	26.9	6.2
	Freedom Party of Austria (FPÖ)	No	26.7	6.1
	Gruene	No	22.9	4.3
	Liberales Forum	No	27.1	4.9
	KPÖ	No	16.0	3.0
	DU–Lugner	No	26.7	6.6
Italy	Fiamma Tricol.	No	23.5	8.4
	AN	No	25.3	8.1
	CCD	No	23.9	6.1
	FI	No	25.7	7.0
	CDU	No	22.3	6.1
	Lega Nord	No	24.5	5.5
	Liste etn. loc.	No	23.3	5.5
	Radicali	No	25.7	4.7
	UDR	Yes	23.1	6.0
	Italian Renewal (RI)	Yes	25.4	5.4
	Italian Popular Party (PPI)	Yes	23.4	5.1
	Democratici	No	22.8	4.7
	SDI	Yes	22.7	3.6
	Verdi	Yes	23.2	4.8

APPENDIX 6A.1. (*Continued*)

Country	Party	In gov?	Ideological index	Left–right self-placement
	Democratici di sinistra	Yes	21.5	3.2
	Party of Italian Communists (PCDI)	Yes	19.0	3.6
	Rifond. comun.	No	18.2	2.9
Spain	PSOE	No	21.0	3.6
	PP	Yes	22.8	6.9
	IU	No	17.5	2.8
	PDNI	No	13.8	2.5
	Green	No	18.3	4.2
	BNG	No	17.7	4.1
	CC	No	25.5	6.3
	UPN	No	17.0	8.0
	HB-EH	No	14.3	2.1
	PNV	No	22.3	4.6
	EA	No	16.0	7.0
	CHA	No	16.5	4.5
	IC	No	15.7	2.3
	CiU	No	24.1	5.4
	ERC	No	26.0	2.0
	PA	No	15.7	4.5
	Unió Valenciana	No	17.0	4.4
Portugal	Bloco de esquerda (Left)	No	23.0	2.6
	CDS/PP (Social Democratic Christians)	No	22.3	7.1
	CDU/PCP (Communists)	No	20.9	2.9
	MRPP (Left-wing)	No	17.0	6.5
	PPD/PSD (Social Democrats)	No	22.0	7.1
	PS (Socialist Party)	Yes	21.6	4.8
	PSR (Left-wing)	No	20.5	5.3
Netherlands	PvdA	Yes	20.5	4.2
	CDA	No	21.5	6.2
	VVD	Yes	23.7	6.5
	D66	Yes	20.7	4.9
	Groen links	No	18.6	3.8
	SGP	No	22.1	7.1
	GPV	No	22.6	7.7
	RPF	No	19.5	6.5
	Socialistische Partij	No	18.5	4.2
	De groenen	No	22.0	5.5
Belgium	Agalev	No	18.9	4.7
	CVP	Yes	20.3	5.8
	VLD	No	22.1	5.9
	SP	Yes	18.0	4.0
	Vlaams Blok	No	20.8	6.5
	VU–ID 21	No	20.3	5.4
	WOW	No	14.3	5.0
	PVDA–AE	No	11.3	2.7
	Vivant	No	20.3	4.9
	PNPb	No	15.0	N/A

APPENDIX 6A.1. (*Continued*)

Country	Party	In gov?	Ideological index	Left–right self-placement
	PS	Yes	20.7	3.6
	PSC	Yes	22.0	6.0
	PRL–FDF–MCC	No	24.7	6.4
	Ecolo	No	20.0	4.5
	Front National	No	19.5	7.1
	AGIR	No	18.7	5.5
	PTB	No	5.5	3.3
Denmark	Social Democrats	Yes	21.7	4.9
	Social Liberals	Yes	23.6	5.2
	Conservatives	No	26.2	6.9
	Center Democrats	No	23.2	5.9
	Socialist People's Party	No	18.3	3.5
	Danish People's Party	No	27.6	7.1
	Christian People's Party	No	22.0	5.8
	Liberals	No	26.8	6.6
	Progress Party	No	21.0	6.2
	Unity List—Red–Green Alliance	No	13.5	2.3
Sweden	Center Party	No	24.9	6.3
	People's Party	No	25.9	6.3
	Christian Democrats (KD)	No	26.9	6.0
	The Green Party (MP)	No	23.2	4.8
	Moderates	No	29.7	7.7
	Social Democratic Party (S)	Yes	24.1	4.0
	Vänsterpartiet	No	21.1	3.0
Finland	Social Democratic Party of Finland	Yes	21.2	4.7
	Centre Party of Finland	No	24.0	6.7
	National Coalition Party	Yes	26.5	7.9
	Left Alliance	Yes	17.0	2.6
	Swedish People's Party in Finland	Yes	25.4	6.4
	Green League	Yes	22.0	5.3
	Christian League of Finland	No	21.3	6.7
	True Finns	No	21.4	5.6
	Reform Group	No	21.4	5.0
Iceland	Progressive Party	Yes	25.7	5.3
	Independence Party	Yes	27.9	7.5
	The Alliance	No	23.3	4.1
	Liberal Party	No	27.5	4.9
	Left—Greens	No	21.2	3.3
	Humanist Party	No	19.0	4.0
	The Christian Party	No	27.0	6.0
	Social Democratic Party	No	28.0	5.1
	People's Alliance	No	25.3	2.5
	Women's Alliance	No	20.0	4.0
Ireland	Fianna Fail	Yes	22.4	6.0
	Fine Gael	No	23.3	6.0
	Labour	No	24.3	4.8

APPENDIX 6A.1. (*Continued*)

Country	Party	In gov?	Ideological index	Left–right self-placement
	Progressive Democrats	Yes	23.3	5.7
	Sinn Fein	No	19.1	5.8
	Green Party	No	21.0	4.8
	Independent	No	21.2	5.3
Estonia	Estonian Social Democratic Labor Party (ESDTP)	No	18.5	5.1
	Estonian Center Party (EK)	No	17.8	5.5
	Estonian Coalition Party (EK)	No	19.8	6.2
	Estonian Christian People's Party (EKRP)	No	19.0	6.6
	Estonian Country People's Party (EME)	No	17.3	5.6
	Association of Pensioners and Families (APF)	No	17.9	6.2
	Estonian United People's Party (EURP)	No	17.0	5.3
	Estonian Reform Party (ER)	Yes	20.6	6.5
	Estonian Blue Party (SE)	No	23.7	5.4
	Pro Patria Union (IL)	Yes	21.1	7.0
	Estonian Rural Union (EM)	No	19.9	5.6
	Moderates (M)	Yes	19.5	6.1
	Farmers' Union (PK)	No	14.9	5.4
	Russian Party in Estonia (VEE)	No	16.0	4.5
	Russian Unity Party	No	18.5	4.9
Latvia	Latvia's Way (LC)	Yes	18.5	5.9
	National Harmony Party (NHP)	No	17.8	5.0
	The New Party (JP)	Yes	18.3	6.4
	Latvian Farmers' Union (LZS)	No	20.4	6.4
	Democratic Party 'Master' (DPS)	No	16.9	4.8
	National Movement for Latvia–Siegerist's Party (TKL–ZP)	No	13.0	6.0
	People's Party (TP)	No	18.9	6.4
	Alliance of Social Democrats of Latvia (LSDSP)	No	16.9	5.6
	For Fatherland and Freedom (TB)/Latvian National Independence Movement Union (LNNK)	Yes	18.0	7.2
Lithuania	Homeland Union/Lithuanian Conservatives (TS/LK)	Yes	26.0	8.6
	Christian Democratic Party of Lithuania (LKDP)	Yes	22.3	7.8
	Lithuanian Democratic Labor Party (LDDP)	No	19.6	3.7
	Lithuanian Center Union (LCS)	Yes	22.8	5.3
	Lithuanian Social Democratic Party (LSDP)	No	21.3	4.4
	Lithuanian Nationalist Party 'Young Lithuania' (LNP-JL)	No	23.9	6.0
	New Democracy–Women's Party (ND–MP)	No	21.4	4.2
	Christian Democratic Union (LKDS)	No	23.4	6.4
	Polish Election Action (LLRA)	No	23.0	5.0
	Lithuanian National Union (LTS)	No	29.5	6.0

APPENDIX 6A.1. *(Continued)*

Country	Party	In gov?	Ideological index	Left–right self-placement
	Lithuanian Democratic Party (LDP)	No	24.4	4.0
	Lithuanian Liberal Union (LLS)	No	22.2	5.4
	Lithuanian Peasants' Party (LVP)	No	21.0	4.8
	Lithuanian Russians Union (LRS)	No	19.0	4.0
	Lithuanian Political Prisoners' and Deported People's Union (LPKTS)	No	22.5	5.5
	Lithuanian Freedom Union (LLS)	No	27.2	5.0
	Lithuanian Party of Economy (LUP)	No	18.5	7.0
	Lithuanian Freedom League (LLL)	No	21.0	5.0
	Lithuanian Socialist Party (LSP)	No	26.5	2.0
	Logic of Life Party (LGLP)	No	6.0	4.7
	Lithuanian People's Party (LLP)	No	19.0	5.0
	Lithuanian Green Party (LZP)	No	23.3	4.7
	Independence Party (NP)	No	20.0	5.0
	Lithuanian Party of Justice (LTP)	No	16.0	6.0
	Movement 'Election 96'	No	19.5	5.0
	New Union—Social Liberals (NS–SL)	No	17.4	4.0
	National Democratic Party	No	18.0	4.0
Poland	Solidarity Election Action (AWS)	Yes	19.9	7.6
	Polish Peasants' Party (PSL)	No	19.6	5.3
	Movement for the Reconstruction of Poland (ROP)	No	20.1	6.1
	Alliance of the Democratic Left (SLD)	No	19.9	3.4
	Union of Real Politics (UPR)	No	25.6	5.2
	Union of Labor (UP)	No	21.8	5.0
	Union of Freedom (UW)	Yes	22.1	6.0
	National Party of Senior Citizens and Pensioners (KPEiR)	No	21.3	5.2
	Non-Party Bloc for the Support of Reforms (BBWR)	No	19.4	7.1
Czech Republic	Czech Social Democratic Party (CSSD)	Yes	21.5	4.7
	Czech People's Social Party (CSNS)	No	21.5	7.0
	Christian Democratic Union—Czechoslovak People's Party (KDU–CSL)	No	22.6	6.9
	Democratic Union DEU	No	22.5	6.3
	Pensioners for a Secure Life (DZJ)	No	21.0	5.6
	Communist Party of Bohemia and Moravia (KSCM)	No	19.4	2.7
	Moravian Democratic Party (MDS)	No	24.0	6.0
	Independents (N)	No	23.6	5.9
	Civic Democratic Party (ODS)	No	25.3	8.0
	Citizens' Coalition–Political Club (OK–PK)	No	28.5	6.5
	Assembly for the Republic—Czechoslovak Republican Party (SPR–RSC)	No	19.1	5.0

APPENDIX 6A.1. (*Continued*)

Country	Party	In gov?	Ideological index	Left–right self-placement
	Green Party (SZ)	No	21.0	6.0
	Freedom Union (US)	No	24.5	7.2
Slovakia	Democratic Party (DS)	Yes	23.8	6.7
	Democratic Union (DU)	Yes	20.9	5.4
	Movement for a Democratic Slovakia (HZDS)	No	18.7	4.9
	Communist Party of Slovakia (KSS)	No	16.0	3.3
	Christian Democratic Movement (KDH)	Yes	19.9	6.2
	Slovak National Party (SNS)	No	19.1	5.6
	Social Democratic Party of Slovakia (SDSS)	Yes	20.5	4.8
	Party of the Democratic Left (SDL)	Yes	18.8	3.5
	Hungarian Coalition Party (SMK)	Yes	19.2	6.2
	Party of Civil Understanding (SOP)	Yes	18.7	5.0
	Party of Entrepreneurs and Professionals (SPZ)	No	29.5	5.0
	Green Party of Slovakia (SZS)	Yes	22.0	6.2
	Entrepreneurs and Farmers Union (UZPR)	No	12.0	3.0
	Association of Workers of Slovakia (ZRS)	No	14.0	5.6
	Slovak Democratic Coalition (SDK)	Yes	21.5	5.6
Hungary	Hungarian Democratic Forum (MDF)	Yes	19.4	6.3
	Alliance of Free Democrats (SzDSz)	No	22.6	5.0
	Independent Smallholders' Party (FKgP)	Yes	21.2	6.2
	Alliance of Young Democrats–Hungarian Civic Party (FIDESZ–MPP)	Yes	22.1	6.1
	Christian Democratic People's Party (KDNP)	No	21.2	4.7
	Hungarian Socialist Party (MSzP)	No	19.9	4.3
	Party of Hungarian Truth and Life (MIÉP)	No	20.0	6.9
	Workers' Party (MP)	No	16.6	4.3
Romania	Democratic Convention of Romania (CDR)	Yes	26.8	7.1
	Romanian Party of Social Democracy (PDSR)	No	21.6	5.1
	Democratic Party (PD)	Yes	22.0	5.7
	National Peasant Christian Democratic Party (PNTCD)	Yes	26.8	7.5
	National Liberal Party (PNL)	Yes	24.0	7.4
	Democratic Alliance of Hungarians in Romania (UDMR)	Yes	23.0	5.0
	Great Romania Party (PRM)	No	21.9	5.1
	Social Democratic Party of Romania (PSDR)	Yes	23.0	3.3
	Romanian National Unity Party (PUNR)	No	24.0	5.0
	Alliance for Romania (ApR)	No	23.0	5.8
	Union of Right Forces (UFD)	Yes	25.0	7.8
	Gypsi (Romani) Party (PR)	No	30.5	8.0
	Socialist Party/Socialist Labor Party (PS/PSM)	No	27.4	1.0
	Ecologists (PER)	Yes	28.0	10.0
	CDR as a whole	Yes	17.7	9.5
Bulgaria	Union of Democratic Forces (SDS)	Yes	24.6	7.7
	People's Union (NS)	Yes	25.5	5.9
	Bulgarian Socialist Party (BSP)	No	18.4	3.3

APPENDIX 6A.1. (*Continued*)

Country	Party	In gov?	Ideological index	Left–right self-placement
	Bulgarian Euro-left (BEL)	No	20.3	4.1
	Bulgarian Business Block (BBB)	No	19.6	4.0
	Movement for Rights and Freedoms (DPS)	No	22.6	6.0
	Bulgarian Communist Party (BKP)	No	33.0	1.0
	Liberal-Democratic Union (LDU)	No	19.0	6.0
	Federation 'Bulgarian Kingdom' (FCB)	No	30.3	6.0
	Bulgarian Social Democratic Party (BSDP)	Yes	20.3	5.0
	Bulgarian Agrarian National Union (BZNS)	Yes	26.0	4.5
	Internal Macedonian Revolutionary Organization (VMRO)	No	20.0	N/A
Croatia	Action of Social Democrats of Croatia (ASH)	No	20.7	4.3
	Dalmatian Action (DA)	No	15.0	2.0
	Croatian Party of Rights (HSP)	No	22.0	10.0
	Croatian Democratic Union (HDZ)	Yes	23.2	6.2
	Croatian Christian Democratic Union (HKDU)	No	25.5	6.4
	Croatian Christian Democratic Party (HKDS)	No	21.8	6.8
	Croatian People's Party (HNS)	No	21.5	5.3
	Croatian Popular Party (HPS)	No	25.0	5.5
	Croatian Peasant Party (HSS)	No	22.6	5.2
	Croatian Social Liberal Party (HSLS)	No	23.9	4.9
	Croatian Party of Rights (HSP)	No	22.6	6.4
	Croatian Party of Rights 1861 (HSP 1861)	No	21.0	7.7
	Croatian Party of Pensioners (HSU)	No	24.8	5.0
	Independent Croatian Democrats (HND)	No	19.0	6.0
	Istrian Democratic Assembly (IDS)	No	23.3	4.0
	Liberal Party (LS)	No	24.4	4.1
	Primorian–Goranian Union (PGS)	No	29.4	4.3
	Social Democratic Party of Croatia (SDP)	No	22.7	4.1
	Social Democratic Union (SDU)	No	21.0	4.0
Greece	Socialistic Party	Yes	20.3	4.7
	Conservative	No	21.2	7.8
	Communists	No	18.0	2.9
	Left-Wing Communists	No	19.0	3.8
	Left-Wing Socialists	No	18.9	4.5
	Right Wing	No	19.5	6.4
Russia	Agrarian Party of Russia (APR)	No	19.1	4.7
	Communist Party of the Russian Federation (KPRF)	No	16.6	3.3
	Liberal-Democratic Party of Russia (LDPR)	No	18.7	5.5
	Our Home is Russia (NDR)	Yes	19.3	6.4
	New Force	No	21.1	5.9
	Fatherland	No	20.0	5.5
	Right-Wing Bloc	No	24.8	7.2
	Russian All-People's Union (ROS)	No	21.7	4.5
	Russian National Unity (RNU)	No	13.2	5.1

APPENDIX 6A.1. (*Continued*)

Country	Party	In gov?	Ideological index	Left–right self-placement
	Working Russia	No	14.8	4.6
	Honour and Motherland	No	19.3	5.1
	Yabloko	No	20.3	5.5
Malta	Nationalist Party	Yes	24.2	6.6
	Malta Labour Party	No	20.3	4.9
	Alternattiva Demokratika	No	22.1	5.6
Luxembourg	Action Committee for Democracy and Justice (ADR)	No	22.0	5.5
	Christian Social People's Party (CSV)	Yes	22.8	6.3
	Green Party	No	20.3	4.5
	Marxist and Reformed Communist Party 'The Left'	No	19.4	3.9
	Democratic Party (DP)	Yes	23.0	5.3
	Luxembourg Socialist Workers' Party (LSAP)	No	21.0	4.5
Slovenia	Democratic Party of Slovenia (DSS)	No	24.2	4.1
	Democratic Party of Pensioners of Slovenia (DESUS)	Yes	22.3	5.1
	Liberal Democracy of Slovenia (LDS)	Yes	22.8	4.4
	Slovene People's Party (SLS)	Yes	21.3	5.6
	Slovene National Party (SNS)	No	22.6	6.1
	Social Democratic Party of Slovenia (SDS)	No	22.7	6.0
	Slovene Christian Democrats (SKD)	No	22.5	6.7
	United List of Social Democrats (SLSD)	No	20.8	3.9
	Green Party (ZS)	No	22.9	5.3
Ukraine	Agrarian Party of Ukraine (APU)	Yes	19.4	5.7
	All Ukrainian Union 'Community' (VOH)	No	28.7	6.0
	Labor Party of Ukraine (PTU)	No	20.1	6.8
	Ukrainian National Assembly (UNA)	No	23.2	6.8
	Democratic Party of Ukraine (DPU)	Yes	20.4	6.4
	Communist Party of Ukraine (KPU)	No	14.2	3.4
	Congress of Ukrainian Nationalists (KUN)	No	9.5	9.3
	Liberal Party of Ukraine (LPU)	No	32.3	5.0
	People's Democratic Party (NDP)	Yes	19.8	6.5
	Rukh—Ukrainian People's Movement (Kostenko, UNR)	No	22.1	6.9
	People's Movement of Ukraine (Udovenko)	No	22.7	7.5
	Forward Ukraine!	Yes	20.0	5.0
	Ukrainian Green Party (PZU)	No	21.8	5.4
	Party of Reforms and Order (PRP)	Yes	23.1	6.7
	Party of Slavonic Unity (PSE)	No	10.0	1.0
	Socialistic Democratic Unity	No	25.6	5.8
	Progressive Socialist Party (PSP)	No	17.0	3.6
	Peasants' Party of Ukraine (SPU)	No	12.7	6.6

APPENDIX 6A.1. (*Continued*)

Country	Party	In gov?	Ideological index	Left–right self-placement
	United Social Democratic Party of Ukraine (SDPU-O)	No	20.3	6.0
	Socialist Party of Ukraine (SPU)	No	19.3	4.7
	Social Nationalist Party (SNP)	No	26.0	5.0
	Ukrainian Republican Party (URP)	No	20.0	5.0
	Ukrainian Christian Democratic Party (UKDP)	Yes	17.7	6.6
Belarus	Party of Communists of Belarus (PKB)	No	17.5	4.8
	Liberal-Democratic Party of Belarus (LDPB)	Yes	23.3	6.2
	Belarusian Women Party 'Hope' (BPZ)	No	20.8	5.5
	Republican Party of Labour and Justice (RPPS)	No	19.8	5.1
	United Civic Party (AGP)	No	25.1	6.9
	Belarusian Social Sport Party	No	23.0	5.5
	Belarusian Party 'Zelyenye'	No	23.1	5.4
	Belarusian Party of Labor (BPP)	No	20.1	4.9
	Communist Party of Belarus (KPB)	Yes	19.3	4.3
	Belarusian Patriotic Movement (BPR)	Yes	25.0	6.7
	Belarusian Social-Democratic Party (BSDP)	No	23.0	6.7
	Party of National Accord (PNZ)	No	25.4	7.2
	Belarusian Social Democratic Union (BSDH)	No	25.5	7.3
	Belarusian Ecological Party (BEP)	No	21.4	6.3
	Agrarian Party (APB)	Yes	25.2	5.6
	Belarusian Popular Front (BNF)	No	20.9	6.2
	Republican Party (RP)	No	16.1	6.0

Notes: For ideological index, 1: Extreme left, 37: extreme right; for left–right self-placement, 1: extreme left, 10: extreme right.

APPENDIX 6A.2. *Coding of Communist parties*

Old Communists	
Bulgaria	Bulgarian Socialist Party (BSP)
	Bulgarian Agrarian National Union (BZNS)[a]
	Bulgarian Communist Party (BKP)
Estonia	Estonian Social Democratic Labor Party (ESDTP)
	Estonian United People's Party (EURP)
	Russian Unity Party
Belarus	Communist Party of Belarus (KPB)[a]
	Party of Communists of Belarus (PKB)
	Agrarian Party (APB)[a]
Lithuania	Lithuanian Democratic Labor Party (LDDP)
	Lithuanian Peasants' Party (LVP)
	Lithuanian Russians Union (LRS)

APPENDIX 6A.2. (*Continued*)

Romania	Romanian Party of Social Democracy (PDSR) Socialist Party/Socialist Labor Party (PS/PSM)
Russia	Agrarian Party (APR) Communist Party of the Russian Federation (KPRF) Working Russia Russian All-People's Union (ROS)
Slovakia	Association of Workers of Slovakia (ZRS) Communist Party of Slovakia (KSS)
Slovenia	United List of Social Democrats in Slovenia (SLSD)
Czech Republic	Communist Party of Bohemia and Moravia (KSCM)
Ukraine	Communist Party of Ukraine (KPU) Socialist Party of Ukraine (SPU) Peasants' Party of Ukraine (SPU) Progressive Socialist Party (PSP)
Hungary	Workers' Party (MP)

Reformed Communists

Croatia	Social Democratic Party of Croatia (SDP)
Latvia	Alliance of Social Democrats of Latvia (LSDSP) National Harmony Party (NHP)
Poland	Polish Peasants' Party (PSL) Alliance of the Democratic Left (SLD)
Romania	Democratic Party (PD)[a]
Slovakia	Party of the Democratic Left (SDL)[a]
Hungary	Hungarian Socialist Party (MSzP)

[a] Government parties.

How Political Institutions Shape Losers' Consent

In this chapter we continue our investigation of how political context shapes losers' consent by considering the ways in which formal political institutions may have an effect on popular views towards government. Specifically, we contend that, aside from differences in democratic experiences, which were the topic of the previous chapter, there are identifiable differences in formal political institutions across countries that systematically affect how winners and losers view the political system. Specifically, we argue that, even when countries have similarly long-standing or brief experiences with democracy, variation in formal political institutions can serve to attenuate or exacerbate the impact of losing on people's views of government.

Institutions can mute or amplify the impact of losing in one of several ways: by defining the rules of the process by which losers are produced in the first place, usually through the electoral system; by determining the substance of government policy, and how close policy is to the preferences of the losers; and, finally, by determining the boundaries of how power, once allocated, can be exercised by the winners—that is, the constraints on the ability of the winners to bring about policy change. Put simply, then, we argue that institutions help determine who becomes a loser—that is, the process by which winners and losers are created—and how losers experience the exercise of power by a government they did not help elect—that is, the outcomes of government action citizens observe.

As it turns out, and as we will try to demonstrate below, different institutions may have quite similar effects on losers' views of the political system. Implicitly this opens up alternatives for institutional designers wishing to minimize the impact of losing. To put it simply, adopting a country's institutions wholesale is unlikely to be the only solution to the problem of maintaining the consent of the losers. There are, of course, many different ways to represent political institutions and, as a starting point, we need some way of making distinctions between them. One simple way of beginning to unbundle these institutions is to divide up institutions into those that concern giving citizens a voice in government and those that limit or constrain the role of government when in power. While having a say in government policy may be related to how much power a government may have, the two are distinct and worth considering separately.

INSTITUTIONS AND ATTITUDES TOWARD GOVERNMENT

Research on citizen views of government has repeatedly observed apparent institutional weaknesses as important influences on citizen support for democratic government. During the 1970s, for example, scholars concluded that democratic systems were suffering from overload because they appeared increasingly incapable of dealing with an expansion in citizens' demands (Huntington 1974; Brittan 1975). Similarly, in the late 1970s and 1980s, analysts found that representative democracy was not responsive enough to demands articulated by a citizenry with increased participatory inclinations (Barnes et al. 1979; Jennings et al. 1990; Cain, Dalton, and Scarrow 2003).

The dissatisfaction with political institutions among western mass publics that followed frequently was viewed as resulting from citizens' perceived inability to provide inputs to the system, to derive outputs generated by it, or both. Either way, scholars identified institutional reasons for democracy's inability to cope with citizen demands. As a consequence, researchers suggested that this structural deficit, which inhibited democratic systems from reacting to current and new problems, could be reduced through an extension of more direct forms of popular participation in democratic decision-making (Barber 1984; Held 1987). Thus, along with a documented trend toward higher levels of citizen political sophistication and political values that emphasize citizen involvement in the democratic process, opportunities for citizens to have input to the political process became a more closely investigated institutional feature of democratic systems in the Western world (Cain, Dalton, and Scarrow 2003).

The connection between political institutions and citizen attitudes toward democracy is a subject of particular relevance to contemporary debates about democratic performance and real-world institutional engineers because it involves the question to what extent citizen attitudes toward democratic reality, and by implication the potential for protest or instability, are mediated by a country's political institutions. Moreover, such questions are relevant to our understanding of both established and new democracies. In our view, opportunities to participate in the democratic process or the quality of political outputs constitute only part of the link between institutions and attitudes in contemporary democracies. In particular, it is not clear that more opportunities for input and access to the system will automatically lead to higher levels of satisfaction with democracy; nor is it self-evident that particular types of democratic institutions necessarily lead to superior outputs (Crepaz 1996; but see Lijphart 1999). In fact, because the same set of democratic

institutions can have different consequences for different groups among those
governed by them, and in particular for those in the minority and majority,
we seek to explore how long-standing and institutionally defined differences across and within political systems mediate citizen support for the
system.

In the absence of, and prior to, knowledge about the specific nature of
the representative process in a democracy, we know that losers tend to exhibit
more negative attitudes toward the political system and its workings. However,
while there are these important individual-level differences between winners
and losers, winning and losing also mean different things in different political systems. In addition to the distinction between old and new democracies
examined in the previous chapter, one way to think about these differences is to
consider the fact that some political systems are designed to protect democratic
minorities from unrestrained rule by the majority.

Research by Lijphart (1984, 1999), Powell (2000), and Colomer (2001)
on the nature of democratic systems serves as a good starting point for our
theory of how political institutions may affect political legitimacy. Lijphart
develops a typology of democratic systems that places countries on a continuum from most consensual to most majoritarian in nature (Lijphart 1984,
1999). At the extremes, majoritarian government is about unfettered rule by
the majority on the basis of an unwritten constitution without provisions for
minority veto, whereas a pure form of consensus democracy is organized on the
basis of a rigid, written constitution with formal veto powers for minorities.
Similarly, Powell's (2000) research comparing the majoritarian and proportional visions of democracy examines the political consequences of different
institutional designs with regard to government responsibility, accountability,
and citizen control. Powell argues that contending visions (and manifestations)
of democratic governance usually entail a tradeoff between accountability and
responsiveness—with majoritarian systems better able to provide citizens with
opportunities to hold policy-makers accountable, while proportional systems
usually are able to be closer to representing the policy interests of most citizens. Along similar lines, Colomer's (2001) research on political institutions
differentiates between political systems that follow single-winner political
rules (institutions) and those that keep to multiple winner rules. According to
Colomer, multiple winner rules turn out to be more 'socially efficient' because
these are institutions that can 'satisfy large groups' interests on a great number
of issues' (Colomer 2001: 2).

Taken together, this and related research on democratic institutions suggests that citizens experience democratic politics differently, depending on
the kind of system they live in. In particular, when it comes to citizen access
to, and participation in, the political process, as well as the translation of
citizens' preferences into policy outcomes, it is important to note that some
countries' institutions are designed to afford greater opportunities for both

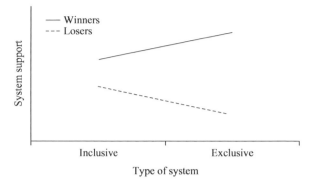

FIGURE 7.1. Interactive effects of institutions and winner–loser status on system support

winners *and* losers of democratic competition to be represented in the political arena and to implement their preferred policies. Moreover, even under identical conditions of access to the political process, systems are designed differently for the exercise of power—and in particular, the extent to which the minority is included in the decision-making process between elections. Given that some systems and thus some institutional features provide more direct and proportionate representational opportunities than others and because some systems afford the minority more of a voice in the democratic decision-making process, we expect that the more inclusive political institutions in a country, the greater the extent to which negative consequences of losing elections are muted. Conversely, the more majoritarian the country's institutions are, the more winners get to have a say and to impose their will on the minority.[1]

It is worth noting, however, that this argument does not imply that citizens in one type of system are, on average or necessarily, more likely to be satisfied with the system than in another, regardless of majority or minority status. Instead, we argue that there is an interactive effect between the nature of a country's institutions and status as part of the majority or minority on satisfaction with democracy. Figure 7.1 plots this hypothesized interactive effect in the context of the theoretical model that guides our inquiry.

In the context of our theoretical model, this interactive effect suggests that the negative influence of losing is muted when individuals encounter inclusive institutions and amplified when the institutions are exclusive in nature (Figure 7.2).

---

[1] Note, however, that this argument does not make predictions regarding the quality of the decisions made, or of the quality of the eventual policy outcomes obtained. For the effects of consensus versus majority democracy on policy outcomes, see Crepaz (1996).

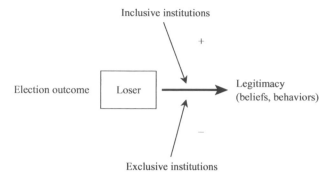

FIGURE 7.2. The mediating role of institutions on legitimacy beliefs among losers

UNBUNDLING INSTITUTIONS: ELECTORAL SYSTEMS, VETO PLAYERS, AND FEDERALISM

There is some evidence that the model we propose here has empirical support. In a study of eleven European democracies that combined data on attitudes toward government and Lijphart's categorizations of countries into consensual and majoritarian ones, Anderson and Guillory (1997) found that losers in more consensual political systems display higher levels of satisfaction with the way democracy works than losers in more majoritarian systems. Conversely, winners in more majoritarian systems exhibit higher levels of satisfaction than winners in more consensual systems. While the study by Anderson and Guillory thus identified and demonstrated the ways in which exclusive and inclusive institutions generated different responses for losers, it also conceptualized and measured institutions in quite general terms. We would argue that it would be a good idea to unpack these ideas a little further, since the comparison between majoritarian and consensus institutions is really one between bundles of institutions rather than a comparison between two specific institutions. Consensus politics, for example, does not simply involve coalition government but also multiparty systems and proportional representation, not just one but all of which give voters a say in the eventual policy output of government. Consensus politics also involves limitations on what that government can do through federal and/or bicameral structures. It is not the case, then, that comparisons between majoritarian and consensus politics means comparing two dimensions of one specific institution, but a more complex comparison across several institutional features—or packages—that are combined.

Such a comparison of bundles of institutions can illuminate important patterns, but it also can blur our understanding of which specific institution is crucial to producing the observed effect. It may be, for example, that we do not need the full set of consensual institutions to produce the same effect; instead, we may need just one or two. Alternatively, of course, it may not be individual institutions that matter—for example, the type of electoral system or federalism—but that we may require combinations of institutions (e.g. PR plus federalism plus multiparty government) to produce the same effect on losers' consent.

If we unbundle some of the properties of these ideal types of political systems, can we still see some of the effects on losers found by Anderson and Guillory but created by individual and specific institutions? This is an important question of institutional design. If one is interested in developing institutions that help reconcile losers to their loss, then scholars such as Lijphart have a whole collection of institutional arrangements and designs to suggest as possible solutions. One recommendation of such scholars might be, essentially, to replicate Belgian or Swiss political institutions. Yet, rather than overhaul a whole system and try to sell a country the whole Belgian constitution, it might be easier to introduce reforms in a more piecemeal manner. Moreover, if it is the case that specific institutions can mitigate the effects of losing then, as a matter of design, it might be possible to introduce constitutions that produce the virtuous properties of the Belgian system without necessarily being a copy of that system.

INSTITUTIONS AND HAVING A SAY

Giving people a say in the decisions being made is one of the surer ways of providing legitimate rule and preventing disaffection. Coalition governments— one component of the Lijphart model—may mean that, in contrast to straight-forwardly plurality systems such as those in the United Kingdom or the United States, governments will be more likely to have the support of a majority of voters. That is, it may be the case that greater numbers of people have something of a say in government under coalitional than non-coalitional settings and so, on average, there will be fewer losers under coalition arrangements. While this may often be true, it is not always the case (Powell 2000). Powell's work also uncovers a subtler property of coalition governments in uncovering the underlying arithmetical properties of different kinds of political systems. Using related but somewhat different terms from Lijphart, Powell shows that multiparty coalition governments are closer to the median voter than are governments in majoritarian systems. Thus, voters in Britain are, on average, further away from the policy of their single party governments than voters in the Netherlands where the 'averaging' of party positions in coalition moves governments closer to the center and, hence, closer to the median voter. That is, once a government gets into power, it may reflect more or less closely what voters want depending, in part, on whether it is a coalition government. We may therefore expect coalition governments to produce generally fewer losers and losers who are comparatively happier with the policy positions of the government.

But coalition governments do not exist in isolation from other elements of the political system. In fact, they are often a product of multiparty systems produced by proportional representation systems. The system itself offers another possibility of reconciling losers to the system. Supporters of PR systems often argue that such systems in and of themselves give people a sense that their vote (and hence their voice) will be heard. Majoritarian systems create too many wasted votes in and of themselves, not just by creating governments that are unsupported by majorities, but by not even allowing candidates from minority parties to win. Proportionality of electoral choice, then, would seem to have a value in and of itself as a process feature that gives people a say, regardless of outcome. This would seem to hold even if the PR electoral system produces a single party or minority government, as occasionally happens in Scandinavia, for example.

Proportionality thus has two effects upon losing and losers: a direct effect in which citizens have their say and an indirect effect by encouraging multiparty governments. Scholarly opinion differs on which of these is the most important. Lijphart does not really say which of these effects should predominate; he also does not distinguish between whether a proportional system is of value in and of itself or is simply a necessary condition for coalition government. For Powell, however, the major importance of proportionality lies in its indirect effect—it is the policy position of the government that matters and to which proportional electoral rules are clearly subordinate.

INSTITUTIONS AND THE POWER OF GOVERNMENT

Once in power, governments may have greater or lesser range to be able to accomplish their goals. As Anderson and Guillory argue, for losers the worst outcome is to have little voice in a system in which the government has a great deal of power to implement policies unchecked. A better outcome (at least for losers) would be to have one in which any government is more constrained. For the purposes of unbundling institutions, then, a reasonable concern of losers is the extent of power of government—how much any government can do once in office. Good examples of countries with more exclusive (or majoritarian) features are the United Kingdom and New Zealand—at least before the former's recent moves toward a more decentralized polity and the latter's experiments with more proportional electoral rules. In these systems, virtually all aspects of institutions—including electoral system, centralization— were primarily majoritarian in nature. Conversely, countries like Belgium and Switzerland are classic examples of states that feature more inclusive systemic properties.

As a number of examples from around the globe attest, it is possible to constrain or limit government power by a range of constitutional devices. Lijphart, for example, specifically noted federalism and bicameralism in the original model of consensus governments. More recently Tsebelis' (2003) work offers a more general look at constitutional–institutional arrangements and limitations and the way they contribute to policy stability or, its obverse, the ease of policy change. More generally speaking, constitutional devices such as federalism can be seen as distributing power among competing institutions. Similarly America's system of 'checks and balances' divides power between President and two houses of Congress and so divides power among competing branches. Presumably the value of devices such as federalism or separation of powers lies in the fact that rival parties may control different branches. If different parties control different levels of government—a right wing party at the state level balancing out a left wing party in the center—then this is a situation broadly analogous to coalition government: citizens from across the political spectrum obtain a share in power if party control is split. Given the relevance of sharing power, these sorts of devices work best (for losers) when party control is split. It would further help that end if staggered electoral cycles or different franchises/electoral systems were in place. Even under a federal system, if all elections were held at the same time under the same franchise and electoral rules, presumably the government of the day would win across the board. Having staggered electoral terms—as in Australian, Canadian, and German federalism—gives opposition parties a chance to capitalize on the unpopularity of the national government and so allow those opposition parties a chance to win power at least at the level of the state, province, or Land.

There is a wide variety of upper houses that exhibit considerable variation in their composition and power (Tsebelis and Money 1997). For those who lose out in helping to form the executive branch of the national government, it is important to have some differences in the method of electing the upper house than the lower house in order to make the composition of the two houses differ from each other. Some of these differences could be quite subtle. In Australia, for example, elections for the upper house are often held at the same time as elections for the lower house, but the electoral system for the Senate is proportional rather than majoritarian. As a result, the composition of the Senate differs in that minor parties are typically much more prominent in the Senate than the House. After it is elected, it is also important that the upper house be powerful in order to balance the power of the government.

For losers an important concern is to constrain what government may do, and there are many ways in which to do so. Winners, however, should be more ambivalent when governments are constrained since they will have won relatively little in a system in which there is a strong version of decentralized federalism and also a bicameralism in which an upper chamber is elected by different franchise and/or at a different time.

In this context, it is worth noting that there is an unresolved normative issue underlying both the consensus model and models ground in spatial analysis on one hand and models grounded in a pluralist tradition on the other. This issue concerns the value placed on having policies that are hard to change. Consensus polities are most open to voters having a say through proportional electoral systems and multiparty governments, but they also are ones where it may be hard for governments to accomplish policy changes if those governments are then constrained by formal limitations such as federalism. As Miller (1983) notes, one of the concerns of the spatial literature on collective decision-making has been a search for policy stability. As the seminal McKelvey–Schofield theorems show, left to their own devices in a purely majoritarian setting, a group of people will rarely be able to make a choice as a group but, instead, any group choice will cycle between alternatives.

In this context, and following on from Shepsle's work on structure-induced equilibrium in the American setting (Shepsle 1979), Tsebelis's work shows how—comparatively—institutions may reduce the possibility of cycling, thus making it harder to change the status quo as a consequence of institutional design. In the American context, for example, separation of powers shrinks the range of possible alternatives to the status quo since any new position has to win the support of both houses of Congress and of the President. Political institutions, then, offer a solution to the 'problem' of policy instability.

Having governments that cannot accomplish much and, hence, having a situation in which the status quo is hard to change, has appeal both for Lijphart and, also, for spatial modelers. But, there is a distinct downside to having a policy that is hard to change, and this is especially the case so far as pluralist conceptions of democracy are concerned. To pluralists, having an unchanging policy can be far from healthy (Miller 1983). In fact, pluralists view policy change as positive because it implies a shift has taken place in the governing coalition. Policy cycling enables losers to become substantive— that is, policy—winners as a consequence of these shifting coalitions (Miller 1983: 743).

Thus, for pluralists institutions that facilitate pure majority rule are satisfying: they do not create permanent losers because they open up the possibility of winning in future periods, especially in settings where politics is multidimensional. Multidimensional settings are ones where (for social choice theorists) cycling is more likely to take place and (for adherents of a consensus model) politics is likely to be split in a divided society. Thus, if the possibility of becoming winners next time ('wait till next year': Miller 1983: 742) is one thing that helps losers give consent to a political system, then the kinds of chaotic instability characteristic of formal models provides a context in which losers can build issue coalitions that will make them winners. One consequence of the lack of cycling is seen in the work of McGann (2002) who argues that constitutional devices such as super-majorities that are aimed at protecting minorities can, in fact, hurt them. Having too large a super-majority requirement means that some minorities will find it almost impossible to change the current policy (status quo). McGann, following on from Miller and the pluralists, therefore argues that simple majorities—pluralities—give minorities a realistic opportunity to be able to bring about change from the status quo. Moreover, as our evidence on the dynamics of losers' consent suggests, occasional change in office means that any one group of losers will not become too troubled with the political system.

For some pluralist scholars, then, policy immobility is not necessarily desirable—even when considering divided societies—because it so heavily privileges the status quo. Presumably even for nonpluralists, complete policy-immobility is not appealing: governments should be able to move policy or (equivalently) move from the status quo at least somewhat even if too much movement (cycling) is seen as problematic. That is, having a say in and of itself may not be enough to satisfy citizens, and it may well make winners significantly less happy with the system as winning becomes less meaningful. Thus, from the perspective of losers, less policy change is good; but from the perspective of the winners, too little change may not be such a good thing.

The cases of Italy and France's IVth Republic provide two examples, albeit often heavily caricatured ones, of systems where multiparty coalition governments cannot seem to make effective policy at all and, in consequence, disappoint their citizens. Between the Scylla of it being too easy to change government policy and the Charybdis of it being too hard lies the Goldilocks of 'just right' amount of policy movement—but we have no sense of that metric or how wide a range 'just right' might encompass. The implicit tendency within both the model of consensus democracy and spatial models is to see policy stickiness as having a positive value and, of the two alternatives of too much change and too little change, having too much change is by far the worse. As Tsebelis shows, there are many institutional designs that can produce policy immobility. Simply, from the point of view of policy immobilism, checks and balances within the American system of separation of powers between President and Congress may well produce very similar lack of policy movement to the pure parliamentary system of Italy. This may also imply that too much coalition government may have a negative impact on policy and consequently legitimacy (Listhaug, Aardal, and Ellis 2002).

This discussion of various institutional forms essentially unpacks the set of institutions at the heart of the work of Anderson and Guillory and Lijphart. The idea of a consensus polity is one that bundles together many different institutions each of which could, in its own right, shape citizen views. The empirical question remains as to whether there is any evidence that individual components of institutional design can help reconcile citizens to the system. We can examine the impact of individual institutions by examining whether opinions of voters towards their political system vary in response to specific institutional attributes. Below, we do this for both Western Europe and North America. Of course, some institutions are difficult to unbundle. The most obvious example here is the bundle consisting of coalition government, multiparty system, and proportional representation. It is hard, though not impossible, to move away from proportionality without affecting the other two. For some institutions, then, their effects are not likely to be individual and additive but rather are interactive and contingent. This is not the case for federalism—an especially interesting institution—since it is entirely compatible with majoritarian-type institutions as the examples of Australia and Canada attest as well as coalition government multiparty proportional representation systems such as Switzerland or Belgium. With federal institutions, then, we can tease out a distinct institution uncorrelated with other institutions to see if federal institutions do help dampen the effects of losing.

We therefore proceed in two steps; first, by examining institutional effects across a range of countries in Western Europe to show that different political institutions may, in fact, have desirable properties, at least so far as losers are concerned. From here we turn to examine the impact of federalism in both the United States and Canada in greater detail.

SATISFACTION WITH DEMOCRACY IN EUROPE

One simple way of beginning our study is to examine citizen satisfaction with democracy across a range of European countries. Table 7.1 displays some simple models of the kind used throughout this study. The first model (shown in column 1) takes as its dependent variable citizen satisfaction with democracy. The other two estimate the degree to which citizens feel they may rely on their national parliament and national government. The data are taken from a standard Eurobarometer survey of European citizens (No. 52, 1999) across the fifteen member states of the EU and, hence, across fifteen different sets of political
institutions.

The models that are reported here are quite straightforward. Evaluations of the political system are modeled as a function of individual attributes, being a loser, and of a series of institutional features.[2] The individual-level

---

[2] Relating to the previous chapter, which shows significant differences in the winner–loser gap between old and new democracies, we include an interaction between losing and a measure for the newer democracies of Europe—East Germany, Greece, Portugal, and Spain. Consistent with the results reported in the previous chapter, we expect losers in new democracies to have a bigger reaction to their loss than voters in more established democracies. While several of these countries have been democracies now for almost a generation this still may not have provided enough time and enough learning experiences for citizens to adjust as easily to losing as their fellow Europeans in countries such as Ireland or Sweden which have been democratic for the lifespan of everyone surveyed.

TABLE 7.1. *Losing and institutional features on attitudes toward government*

	Satisfaction with democracy	Can you rely on the national parliament?	Can you rely on the national government?
Loser	−0.140***	−0.592***	−0.869***
	(8.92)	(13.26)	(18.84)
New democracy	0.143***	0.158**	0.398***
	(5.13)	(1.98)	(4.84)
Loser * new democracy	−0.149***	−0.126*	−0.238***
	(6.01)	(1.76)	(3.23)
Parties in government	0.141***	0.588***	0.653***
	(5.43)	(8.06)	(8.66)
(Parties in government)^2	−0.024***	−0.092***	−0.097***
	(6.57)	(8.98)	(9.10)
Electoral system	−0.018***	−0.166***	−0.150***
	(2.60)	(8.64)	(7.54)
Federal system	0.001	0.205***	0.123**
	(0.04)	(4.21)	(2.43)
Life satisfaction	−0.221***	−0.303***	−0.274***
	(22.19)	(10.65)	(9.35)
Age	−0.022***	0.105***	0.089***
	(3.02)	(5.11)	(4.22)
Education	0.000	0.202***	0.148***
	(0.00)	(8.66)	(6.17)
Sex	0.001	−0.128***	−0.047
	(0.04)	(3.45)	(1.21)
Left wing	−0.085***	−0.086*	−0.145***
	(4.80)	(1.71)	(2.78)
Right wing	−0.046**	0.168***	0.001
	(2.34)	(3.01)	(0.01)
Sociotropic evaluations	0.173***	0.370***	0.434***
	(16.50)	(12.41)	(14.09)
Pocketbook evaluations	0.041***	0.032	−0.000
	(3.31)	(0.92)	(0.00)
Will not vote	−0.121***	−0.807***	−0.688***
	(3.98)	(9.24)	(7.69)
Constant	2.726***	4.925***	4.869***
	(39.45)	(25.09)	(24.05)
N	11,815	11,676	11,780
R-squared	0.12	0.09	0.11

*$p < 0.1$.
**$p < 0.05$.
***$p < 0.001$.

Notes: Absolute value of t statistics in parentheses.

Source: Eurobarometer 52, 1999.

demographic attributes are introduced as control variables and are of little substantive interest.[3] The institutional variables that constitute the focus of this chapter tap a number of the different ideas we advanced above. Included are measures of: federalism; of the number of parties in power as well as the number of parties squared (to capture potential curvilinear effects); and the electoral system (with higher values indicating more disproportionality in the translation of votes into seats). Also included is a measure of losing based on the respondent's intended vote at the next election.

A number of things are apparent from this simple model. First, as we see throughout this study, losers are significantly less happy with the political system—less satisfied with the way democracy works and also less likely to think one can rely on the major political institutions of the country—than other voters even after we include a range of individual attributes and attitudes that control for a possible general level of dissatisfaction with life in general. Moreover, as shown in the previous chapter, we see that the winner–loser gap is larger in the newer democracies, indicating that losers are, indeed, less satisfied and hold their political institutions in lower regard than winners in the more established democracies.

In terms of institutional effects we see, as predicted by Anderson and Guillory, the similar effects of both electoral system and coalition government. Thus, less proportional electoral systems reduce citizens' faith in the political system, while coalition government tends to increase it. Since these are, by now, familiar findings we will not dwell on them except to make two further points. First, there is evidence to suggest that too much coalition government may well, in general, depress satisfaction with the political system. Alongside the simple number of parties in government we included a squared term. The sign on this squared term suggests that, while satisfaction with government may increase as the number of parties in the coalition grows, after some point (approximately five parties) there can be too many parties in the coalition—at least so far as voters are concerned.[4] It is easy to make too much of this one coefficient, but it is consistent with the argument that policy immobilism brought about by large coalitions does frustrate voters.

Second, and more important, the various institutions of consensus democracies seem to have an impact in and of themselves: that is their impact

---

[3] In addition to standard variables for age, education, and political extremism they include, for example, whether an individual thinks the economy (either of the nation or their own pocketbook) is doing well or poorly and whether the individual intends to vote in the next election. They also include the individual's sense of satisfaction with life in general. Presumably citizens who think their own life is going poorly are less likely to think well of the political system.

[4] Given the number of cases involved it is too easy to make too much of the standard levels of significance. Our interpretation here rests upon the signs of the parameters.

TABLE 7.2. *Changes in the effect of losing on satisfaction with democracy for subsets of respondents*

	Coefficient on 'Loser' variable	Constant
Satisfaction with democracy		
Federal system	−0.08	2.9
Not federal system	−0.19	2.6
Electoral system = 1	−0.18	2.62
Electoral system = 2	−0.12	3.27
Electoral system = 3	−0.08	2.05
Electoral system = 4	−0.17	2.55
Parties in government = 1	−0.21	2.71
Parties in government = 2	−0.14	3.07
Parties in government = 3	−0.13	2.93
Parties in government = 5	−0.16	3.07
Parties in government = 6	−0.07 ns	2.43
Can you rely on national government		
Federal system	−0.62	5.17
Not federal system	−0.89	5.4
Electoral system = 1	−0.88	5.11
Electoral system = 2	−0.75	3.79
Electoral system = 3	−0.90	5.97
Electoral system = 4	−0.86	5.32
Parties in government = 1	−1.17	5.51
Parties in government = 2	−0.75	5.77
Parties in government = 3	−0.36	6.06
Parties in government = 5	−0.55	5.14
Parties in government = 6	−0.66	3.88

Notes: Calculations based on estimations shown in column 1, Table 7.1.
ns: not significant.

is separable and additive and therefore not necessarily dependent on being bundled together. Furthermore, one of the main effects of interest—that of federalism—does operate in the hypothesized way: federal states are associated with both higher levels of satisfaction with the performance of democracy and higher levels of regard for political institutions. Simply dividing up the power of central government, then, seems to help people think well of institutions.

Of course this does not speak directly to how losing and institutions interact. One way to show this is to divide the sample into federal states and non-federal states and examine the size of the parameter attached to being a loser: if the institutions do have the anticipated effect then the impact of losing should be greater under unitary than federal systems.

Table 7.2 reports results from estimating the model in the first column of Table 7.1 subsetting the data in a number of ways. Most of the statistical output has been suppressed and the table only displays the parameter associated with losing.[5] As can be seen from Table 7.2, the impact of losing under unitary states is bigger, indeed twice as large, as in federal states. The remainder of the table adopts a similar approach to parties in government, for example. Here the results show that losers' reactions are biggest under single party governments. Electoral system effects are apparent as well: greater proportionality does help alleviate the impact of losing although the effects are mostly seen in shifts in the intercept (in the average level of dissatisfaction) than in the parameter. A similar approach is used to show the changing reaction of losers to the national government (i.e. subsetting the data by type of electoral system or federalism and estimating the model in column 3 of Table 7.1); this produces a very similar pattern of results.

FEDERALISM: EVIDENCE FROM CANADA

On the basis of this kind of approach, then, federalism would seem to help moderate the effect of losing presumably by allowing the sharing of power. We can show this effect rather more directly, by looking in greater depth at a specific example of federalism to see if there is a difference in attitudes between winners and losers at the state or provincial level, even after we control for national factors.

To do so, we focus on Canada. Canada is an especially interesting example of federalism because it exists alongside a majoritarian system. European examples of federalism—Austria, Belgium, Germany, and Switzerland—all operate with proportionality, multiparty systems, and coalition governments. Thus, the kinds of positive effects we saw in Table 7.1 and even Table 7.2 might be dismissed as being confounded by the beneficial effects of proportionality. For Canada such confounding is not possible since governments at both provincial and national level are parliamentary and majoritarian. As it turns out, the results of an analysis of Canadian data do, in fact, indicate that it is, in fact, federalism that drives the effect we observe.

Table 7.3 shows results from a simple model of satisfaction with democracy controlling for both national level party identification (national level loser effects), economic dissatisfaction, and language group using data from the 2000 Canadian National Election Study (CNES). Since there is no institutional variation across the provinces of the kinds we saw in Europe—for example, no variation in electoral system—we have no need to control for such effects. As can be seen, those voters whose party won at the federal level— Liberal Party identifiers—were generally more satisfied with the performance of democracy in Canada than other voters, even after we control for their orientations towards the national government. Moreover, as importantly, being a

---

[5] The parameters were produced by estimating the same model in column 1 of Table 7.1 subset by the relevant institutional variable, for example, the model was estimated for both federal and unitary states.

TABLE 7.3. *Satisfaction with democracy in Canada, 2000*

	All respondents		Canada excluding Quebec		Quebec only	
	Unstandardized coefficients	Std. error	Unstandardized coefficients	Std. error	Unstandardized coefficients	Std. error
Liberal ID	0.447***	0.035	0.395***	0.040	0.548***	0.070
Winner at provincial level	0.076*	0.037	0.130**	0.041	−0.075	0.079
Alliance ID	−0.337***	0.052	−0.365***	0.054	−0.160	0.189
Bloc Quebecois ID	−0.069	0.063	−0.030	0.040		
Female	0.019	0.031	0.042	0.037	−0.027	0.055
French speaker	−0.188***	0.039	0.014	0.216	−0.230*	0.110
Economic satisfaction	0.180***	0.024	0.192***	0.028	0.143**	0.045
University education	0.006	0.034	−0.048	0.056	0.100	0.066
High school dropout	−0.076	0.046	0.006	0.006	−0.148	0.082
Age	0.005	0.005	−0.000	0.000	0.006	0.009
Age squared	−0.000	0.000	0.073*	0.030	−0.000	0.000
Intend to vote	0.097***	0.025	0.130**	0.041	0.136**	0.043
Constant	1.907	0.155	1.973	0.184	1.802	0.301
N	2,726		1,820		906	
Adj. R^2	0.138		0.14		0.13	

***$p < 0.001$.
**$p < 0.01$.
*$p < 0.05$.

Notes: Dependent variable (1–4 scale, where 4 = satisfied).

Source: Canadian National Election Study (2000).

winner at the provincial level significantly increases voters' satisfaction with the way democracy works. Thus, federal institutions allow voters to offset a loss at the federal level with being a winner at the provincial level, and vice versa. The patterns of Tables 7.1 and 7.2 showing the scope for federalism in and of itself to have positive effects are not, then, confined to those data and models.

Before moving on we should note some additional nuances within the Canadian data, however. Some are relatively specific issues and we will not dwell on them here, but one issue is worth noting. That is the distinct community of Quebec.[6] Estimating the model separately for the province of Quebec and

[6] Broadly speaking, the result of Table 7.3 can be replicated using data from the 1997 CNES and is found across different waves of interviewees pre- and post-election. There is some sensitivity to the definition of winner—whether it is defined in terms of provincial vote last time, or

the rest of Canada shows that the positive effect of being a winner at the provincial level is not present for Quebeckers who have long been more hesitant to extend legitimacy to the political system than other Canadians.[7] As the results shown in columns 2 and 3 in Table 7.3 indicate, being a winner at the national level (Liberal party support) translates into more positive evaluations of the political system in both Quebec and the rest of Canada. What is more, being a winner at the provincial level does not translate into more positive evaluations of the political system in Quebec, though it does elsewhere in the Canadian federation. Thus, there are clear limits to the palliative effect of federalism when political divisions are extreme (see Nadeau and Blais 1993).

THE POWER OF GOVERNMENT: EVIDENCE FROM THE AMERICAN STATES

Notwithstanding the case of Quebec, the results so far have been encouraging. Even within a majoritarian setting like Canada's, and even controlling for the impact of proportionality, it is possible to see that federal institutions can help salve the wounds of losing. Moreover, individual component parts of a consensus model clearly have independent effects on citizen assessments of the system. However, given that provincial institutions in Canada do not vary significantly, one question raised by the results in Table 7.3 is what happens when we combine the effects of winning and losing at the state or provincial level with variations in subnational institutions. To examine this question, we turn to the US case, where the fifty states provide a setting with substantial variation in electoral context. This allows us to test how variation in context, and in the power of government, conditions the effect of losing on trust in government. In contrast to Canada, then, US federalism provides greater variety in the range of different institutional combinations. We can therefore exploit variation in federal institutions to focus even more sharply on questions of institutional design.

In this section, we test how the electoral context affects the relationship between losing and trust in the United States. In particular, we assume that the stakes of an election matter; that is, the extent to which government is granted power to implement preferred policies. As our model predicts, when the stakes are greater, so too should be the effects of losing. In other words, the impact of losing should vary by the importance of an electoral office, and these perceptions are likely to be shaped by the context of the electoral choice. While few surveys provide questions that measure trust in government at the

provincial party identification or national party identification across the two sets of data and the various panels but the pattern of coefficients is of a significant and consistent effect.

[7] Indeed, there is some evidence in the 1997 data to suggest that those who won in Quebec provincial elections were in fact among the most dissatisfied of all of Canada's voters.

state or local level, data on perceptions of state governments were available in a survey commissioned by the Kennedy School of Government and National Public Radio (NPR). We use these data to estimate models of trust in state government.

Our estimates of trust (or distrust, in this case) in state governments control for several demographic factors, evaluations of the federal government, and include a measure of whether the respondent identified with the party of the state's governor. We have two measures of electoral context that provide variation in how voters might perceive the stakes of an election—the formal powers granted to a state's governor, and whether the state has unified or divided government. One of our hypotheses is that citizens will perceive that more is at stake when electing a Governor with strong executive powers. As a result, the effect of losing on trust is expected to be greater among respondents in states with strong governors than those in states where governors have few formal powers. Likewise, we anticipate that voters living in states where one party controls both the legislature and the governor will see more at stake, and consequently will be more affected by losing. At the individual level, we also expect that the effect of losing on distrust is likely to be greater among the highly interested and strong partisans, when compared to those less interested and less partisan.

To account for how voters respond to elections where more was at stake and to test how different types of voters might be affected by losing, we estimate models of distrust in state government with different subsets of the data. We do this by estimating how support for a losing party affects trust among respondents who live in states where governors have strong powers and then estimate the same model with respondents who live in other states. We follow this same procedure and estimate our model with respondents who live in states with unified government, and then again with those who reside in places with divided government. Finally, we estimate the effect of losing on trust among strong partisans, weak partisans, those interested in politics, and those not interested. Table 7.4 simply reports the coefficient for the effect of losing on trust, for models estimated with these eight subsets of the data. Higher scores on the dependent variable reflect more distrust.

The results demonstrate that electoral context conditions how losing affects trust in government. Once again, we see that the relationship between losing and distrust of state government is greater among individuals who have stronger identification with political parties, and also among those most interested in politics. As expected, the relationship between losing and distrust is also more robust among respondents who live in states where governors have stronger powers. Likewise, the effect is greater in places where a single party has control of the legislative and executive branches. The 2003 California gubernatorial recall election—spearheaded by Republicans who ended unified Democratic control of state government by ushering Arnold Schwarzenegger

TABLE 7.4. *Distrust in state government: the effect of identifying with a losing party in the American states, across different state electoral contexts*

	Effect of supporting losing party in state
Lives in state with strong governor	0.44
Lives in state with a weak governor	0.24
Lives in state with unified government	0.37
Lives in state with divided government	0.24
Strong party identification	0.38
Weak/no party identification	0.13
Very interested in politics	0.31
Response other than very interested	0.24

Notes: OLS coefficients estimated from models predicting distrust in state government, controlling for age, education, gender, race (black), ethnicity (Latino/a), change in personal finances, and evaluations of the federal government. All coefficients are statistically significant. Dependent variable is coded such that higher scores reflect more distrust in the respondent's state government. Respondents were asked 'how often do you trust [your] state government'. The variable is coded 1: always, 2: mostly, 3: sometimes, 4: never.

Source: Kennedy School of Government/NPR Survey, 1999.

into office—provides a potent illustration of how unified control of government may generate bitterness among losers.

These results from the United States further illustrate how the effects of losing on citizens' overall assessment of their political system might be affected by federalism. In previous chapters, we demonstrated that supporters of the party not controlling the White House—particularly strong partisans—were less trusting of the federal government. Table 7.4 illustrates the same effects with evaluations of state governments. Once again losers are more distrusting of their state government if their party is out of power there, and this effect is larger among strong partisans. It is important to note, however, that US federalism allows citizens to lose on one level while winning on others. Put differently, strong Democrats' trust in the federal government soured after losing the 2000 presidential election (see Chapter 5), but Democrats living in states controlled by Democrats, nonetheless, may have found reasons to trust their state governments. This effect could be even larger if they lived in places with unified Democratic control of government or in places with Democratic governors who possess strong executive powers, like Georgia, Oregon, and Vermont. This dispersion of the effects of winning and losing across different levels of government in the United States may be part of the reason why the effects of the 2000 US presidential election do not appear to be particularly severe when the country is considered as a whole.

CONCLUSION

There are identifiable and relatively stable features of democratic life that serve to organize and constrain citizens' political experiences, and which allow them to develop attitudes about the workings of the political system. Citizens form attitudes about politics in systemic contexts whose institutional structures mediate preferences, define the choices that are available, and provide citizens with opportunities to be heard in the political process (Powell 1982, 1989). One feature of democratic life that is important for citizen attitudes toward the system is how democratic institutions treat those who are in the majority and those who belong to the minority.

In this chapter we have shown that responses to losing are mediated by institutions and, further, that specific institutions, and not just combinations of institutions, help to shape the response of losers. Losers express less negative views about the political system than winners when electoral rules are more proportional, when the political system has a greater number of veto players, and when power is shared within the political system. Thus, the size of the winner loser gap depends on whether institutions are exclusive or inclusive. We also show that federalism, as a stand-alone institution that can be part of either a majoritarian or consensus bundle of institutions is effective in allowing losers some say in the system, and therefore helps make losers more positive towards the system. Put simply, then, having a say and sharing in power, even when in the opposition at the national level, enhances losers' consent.

The findings presented here provide additional evidence that institutional variation is an important mediator of public opinion toward political authorities. As recent research on government support has shown, institutional variation is an important element for understanding citizens' ability to assign credit and blame to incumbents for economic performance (Anderson 2000). Regarding the study of democratic institutions, our analyses also document important and systematic consequences of different kinds of democracies at the level of mass publics. Aside from affecting policy outcomes (Lijphart 1994; Crepaz 1996), cabinet stability and conflict (Powell 1986), or the congruence of elite and mass policy preferences (Huber and Powell 1994), to name just a few examples, our results show that different forms of democratic organization also have consequences for public attitudes toward democracy as a form of government.

Whether citizens evaluate the functioning of their democracy based on the recent performance of their electoral institutions and organization or based on the more lasting institutions, such as electoral laws, holds importance for the broader scholarly debate about the design of democratic institutions. Specifically, political theorists have debated whether it is more important that the institutions produce superior outcomes or that the institutions are designed in a way that produces maximum process fairness to all participants. Our results add to these debates by showing that institutions have varying effects, depending on whether citizens are among the winners or losers. This suggests that it is important to consider not simply the direct, aggregate effect of institutions on the behavior of all citizens, but also their effects on particularly important subgroups within the electorate.

While much of our study up to this point has focused on comparing winners and losers, we now turn to examining losers in greater detail. That is, we focus on comparing losers only: why are some losers in some countries more sanguine about the political system while other losers in other countries are more displeased with the political process? This is the question we turn to in the next chapter.

Comparing Losers' Assessments of Electoral Democracy

In the chapters so far, the evidence we have presented shows that losers and winners differ systematically in how they view various aspects of democratic governance. To recap, we have documented a gap in the legitimacy beliefs of the winners and losers, and this gap exists with regard to different dimensions of support for democratic political systems, over time, and across countries. We also have shown that there are a number of factors, both at the level of individual voters and different political contexts that serve to attenuate or exacerbate the impact that losing has on citizens and, by implication, help shape the size of the gap in legitimacy beliefs between winners and losers.

Theoretically speaking, this evidence suggests that, while there may be cross-national differences in the size of the winner–loser gap, the relevant comparison is that of winners and losers. Such a perspective is revealing when we are interested in understanding which countries experience the greatest tensions between winners' and losers' understandings of the political system and its processes. As such, this approach helps us to pinpoint variations in intra-country differences and political dynamics. However, such a perspective is not necessarily designed to specify the conditions under which some losers in some countries are happier with the political process than others—that is, why we may see differences in attitudes toward the system among different sets of losers. This is the topic we turn to next.

COMPARING WINNERS AND LOSERS VERSUS COMPARING JUST LOSERS

Electoral democracy is designed to settle political disagreements peacefully. The principle is to let the party or parties with more votes, rather than the group(s) with more military might, govern. The principle is attractive and compelling both for normative and practical reasons. An election is much less costly and less ethically challenging than a civil war. Yet, as attractive as it may be, electoral democracy raises a number of problems. First, not any type of election will do. To be acceptable to all, the election must be perceived to be fair and honest. Second, those who feel that their vital interests are threatened by the elected government are likely to be highly skeptical about the virtues of the electoral process. Third, it is easier for supporters of the party or parties that form the government than for supporters of the parties that form the opposition to accept the outcome of an election. Furthermore, supporters of parties that systematically lose, election after election, may come to question the legitimacy of electoral democracy.

It is tempting to think positively about electoral democracy when one wins and to become skeptical when one loses. And indeed the previous chapters have shown that winners are generally more positive about electoral institutions and about the political process more generally, than losers. Viewed from this perspective, losers are a crucial group, in particular because, as we have pointed out above, elections frequently produce more losers than winners. It is not difficult to convince winners that elections are 'good'; after all, their party is in power. It is more of a challenge to convince losers, given that their expressed preference is for someone else to govern. Ultimately, the hope is that somehow most of the losers will accept the outcome.

Instead of comparing winners and losers, as we have done up till now, this chapter focuses on losers—more precisely those who voted for parties that were not part of the government that was formed after the election. That is, instead of investigating the size of the winner–loser gap, we turn to understanding differences across different kinds of losers across different countries. In particular, we take a look at how losers assess electoral democracy and we identify the factors that make them willing or unwilling to accept the legitimacy of elections. Following our theoretical model and the evidence we have assembled so far, we assume that losers' reactions depend on three groups of factors: (1) macro-level factors—that is, the kind of *country* losers live in; (2) meso-level factors—that is, the kind of *party* they support; (3) micro-level factors—that is, the kind of *person* they are. Put simply, we presume that it is easier for losers to think positively about elections in some countries than in others, for some party supporters than for others, and for some types of voters than for others. The objective of this chapter, then, is to determine how these various factors combine to enhance or diminish losers' appreciation of the functioning of electoral democracy.

COMPARING SIMILAR LOSERS' ATTITUDES TOWARD ELECTORAL DEMOCRACY

For the analyses described below, we use the *Comparative Study of Electoral Systems* (CSES) data set. The CSES data set comprises election studies conducted in thirty-two countries between 1996 and 2001. The major advantage of this data set is that it covers a wide range of countries and a very wide range of party supporters, enabling us to examine the impact of country-level and party-level as well as individual-level factors. To make losers directly comparable across countries—that is, to compare similar kinds of losers— we focus on losers in *legislative* elections.[1] Furthermore, legislative elections are more directly relevant to the concerns of this chapter, given our interest in party-level factors, which we will discuss in more detail below.[2] Winners and losers were coded on the basis of a recall question that asked respondents which parties they voted for (the surveys were conducted immediately after the election). If respondents voted for a governing party, they were coded as winners; otherwise, they were categorized as losers.

We examine three dimensions of losers' assessments of electoral democracy: their level of satisfaction with the way democracy works in their country, their evaluation of the fairness of the most recent election, and their evaluation of the responsiveness of elected representatives.

Satisfaction with democracy was measured by the standard question: 'On the whole, are you satisfied, fairly satisfied, not very satisfied, or not at all satisfied with the way democracy works in (country)?'. Evaluation of fairness was tapped by the following question: 'In some countries, people believe their elections are conducted fairly. In other countries, people believe that their elections are conducted unfairly. Thinking of the last election in (country), where would you place it on this scale of one to five, where one means that

---

[1] The CSES data set includes seven studies conducted after concurrent presidential and legislative elections (Chile, Mexico [2000], Peru, Romania, Russia, Taiwan, and the United States), one after concurrent prime ministerial and legislative elections (Israel) and two after presidential elections (Belarus and Lithuania). These studies have been excluded. In the case of concurrent elections, we would have had to distinguish those who lost in both elections, those who lost only in the presidential election and those who lost only in the legislative election (see Anderson and LoTempio 2002) and to distinguish all of them from those who were involved in only one election. There were only two non-concurrent presidential elections, both in post-communist states, which make generalizations uneasy. Moreover, we had to exclude several countries with parliamentary systems because the surveys were conducted when it was unclear who would form the new government (e.g. Hungary).

[2] The 1998 and 2000 Hong Kong legislative elections had to be excluded because the identity of the winners was ambiguous: the Democratic Party won a majority of the seats that were contested under universal suffrage but the party was in a minority position in the whole legislative assembly. The 1998 Ukraine election study was also excluded. The Communist party won a plurality of seats but the president selects the prime minister and he nominated a person from his own party, the People's Democratic party. In this case as well, it is not clear exactly who are the winners and losers. Finally, the 2000 Thailand election study could not be considered because it did not provide information about which party respondents voted for (the survey provided information about vote intentions). All in all, the final data set we are able to make use of for the analyses that follow included twenty legislative election studies conducted in nineteen different countries (Spain has two election studies included in the data set, in 1996 and in 2000): Australia (1996, not included in Fairness), Canada (1997), Belgium (not included in Fairness), Czech Republic (1996), Germany (1998), Denmark (1998), Spain (1996, 2000), Great Britain (1997), Iceland (1999), Japan (1996), Mexico (1997), Netherlands (1998), New Zealand (1996), Norway (1997), Poland (1997), Portugal (2002), Slovenia (1996), Sweden (1998), and Switzerland (1999).

the last election was conducted fairly and five means that the election was conducted unfairly?'.[3]

Three questions were used to form an index designed to measure people's sense of the responsiveness of the political system. The first has to do with the capacity of elected representatives to understand the concerns of ordinary voters: 'Some people say that members of Parliament know what ordinary people think. Others say that members of Parliament don't know much about what ordinary people think. Using the (one to five) scale, where would you place yourself?'. The second concerns the willingness of parties to respond to voters' concerns: 'Some people say that political parties in (country) care what ordinary people think. Others say that political parties in (country) don't care what ordinary people think. Using the (one to five) scale, where would you place yourself?'. The third question ascertains the system's perceived responsiveness: 'Some people say it makes a difference who is in power. Others say that it does not make a difference who is in power. Using the (one to five) scale, where would you place yourself?'. These three questions are combined to form a responsiveness index.[4] The following analysis thus utilizes three dependent variables: 'satisfaction', 'fairness', and 'responsiveness', which constitute three dimensions of voters' overall assessment of how electoral democracy works in their country. Each of these three dimensions is measured on a scale where -1 represents the most negative evaluation and $+1$ represents the most positive evaluation.

LOSERS' OVERALL VERDICT

Figures 8.1–8.3 present the mean scores for each of the three dimensions observed among losers in each country (see also Appendix 8A.1). The data show that more losers are satisfied with the functioning of democracy than are dissatisfied, an overwhelming majority believes that the most recent election was fair, and more losers say that the political system is responsive than the opposite. In fact, losers' evaluations are particularly positive on each of the three dimensions in Denmark, the Netherlands, and Norway, and least positive in Japan, while evaluations are more mixed across countries and dimensions otherwise. What, then, accounts for differences in losers' attitudes toward the political system across the countries included in our sample?

ACCOUNTING FOR SYSTEMIC DIFFERENCES IN LOSERS' JUDGMENTS

The first step of our analysis consists of explaining variations among countries in losers' overall evaluations of the functioning of electoral democracy.

---

[3] This question was not asked in Australia and Belgium, and so the number of cases is slightly reduced with respect to that dimension.

[4] Cronbach's alpha was 0.49.

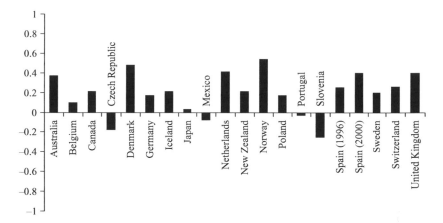

FIGURE 8.1. Losers' satisfaction with democracy

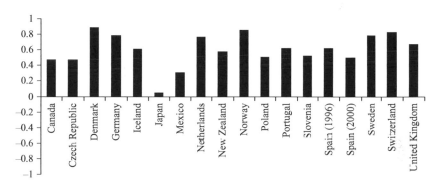

FIGURE 8.2. Losers' evaluations of fairness of election

Specifically, in line with our previous analyses and theoretical priors, we expect the following systemic factors to make losers feel more positive or negative about the political process. The first two hypotheses concern the degree of democracy and the length of the democratic experience. To test these, we distinguish among three groups of countries: those that were clearly democratic at the time of the election and had a long experience with democratic elections (established democracies); those that were clearly democratic at the time of the election but with a short experience with democracy (non-established democracies); and finally, those where the degree of democracy was more dubious (weak democracies).

As before, we use the Freedom House ratings of political rights as an indicator of degree of democracy. Eighteen of the nineteen countries examined here obtained the 'maximal' score of 1 at the time their legislative election

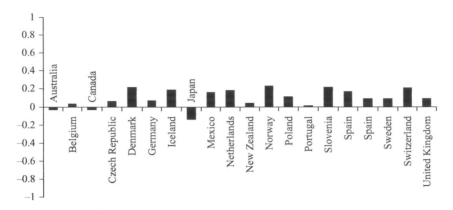

FIGURE 8.3. Losers' evaluations of responsiveness

was held. Among these eighteen, thirteen can be considered as 'established' democracies; that is, they have had systematically high scores (1 or 2) on Freedom House ratings of political rights over the previous twenty years: Australia, Belgium, Canada, Denmark, Germany, Iceland, Japan, Netherlands, New Zealand, Norway, Britain, Sweden, and Switzerland. And five countries can be construed as 'non-established' democracies: Spain, Portugal, Poland, Slovenia, and the Czech Republic. These five countries were coded as 1 on our 'non-established' democracy variable. Mexico, finally, is the only country which did not get the 'highest' score and is therefore coded 1 on our 'weak' democracy variable (see Appendix 8A.2).

The first hypothesis is that losers' judgments should be more negative in 'weak' democracies. We expect that, in countries where basic political rights are strongly respected, even losers are willing to recognize that elections are conducted fairly, that politicians care about voters, and that elections matter. The proposition may appear tautological, though it must be kept in mind that judgments are subjective by their very nature, and that citizens' expectations about the proper functioning of democratic institutions may actually be higher in more democratic countries. These higher expectations, in turn, may sometimes feed disappointment among those with the least to complain about in terms of democratic performance when considered from a cross-national perspective. There is some evidence to support this view, as recent studies have shown that disenchantment with the political system in more democratic countries frequently is felt most acutely among those with the most democratic inclinations (Dalton 2004).

And as we have noted in our chapter comparing losers' consent in old and new democracies, it may well be that it is not only the degree of democracy that matters but the length of experience with the democratic process. After all, democracy entails, among other things, making compromises in order to please different segments of the population. As a consequence, the democratic process is designed to be somewhat messy. It may take time for citizens to appreciate that such messiness is valuable and produces good outcomes. In particular, it may take time for losers to understand that there are many viewpoints in society, that it is unfortunately impossible to satisfy every one of them, and that it is impossible for everyone to win every time. Thus, in addition to a more sizable gap between winners' and losers' evaluations of the political system in weak democracies, as a second hypothesis we posit that the evaluations of losers in non-established democracies will be more negative than in established democracies.

This expectation is open to challenge, at least a priori. We suspect that the opposite pattern could also occur as citizens who have experienced how bad things can be when certain basic political rights are not respected might well be more appreciative of the benefits of democracy and more prone to accept its shortcomings. That is, citizens may value democratic rights and practices more highly when the contrast with the most immediate past experience of authoritarian rule is particular stark: if this is the case, losers in new democracies may evaluate democratic politics, however imperfect, more positively.

The third macro-level factor that may lead to cross-national differences in losers' consent deals with the kind of rules that govern the election of representatives. Four basic types of electoral systems can be distinguished (Blais and Massicotte 2002): plurality (the candidate with the most votes is elected), majority (the candidate with more than 50 percent of the vote is elected), proportional representation (the number of seats a party wins depends on the number of votes obtained), and mixed (some combination of the former). There is only one instance of a majority system (Australia) in the group of countries, and only two of a plurality system (Britain and Canada). The great majority of countries included in the analysis are either PR or mixed, and many of the mixed systems are corrective, which make them similar (with respect to the seats/votes ratio) to PR. Under such circumstances, one practical solution is to use a scale to ascertain the degree of proportionality or disproportionality of the electoral system, such as Gallagher's least-squares index of disproportionality (Gallagher 1991), which allows us to distinguish the most proportional from the least proportional systems (see Appendix 8A.3).

As we emphasized in Chapter 7, the degree of proportionality of the electoral system basically has two effects upon losing and losers: a direct effect, by giving citizens a say in how governments are elected, and an indirect effect by making multiparty governments more likely. Following the earlier results, we would expect that losers feel more negative about electoral democracy in more disproportional systems. The logic is that losing parties get 'fairer' representation in more proportional systems because their share of seats corresponds more or less to their vote share. Supporters of these parties may dislike the outcome of the election but they can reason that 'their' party was not treated unfairly. Similarly, following the logic outlined in Chapter 7, a larger number of parties in government may mean less movement in policy outcomes and thus less dissatisfaction among the losers.

The fourth macro-level factor deals with the impact of the economy—specifically, a nation's wealth—on voters' judgments. Lipset (1959), especially, has argued that a substantial level of economic development is a prerequisite to support for democracy. Similarly, as Przeworski (2001: 11) points out '... in affluent countries even the electoral losers have too much at stake to risk being defeated in a struggle over dictatorship. In poor societies there is little to distribute, so that a party that moves against democracy and is defeated has relatively little to lose'. Following this, we expect losers in more economically developed countries to feel more positive about electoral democracy.[5] The impact of the economy on people's evaluation of democracy has been seriously questioned especially with respect to the democratization process in Eastern Europe (see Hofferbert and Klingemann 1999; Evans and Whitefield 2001). It remains to be seen whether a systematic pattern emerges among political losers in the countries examined here.

To examine our hypotheses, we thus estimate the impact of the variables representing 'weak' and 'non-established' democracies, Gallagher's index of disproportionality, and the human development index on satisfaction with democracy and evaluations of fairness and of responsiveness. As previously (Chapter 7), we also control for the number of parties in government and whether the country has a federal form of government. Table 8.1 shows the results.

The results clearly confirm the hypotheses concerning democratic experience with respect to the first two indicators. Losers from non-established democracies are more likely to express dissatisfaction with the functioning of democracy in their country, and they are less likely to believe that the most recent election had been conducted fairly. Moreover, this effect is most pronounced in the least democratic case in our sample (Mexico). Interestingly, however, losers in less democratic countries are less prone to complain about a lack of responsiveness. In fact, their evaluations of responsiveness are more positive than in established democracies, and higher still in the weakest democracy in our sample (Mexico). This speaks to the notion that voters in countries with recent histories and perhaps remnants of authoritarian government are appreciative of the new rules of the game.

The expectation that evaluations of electoral democracy are more negative when and where there is only weak correspondence between seat shares and vote shares is also supported. We find that losers in more disproportional systems are more prone to say that the election was unfair, and they are also more

---

[5] The indicator of economic development is the United Nations Human Development Index (see Appendix 8A.4).

TABLE 8.1. *Determinants of losers' assessments of democracy: systemic variables*

Independent variables	Satisfaction with democracy	Evaluation of fairness	Evaluation of responsiveness
Weak democracy	−0.32**	−0.43**	0.22**
	(0.04)	(0.04)	(0.03)
Non-established democracy	−0.18**	−0.18**	0.06**
	(0.02)	(0.02)	(0.01)
Human development index	1.11**	−0.84*	0.81**
	(0.32)	(0.30)	(0.22)
Disproportionality	−0.22	−1.69**	−0.59**
	(0.14)	(0.13)	(0.09)
Federalism	0.01	0.07**	−0.03**
	(0.01)	(0.01)	(0.01)
Parties in government	0.04	0.07*	0.12**
	(0.02)	(0.03)	(0.02)
(Parties in government)^2	−0.01**	−0.01	−0.02**
	(0.00)	(0.01)	(0.00)
Constant	−0.76*	1.45**	−0.78**
	(0.31)	(0.30)	(0.21)
N	15,287	13,621	15,414
Adj. R^2	0.04	0.06	0.02

** $p < 0.01$.
* $p < 0.05$.

inclined to think that the political system does not care about ordinary citizens. Moreover, these negative assessments seem to nurture dissatisfaction with the functioning of democracy (this coefficient is significant at the 0.10 level when a one-tailed test of statistical significance is employed).

The findings concerning human development are mixed. Losers in more developed countries appear more satisfied with the way democracy works and have more positive evaluations of the political system's responsiveness, but they emerge as more critical when it comes to ascertaining the fairness of elections. In our view, the most plausible interpretation for this negative effect is that citizens in more developed countries have adopted higher standards of fairness than those in less developed ones. They expect an election to be fair and have become less tolerant of rules or practices that jeopardize that goal.

Finally, the results for the number of parties in government as well as the federalism variable are broadly consistent with what we found in Chapter 7. Generally speaking, the results for the variable 'number of parties in government' indicates that a greater number of parties enhances positive attitudes toward government, while the squared term suggests that this effect is curvilinear. The results for federalism are somewhat more equivocal, with federalism producing more positive evaluations of fairness and more negative evaluations of responsiveness (though the coefficients are small). While these results are broadly similar to those found in Chapter 7, it is possible that potential differences in the two sets of results are driven by the fact that our exclusive focus on losers reduces the variability in attitudes in our data set. Moreover, while the results in Chapter 7 are based solely on a sample of West European countries, the analyses in this chapter are based on a sample of countries that includes a more varied set of populations. It is therefore plausible that some of the differences in the effects are due to different reactions of losers in differently situated democracies and therefore not necessarily inconsistent with the results we showed earlier. Since we do not primarily focus on these effects for the purposes of this analysis, we do not comment on these effects in the remainder of this chapter.

DOES THE PARTY ONE SUPPORTS MAKE A DIFFERENCE?

The evidence so far suggests that losers in some countries are more positive in their evaluations of electoral democracy than losers in other countries—put simply, losers react differently depending on the kind of political system they live in. Going beyond cross-national differences in losers' consent, we turn next to differences in the kinds of parties losers support. Specifically, we expect that losers' assessments of electoral democracy in part also hinge on the kind of party they support. While the voters who are the subject of this chapter all supported a party that lost the election, not all losing parties were in the same situation.

The first distinction to be made is between the parties that were in government at the time the election was held and those that were not. We expect supporters of 'incumbent' parties to be more supportive of electoral democracy than those of parties that were not in government before the election. After all, the former had enjoyed the pleasure of winning in the previous election and of having their party in government for a certain period of time. Thus, our expectation is that supporters of losing parties that formed the government at the time of the election should feel more positive about electoral democracy than those of parties that were not in government.

This is not an obvious prediction. In some sense, losing an election when one's party was in power should be a more disappointing experience than losing when one's party was not in power. In the former case, one's party is clearly worse off, whereas in the latter case, there is no change in the status quo. At the same time, however, we would assume it is more difficult to express dissatisfaction with democracy and to say that the election was unfair when one's party was actually in charge of government and, indirectly at least, of the very election that it lost.

We should add an important caveat at this point. The information we have concerns vote choice in the most recent election (time t). Some of the people who voted for the losing 'incumbent' party may not have voted for that party in the prior election ($t-1$), and these 'new' supporters may have fewer reasons to 'feel good'. Fortunately, these new supporters are unlikely to be numerous since a losing governing party usually loses ground and does not attract many new voters.

Going beyond the simple in- and out-party dichotomy, it is useful to distinguish major and minor incumbent parties further. Supporters of major governing parties should be more inclined to provide positive assessments of electoral democracy than supporters of minor governing parties. After all, whenever there is a coalition government, the major party in the coalition obtains the greatest amount of power, and the minor partners may have more mixed feelings about the coalition experience. As a consequence, supporters of these minor governing parties may be less prone to say that democracy is working well or that politicians are responsive to their concerns.

Two additional distinctions need to be made among 'non-incumbent' parties. The first distinction is between those parties that have never been in government and those that have had prior experience as part of the executive branch. The idea that power alternates between different groups and parties is crucial in democratic theory, so much so that questions are raised whenever there is no alternation over a period of time. Powell (1982: 6), for instance, asked 'Did the competitive electoral process result in a change in the party or party coalition controlling the chief executive during these two decades?' when ascertaining which countries should be deemed to be democratic. Based on this theoretical premise, we expect supporters of parties that have never been in government to be particularly skeptical about the virtues of electoral democracy.[6]

Finally, it is worth noting that particular attention should be given to new parties—that is, parties that are recent entrants into the electoral arena. We expect supporters of these new parties to have a longer time horizon and not to expect 'their' party to win an election in the short term. As a result, many of them may be satisfied if their party is making some progress in terms of vote support or simply contesting the election and may be willing to accept not being in government for some time. Thus, we anticipate supporters of new parties to remain relatively positive in their evaluations of electoral democracy. For the purposes of our analysis, we define a new party as one that is running in an election for the first or second time.

Taken together, then, we distinguish among five types of losing parties and hence five types of electoral losers: major incumbent parties, minor incumbent parties, and among non-incumbents those that have never been in government in the past (non-incumbent/never), those that have previously been in

---

[6] Again, it would be nice to be able to distinguish people who have always supported these 'constant losers' from new supporters but unfortunately the data do not provide that information.

TABLE 8.2. *Types of losing parties*

Type	Parties	Voters
Major incumbent	8.3%	29.03%
	(8)	(4,224)
Minor incumbent	7.3%	3.9%
	(7)	(571)
Non-incumbent/Never	49.0%	36.2%
	(47)	(5,261)
Non-incumbent/Previous	19.8%	28.1%
	(19)	(4,084)
Non-incumbent/New	15.6%	9.6%
	(15)	(1,400)
Number of cases	96	14,550

Notes: Number of parties/respondents shown in parentheses.

government (non-incumbent/previous), and new parties (non-incumbent/new). We expect evaluations to be most positive among supporters of new parties and major governing parties and most negative among supporters of non-incumbents that have never been in government.

Table 8.2 presents the distribution of these five types of losing parties (see Appendix 8A.5 for the list of parties in each country). It can be seen that the most frequent category, corresponding to forty-seven of the ninety-six 'losing' parties considered here, is the party that has never been in government in the past. These parties tend to be smaller, however, so that their supporters represent about one-third of losing voters. Then there are fifteen new parties and nineteen parties that had been in government in the past though they were not incumbent. The latter tend to be bigger and their supporters constitute about one-quarter of losing voters. Finally, there are a few incumbent parties among the losers, but their supporters represent (collapsing major and minor partners) about one-third of losers.

The question, of course, is whether those who voted for these different kinds of parties assessed electoral democracy in systematically different ways. The estimations reported in Table 8.3 allow us to address this question. The estimation model now includes the systemic variables discussed in the previous section plus the four dummy variables corresponding to four types of parties (the reference category is the group of parties that had never been in government).

We expect supporters of the parties that had never been in government to be the most negative in their evaluations. This category is the reference category in the model, and so the prediction is that the four dummy 'party type' variables will be positive. This is basically what we find in Table 8.3 with respect to two of the indicators of system support, overall satisfaction

TABLE 8.3. *Determinants of losers' assessments of democracy: systemic and party variables*

Independent variables	Satisfaction with democracy	Evaluation of fairness	Evaluation of responsiveness
Major incumbent	0.29**	0.17**	0.14**
	(0.01)	(0.01)	(0.01)
Minor incumbent	0.20**	−0.01	0.10**
	(0.03)	(0.03)	(0.02)
Non-incumbent/Previous	0.14**	−0.02	0.06**
	(0.01)	(0.01)	(0.01)
Non-incumbent/New	0.09**	−0.07**	0.07**
	(0.02)	(0.02)	(0.01)
Weak democracy	−0.32**	−0.57**	0.22**
	(0.04)	(0.04)	(0.03)
Non-established democracy	−0.14**	−0.22**	0.09**
	(0.02)	(0.02)	(0.01)
Human development index	2.02**	−1.03**	1.30**
	(0.32)	(0.30)	(0.22)
Disproportionality	−0.40*	−2.33**	−0.67**
	(0.14)	(0.13)	(0.10)
Federalism	−0.04*	0.02*	−0.05**
	(0.01)	(0.01)	(0.01)
Parties in government	0.02	−0.06	0.11**
	(0.02)	(0.03)	(0.02)
(Parties in government)^2	−0.01**	0.02*	−0.02**
	(0.00)	(0.01)	(0.00)
Constant	−1.69**	1.80**	−1.28**
	(0.31)	(0.30)	(0.21)
N	15,287	13,621	15,414
Adj. R^2	0.07	0.08	0.04

**$p < 0.01$.
*$p < 0.05$.

with democracy and assessments of responsiveness. All eight coefficients are positive and significant. The hypothesis that supporters of parties that have never been in government are most critical is thus clearly supported for these two indicators.

Table 8.3 also shows that the most 'positive' group is made up of those who voted for 'major' incumbents. This supports the hypothesis that supporters of major governing parties are the 'best' losers of all. They may be disappointed by the outcome of the election, but 'their' party had just been in power. As a consequence, they are not as critical of the system as other losers. The variable coefficients also confirm the prediction that supporters of major incumbents provide more positive assessments than supporters of minor incumbents.

We had also predicted that supporters of new parties would emerge as relatively positive in their assessments of electoral democracy. This prediction is only partly borne out. Supporters of new parties tend to be more satisfied with democracy and to perceive the system to be more responsive than supporters of 'old' parties that have never been in government. However, these differences are modest, and supporters of new parties are not more positive in their feelings about the system than those of voters who supported old parties that had been previously in government.

All in all, though, the differences between types of parties fit with theoretical predictions as far as satisfaction with democracy and evaluations of responsiveness are concerned. The findings are somewhat different when it comes to perceptions of fairness. There is one common pattern, and that is the propensity of supporters of incumbents to be quite positive. After all, 'their' party was in charge of the election and it would be surprising if they were to conclude that the election was unfairly conducted. With respect to fairness, however, the most critical group can be found not among those who voted for old parties that had never been in government, but rather among those who supported new parties.

To examine whether the differences among these types of losing parties are more pronounced in certain kinds of countries, we created interaction variables to sort out the impact of party types according to the level of human development. Table 8.4 shows a very clear pattern: for the majority of the measures of type of incumbent party, after taking account of the interaction with human development, there is little difference from those losers who voted for the reference group (non-incumbents who have never been in office). The one interaction that is significant for two of the three support measures is of non-incumbent/previous, suggesting that losers of out parties that had previously been in office were particularly critical in more developed democracies.

DISTINGUISHING TYPES OF VOTERS

Taken together, the evidence assembled so far suggests that type of country and type of party both affect losers' evaluations of electoral democracy. Following our theoretical model, losers' evaluations of electoral democracy should also depend on personal characteristics. We focus on two of these characteristics: education and ideological orientation. We expect the better educated to provide more positive evaluations of electoral democracy. It is well known that education makes people more open-minded and tolerant of opposing viewpoints (Hyman and Wright 1979). Tolerance, in turn, is related to support for democratic values (Gibson 2002). Furthermore, the better educated are more likely to have been exposed to the dominant norm that in a democracy one should lose gracefully (McClosky and Zaller 1984).[7]

But it is also easier to lose when one does not have strong views about what government should and should not do. If governments are eager to find

---

[7] Education is coded from 0 for those with no schooling at all to 7 for those with a university degree.

TABLE 8.4. *Determinants of losers' assessments of democracy: systemic and party variables with interactions*

Independent variables	Satisfaction with democracy	Evaluation of fairness	Evaluation of responsiveness
Major incumbent	−0.13	−0.19	−0.5
	(0.40)	(0.35)	(0.28)
Minor incumbent	1.70*	1.04	0.48
	(0.78)	(0.64)	(0.52)
Non-incumbent/Previous	1.42**	0.62	1.64**
	(0.51)	(0.44)	(0.35)
Non-incumbent/New	0.71	0.75	−0.21
	(0.64)	(0.54)	(0.44)
Major incumbent * HDI	0.45	0.40	0.77*
	(0.44)	(0.38)	(0.30)
Minor incumbent * HDI	−1.63	−1.14*	−0.42
	(0.85)	(0.70)	(0.56)
NI previous * HDI	−1.37*	−0.69	−1.70**
	(0.55)	(0.47)	(0.38)
NI new * HDI	−0.67	−0.88	0.30
	(0.69)	(0.58)	(0.47)
Weak democracy	−0.29**	−0.54**	0.25**
	(0.04)	(0.04)	(0.03)
Non-established democracy	−0.15**	−0.22**	0.07**
	(0.02)	(0.02)	(0.01)
Human development index	2.19**	−0.90*	1.18**
	(0.43)	(0.39)	(0.30)
Disproportionality	−0.42**	−2.30**	−0.68**
	(0.14)	(0.14)	(0.10)
Federalism	−0.04**	0.02*	−0.05**
	(0.01)	(0.01)	(0.01)
Parties in government	0.02	−0.05	0.11**
	(0.02)	(0.04)	(0.02)
(Parties in government)^2	−0.01**	0.01*	−0.02**
	(0.00)	(0.01)	(0.00)
Constant	−1.83**	1.66**	−1.16**
	(0.41)	(0.38)	(0.28)
N	15,287	13,621	15,414
Adj. R^2	0.07	0.09	0.04

$**p < 0.01.$
$*p < 0.05.$

compromises that are bound to displease those who favor substantial changes to the status quo, we should find individuals who hold 'radical' views to be particularly critical of electoral democracy. Everything else being equal, therefore, citizens who are on the extreme right and those who are on the extreme left of the political spectrum should provide more negative assessments of representative democracy.

To measure ideological extremism, we rely on the following question: 'In politics people sometimes talk of left and right. Where would you place yourself on a scale from 0 to 10 where 0 means the left and 10 means the right?'. Those who placed themselves at 0, 1, or 2 on the scale, who also constitute 15 percent of the losers, are construed to be on the 'extreme left', and those who placed themselves at 8, 9, or 10, who represent 16 percent of the sample, are considered to be on the 'extreme right'. All others, 69 percent of losers, constitute the reference group.[8]

We estimated models that included the country-level as well as party-type variables employed before alongside education and ideology. The results, shown in Table 8.5 indicate that, as expected, the better educated are more satisfied with democracy, that they are more likely to indicate that the election was fair, and that the political system is responsive. The results concerning ideological orientation are more difficult to pin down, however. We find that respondents on the extreme right are systematically more positive in their evaluations of electoral democracy. The differences are not colossal, but they appear to be systematic, and they are consistent with what we found in Chapter 6, using a different data set and a different sample of countries. At this point, we have no simple explanation for this surprising finding. We speculate that, to the extent that right-wing voters are more patriotic or nationalistic, support for the country's institutions in part is an expression of support for the political community. In contrast, people on the extreme left do come out, as expected, as less satisfied with democracy, and as more skeptical about the fairness of the election. They also appear, however, to be slightly more positive about the system's responsiveness. But again, these differences are substantively small.

In the last stage of the analysis, we sought to determine whether these personal characteristics matter differently in different kinds of countries. As Table 8.6 shows, there is indeed evidence for such interaction effects. With respect to evaluations of the fairness of the electoral process, the gap between the better and the lesser educated is most pronounced in less developed countries. Specifically, in these less developed countries the better educated emerge as most positive about the fairness of the most recent election (readers should keep in mind that overall evaluations are quite positive to start with), a reflection perhaps of their strong adherence to the value of representative democracy and of their willingness to tolerate some shortcomings in the conduct of elections.

The situation is reversed when it comes to evaluations of responsiveness. Here, we find a more sizable gap in the effects of education among the more developed countries. The better educated do not appear to be more sanguine in their assessments of the system's responsiveness than the less educated in less

---

[8] The left/right question was not asked in Japan, and the following analyses therefore do not include Japanese respondents.

TABLE 8.5. *Determinants of losers' assessments of democracy: systemic, party, and individual-level variables*

Independent variables	Satisfaction with democracy	Evaluation of fairness	Evaluation of responsiveness
Education	0.02**	0.03**	0.03**
	(0.00)	(0.00)	(0.00)
Left	−0.11**	−0.05**	0.03**
	(0.01)	(0.01)	(0.01)
Right	0.03*	0.02*	0.08**
	(0.01)	(0.01)	(0.01)
Major incumbent	0.24	−0.13	−0.60*
	(0.42)	(0.34)	(0.28)
Minor incumbent	0.69	−0.85	0.16
	(0.81)	(0.66)	(0.54)
Non-incumbent/Previous	1.12*	0.04	1.46**
	(0.53)	(0.44)	(0.36)
Non-incumbent/New	1.34*	1.26*	0.15
	(0.67)	(0.55)	(0.46)
Major incumbent ∗ HDI	0.04	0.31	0.81⁺
	(0.45)	(0.37)	(0.31)
Minor incumbent ∗ HDI	−0.48	1.06	−0.04
	(0.89)	(0.73)	(0.59)
NI previous ∗ HDI	−1.04	−0.05	−1.50**
	(0.58)	(0.48)	(0.39)
NI new ∗ HDI	−1.37	−1.45*	−0.09
	(0.73)	(0.60)	(0.50)
Weak democracy	−0.25**	−0.54**	0.30**
	(0.05)	(0.04)	(0.03)
Non-established democracy	−0.11**	−0.20**	0.11**
	(0.02)	(0.02)	(0.01)
Human development index	2.66**	−0.58	1.52**
	(0.45)	(0.39)	(0.31)
Disproportionality	−0.00	−1.72**	−0.42**
	(0.15)	(0.14)	(0.10)
Federalism	−0.05**	−0.02	−0.06**
	(0.01)	(0.01)	(0.01)
Parties in government	0.02	−0.18**	0.10**
	(0.02)	(0.04)	(0.02)
(Parties in government)^2	−0.01**	0.04**	−0.01**
	(0.00)	(0.01)	(0.00)
Constant	−2.26**	1.42**	−1.61**
	(0.41)	(0.38)	(0.29)
N	13,196	11,681	13,228
Adj. R^2	0.09	0.08	0.06

**$p < 0.01$.
*$p < 0.05$.

TABLE 8.6. *Determinants of losers' assessments of democracy: systemic, party, and individual-level variables with interactions*

Independent variables	Satisfaction with democracy	Evaluation of fairness	Evaluation of responsiveness
Education	−0.01	0.30**	−0.27**
	(0.10)	(0.08)	(0.07)
Left	−0.85*	−0.93**	−0.55
	(0.43)	(0.35)	(0.30)
Right	0.07	−0.39	0.86**
	(0.47)	(0.38)	(0.32)
Education * HDI	0.03	−0.29**	0.32**
	(0.11)	(0.09)	(0.07)
Left * HDI	0.81	0.97**	0.64*
	(0.47)	(0.38)	(0.32)
Right * HDI	−0.04	0.45	−0.84*
	(0.51)	(0.41)	(0.35)
Major incumbent	0.32	0.04	−0.58*
	(0.42)	(0.35)	(0.29)
Minor incumbent	0.63	−0.76	−0.05
	(0.82)	(0.66)	(0.54)
Non-incumbent/Previous	1.08*	0.04	1.40**
	(0.53)	(0.44)	(0.36)
Non-incumbent/New	1.24	1.18*	−0.02
	(0.67)	(0.55)	(0.47)
Major incumbent * HDI	−0.04	0.12	0.79**
	(0.46)	(0.38)	(0.31)
Minor incumbent * HDI	−0.41	0.96	0.19
	(0.89)	(0.73)	(0.60)
NI previous * HDI	−1.00	−0.04	−1.43**
	(0.58)	(0.48)	(0.39)
NI new * HDI	−1.26	−1.36*	0.09
	(0.73)	(0.60)	(0.51)
Weak democracy	−0.27**	−0.53**	0.26**
	(0.05)	(0.04)	(0.03)
Non-established democracy	−0.11**	−0.20**	0.11**
	(0.02)	(0.02)	(0.01)
Human development index	2.37**	0.36	0.21
	(0.63)	(0.53)	(0.43)
Disproportionality	0.02	−1.64**	−0.44**
	(0.15)	(0.14)	(0.10)
Federalism	−0.05**	−0.01	−0.07**
	(0.01)	(0.01)	(0.01)
Parties in government	0.03	−0.17**	0.10**
	(0.02)	(0.04)	(0.02)
(Parties in government)^2	−0.01**	0.04**	−0.01**
	(0.00)	(0.01)	(0.00)
Constant	−1.99**	0.54	−0.40
	(0.57)	(0.51)	(0.40)
N	13,196	11,681	13,228
Adj. R^2	0.09	0.08	0.06

**$p < 0.01$.
*$p < 0.05$.

developed countries perhaps because they are more aware of actual instances where elected officials did not respond to voters' concerns.

Table 8.6 also shows that 'extreme' left voters are more positive in their evaluations of the fairness of the most recent election and the responsiveness of the system, the more highly developed the country. In contrast, extreme right voters are more critical of the system's responsiveness in more developed countries. Why this is the case remains to be elucidated.

Taken together, these findings confirm that individual level characteristics matter. As expected, better-educated losers provide more positive assessments of representative democracy than their less educated counterparts. But the results also indicate that individual level characteristics play differently in different contexts. The better educated are particularly positive with respect to fairness in less developed countries and more sanguine with respect to responsiveness in less developed countries.

The findings concerning 'extremist' voters are more intriguing and require further analysis to be considered definitive. Contrary to expectations, voters on the extreme right had more positive, not more negative, evaluations. As for those on the extreme left, it is only among less developed countries that they emerge as more critical.

CONCLUSION

The objective of this chapter has been to compare losers with losers; specifically, to examine losers' evaluations of electoral democracy and to identify the factors that affect these evaluations. Based on data measuring losers' evaluations of electoral democracy in twenty countries, several findings are worth recapitulating. The first observation to be made is that with respect to the three indicators retained—overall satisfaction with democracy, evaluation of fairness and responsiveness—losers emerge as quite positive. While previous chapters have shown that they are almost uniformly less positive in their evaluations than winners, our data also show that more losers are satisfied with the functioning of democracy than dissatisfied, an overwhelming majority believes that the most recent election was fair, and more people say that parties care what ordinary people think than the opposite. There is no evidence of widespread malaise here.

Following the notion that both context and individual characteristics help determine the level of losers' consent, we sought to ascertain, sequentially, the impact of systemic, party, and individual level characteristics on these three types of evaluations. Our results show that losers' evaluations of satisfaction and fairness are lower in non-established democracies, and lower still in Mexico. However, their evaluations of responsiveness are higher in non-established democracies, and higher still in the weak democracy (Mexico).

We also found that losers evaluate all three aspects of electoral democracy more positively in countries with more proportional electoral systems. Moreover, our results indicate that losers in more developed countries are more satisfied with democracy but less positive in their assessments of the fairness of the most recent election. This suggests to us that wealth is indeed an important lubricant for keeping people happy with the political system, but that it also is associated with higher expectations regarding the performance of democratic political institutions.

When we looked at differences across losers' evaluations of electoral democracy with an eye toward the kinds of parties they supported, we found that supporters of losing parties that had never been in government were the most critical of representative democracy, while supporters of the major losing party that formed the government at the time of the election felt most positive. Moreover, the data show that such differences between types of losing parties are more pronounced in less developed countries. These results are consistent with our results on the dynamics of losers' consent—where long-term losers are particularly negative in their evaluations of the political system—and our findings regarding the winner–loser gap in old and new democracies—where the gap was found to be larger in newer (and usually less economically developed) democracies.

Regarding differences across losers' responses that may be driven by individual-level factors, our analyses show that more highly educated losers are more satisfied with the functioning of democracy, more positive about the fairness of the election in less developed democracies, and more sanguine about the system's responsiveness in more developed countries. Aside from levels of education, which can be taken to be a proxy for democratic values and tolerance, our results also show that losers' ideology matters: while those who are on the 'extreme' right are not more critical towards representative democracy—in fact, they tend to be slightly more positive—voters on the extreme left were more negative in their evaluations of the political system. This latter effect is particularly pronounced in less developed democracies, where those who are on the extreme left are more negative while no such pattern emerges among more developed countries.

Up to this point we have focused on documenting the contours of losers' consent. That is, we have investigated the winner–loser gap in attitudes about the political system by examining whether and why such a gap exists, and why it varies across countries and different kinds of voters. Moreover, we have taken a look at different kinds of losers—who differ because of who they are, which parties they support, and what kind of polity they live in. One theme that has been underdeveloped so far, however, has been the question of whether losing makes voters more likely to support changes to the rules of the game. This is the topic we turn to in the next chapter.

APPENDIX 8A.1. *Electoral losers' evaluations of electoral democracy*

Country (year)	Satisfaction with democracy	Evaluation of fairness	Evaluation of responsiveness
Australia (1996)	0.37 (811)	—	−0.03 (806)
Belgium (1999)	0.10 (1,119)	—	0.03 (1,070)
Canada (1997)	0.21 (901)	0.47 (895)	−0.03 (881)
Czech Republic (1996)	−0.18 (516)	0.47 (523)	0.06 (509)
Denmark (1998)	0.48 (1,166)	0.89 (1,184)	0.22 (1,184)
Germany (1998)	0.17 (809)	0.78 (816)	0.07 (800)
Iceland (1999)	0.21 (467)	0.61 (482)	0.19 (482)
Japan (1996)	0.03 (537)	0.05 (581)	−0.14 (581)
Mexico (1997)	−0.08 (522)	0.31 (562)	0.16 (559)
Netherlands (1998)	0.41 (599)	0.77 (584)	0.18 (583)
New Zealand (1996)	0.21 (2,048)	0.58 (2,035)	0.04 (2,029)
Norway (1997)	0.54 (1,274)	0.85 (1,264)	0.23 (1,263)
Poland (1997)	0.17 (474)	0.51 (537)	0.11 (537)
Portugal (2002)	−0.03 (393)	0.62 (412)	0.01 (412)
Slovenia (1996)	−0.25 (464)	0.52 (485)	0.22 (485)
Spain (1996)	0.25 (613)	0.62 (614)	0.17 (614)
Spain (2000)	0.40 (402)	0.50 (416)	0.09 (414)
Sweden (1998)	0.20 (549)	0.78 (557)	0.09 (556)
Switzerland (1999)	0.26 (183)	0.83 (184)	0.21 (182)
United Kingdom (1997)	0.40 (1,206)	0.67 (1,215)	0.09 (1,200)
Total	0.23 (15,053)	0.63 (13,390)	0.09 (15,194)

Notes: Entries are means. The variables range between −1 and +1. The number of respondents is indicated in parentheses.

Source: Comparative Study of Electoral Systems surveys (1996–2000).

APPENDIX 8A.2. *Types of democracies*

	Countries	Number of countries
Weak democracy	Mexico	1
Non-established democracies	Czech Republic, Spain, Poland, Portugal, Slovenia	5
Established democracies	Australia, Belgium, Canada, Denmark, Germany, Great Britain, Iceland, Japan, Netherlands, New Zealand, Norway, Sweden, Switzerland	13

APPENDIX 8A.3. *Disproportionality index*

Country	Disproportionality index
Australia	0.113
Belgium	0.026
Canada	0.132
Czech Republic	0.029
Denmark	0.008
Germany	0.027
Great Britain	0.165
Iceland	0.009
Japan	0.131
Mexico	0.064
Netherlands	0.012
New Zealand	0.040
Norway	0.034
Poland	0.103
Portugal	0.051
Slovenia	0.037
Spain (1996)	0.055
Spain (2000)	0.061
Sweden	0.009
Switzerland	0.029

APPENDIX 8A.4. *United Nations Human Development Index*

Country	HD index
Australia	0.931
Belgium	0.923
Canada	0.960
Czech Republic	0.882
Denmark	0.928
Germany	0.925

APPENDIX 8A.4. (*Continued*)

Country	HD index
Great Britain	0.931
Iceland	0.919
Japan	0.940
Mexico	0.853
Netherlands	0.941
New Zealand	0.937
Norway	0.943
Poland	0.834
Portugal	0.880
Slovenia	0.886
Spain (1996)	0.934
Spain (2000)	0.889
Sweden	0.936
Switzerland	0.914

APPENDIX 8A.5. *Types of losing parties*

Major incumbents

Australia	Labour Party
Belgium	Christian People's Party (CVP)
Germany	Christian Democratic Union (CDU)
Great Britain	Conservative Party
Mexico	Institutional Revolutionary Party (PRI)
Norway	Labor Party (DNA)
Poland	Democratic Left Alliance (SLD)
Portugal	Socialist Party (PS)
Spain (1996)	Spanish Socialist Workers Part (PSOE)

Minor incumbents

Belgium	Christian Social Party (PSC)
Germany	Christian Social Union (CSU), Free Democratic Party (FDP)
Japan	Social Democratic Party (SDP), Sakigake
New Zealand	United
Poland	Polish Peasants' Party (PSL)

Parties that have never been in the government (non-incumbent/never)

Australia	Democrats
Belgium	Flemish Bloc (VB), Confederated Ecologists, Agalev, Front National (FN)
Canada	New Democratic Party (NDP), Reform Party (RP)
Czech Republic	Social Democrats (CSSD), Communists (KSCM), Association for the Republic (SPR–RSC)
Denmark	Socialist People's Party (SF), Unity List Red Green (EL), Progress Party (FP)
Germany	Greens, Democratic Socialists (PDS)
Great Britain	Liberal Democrats, Scottish National Party, Plaid Cymru

APPENDIX 8A.5. (*Continued*)

Japan	Communist Party
Mexico	Labor Party (PT), Mexican Ecological Party (PVEM)
Netherlands	Green Left (GL), Reformed Political Alliance (GPV), Socialist Party (SP), Political Reformed Party (SGP), Reformed Political Federation (RPF)
New Zealand	New Zealand First, Alliance
Norway	Socialist Left Party (SV), Progress Party (FRP)
Portugal	Unitarian Democratic Coalition (CDU)
Slovenia	Slovenia: Democratic Party of Retired Persons (DESUS), Slovenian National Party (SNS)
Spain	United Left (IU), Convergence and Union of Catalonia (CiU), Basque nationalist Party (PNV)
Sweden	Left Party (VP), Green Party (MP)
Switzerland	Green Party (GPS), Liberal Party (LPS), Protestant People's Party (EVP), Swiss Democrats (DS), Labour Party (PdA)

Parties that have held cabinet position since 1960 but are not incumbent (non-incumbent/previous)

Belgium	People's Union (VU)
Canada	Progressive Conservative Party (PCP)
Denmark	Radical Left (RV), Left Denmark Liberal Party (V), Conservative Peoples Party (KF), Social Democrats (SD)
Great Britain	Conservative Party
Japan	New Frontier
Netherlands	Christian Democratic Appeal (CDA)
New Zealand	Labour
Norway	Conservative Party
Poland	Freedom Union (UW), Union of Labor (UP)
Slovenia	Social Democrats (SDS), United List of Social Democrats (SLSD)
Spain (2000)	Spanish Socialist Workers Part (PSOE)
Sweden	Moderate Rally Party (M), Christian Democrats (KD), Center Party, People's Party Liberals (FP)

New parties in the last two elections (non-incumbent/new)

Australia	Green Party
Canada	Bloc Quebecois
Czech Republic	Democratic Union (DEU)
Denmark	Danish People's Party (DF)
Iceland	Alliance (S), Left-Green (VG), Liberal Party (FF)
Japan	Democratic Party of Japan
New Zealand	ACT NZ, Christian Coalition
Poland	League of Polish Families (LPR)
Portugal	Left-Bloc Communists (BE)
Slovenia	Slovenia Nationalist Party (SNS)
Spain (1996)	Galician Nationalist Bloc (BNG), Canarian Party (CC)

9

Losing and Support for Institutional Change

Up to this point, our analyses have focused mainly on people's attitudes toward government; in particular, how winners and losers differ in their attitudes or how losers differ from one another. In this chapter, we take up the question of whether losing means that citizens will either try to change the rules of the game or stop playing the game altogether. The work of Hirschman (1970) is especially useful in giving us a way to think about those reactions more abstractly. We have seen that voters may exhibit a number of different reactions to losing; they may lose faith in some aspects of the political system but not others, and some losers in some countries may be more likely to lose faith than others.

When it comes to behavior, however, in reacting to decline actors may choose either exit or voice, and losers should be no different in this regard. In the setting we are concerned with, the choice of exit may mean that losers stop believing that they are able to win within the current system and give up. In this case, the belief or expectation of continuing loss will preface disengagement from the system. Losers, in other words, may 'exit' by simply giving up participating in politics. In contrast, losers may express 'voice' by working hard to become winners, possibly by working for change of the political system itself. Even from this brief description it is apparent that, as Hirschman notes, the choices of exit and voice are related. For him

exit will often be taken *in the light of the prospects for the effective use of voice.* If [actors] are sufficiently convinced that voice will be effective they may well *postpone* exit. … [I]f deterioration is a process unfolding in stages over a period of time, the voice option is more likely to be taken at an early stage. Once you have exited, you have lost the opportunity to use voice, but not vice versa: in some situations, exit will therefore be a reaction of *last resort* after voice has failed. (Hirschman 1970: 37, emphasis in original)

Or, as Miller puts it,

losers (both politicians and their followers) can likewise console themselves with the thought: 'Wait till the next election'. But once again this prospect is comforting to the losers only insofar as there is some reasonable prospect that the next election may produce a different outcome with different winners and losers. (Miller 1983: 743)

Key to the choice of exit over voice is voters' belief that there is a possibility of winning: with no possibility of winning exit is preferred over voice; with some possibility of winning, voice is likely to be the preferred option. This is consistent with Colomer's conjecture that

[a]ctors' support for either the existing or the newly established institutions depends on the corresponding distribution of power. If significant actors are and expect to be permanently (that is, for a very long period) excluded from power—as may happen in institutional frameworks producing absolute winners and absolute losers—they may prefer to challenge the existing institutions and try to replace them with alternative formulas. (Colomer 2001: 211)

Translating these arguments into our discussion of losers is straightforward. We should expect losing to imply disengagement only if losing occurs repeatedly over the longer term or if the loss is clearly foreseeable. In the short term it is conceivable that losing may even have a stimulative effect as losers exercise their voice. We can see supportive evidence of this claim in several areas of reaction to loss. In previous chapters we have shown the attitudinal consequences of losing; below we examine the consequences of losing, and especially those consequences that relate to citizens' willingness to engage the current political system. In this chapter we look at the impact of losing on citizens' willingness to vote, their sense of efficacy, and their willingness to replace current institutions with new ones.

One difference between what follows and our earlier discussion is the emphasis in this chapter upon the role of expectations. Up until now we have considered the impact that the status of loser has upon a range of attitudes and opinions. But, as noted in the quotations by both Hirschman, Miller, and Colomer, expectations and, more specifically, expectations of future loss, are likely to have an important impact. That is, there is a prospective component when citizens consider their future behavior. This is especially clearly seen when we consider institutional change. Here voters are being asked to consider replacing the current status quo institutions with another set. Everything else being equal, it is likely that losers will be dissatisfied with their current institutions, but this is not to say that replacement institutions will make losers better off. In fact they could well make the losers even worse off. Even aside from the question of institutional change, however, expectations of future loss, as well as current status as a loser, can color attitudes.

WILLINGNESS TO VOTE

Given the importance of expectations, actors who anticipate having no opportunity for voice should exit or disengage from politics. One hypothesis, then, is that those losers who have very low expectations of winning anything in an upcoming election should simply not be bothered to vote in that election.

After all, if there is no chance of winning, why bother? Districted electoral systems allow us to test this hypothesis directly. Specifically, in countries with electoral systems based on geographic districts—such as Britain, Canada, or in elections to the US Congress—losing can be experienced in two different ways: at the level of the nation and the level of electoral districts. This means that, in fact, some voters can be double losers—their least preferred party may win both the national election and the district they live in. As a result, those losers who live in districts in which they expect the rival party to win, in an election in which that rival party won the last national contest, should be less keen on voting. And we find that this is, in fact, the case.

A simple model of citizens' intention to vote using the 2000 Canadian pre-election survey shows some of this (Table 9.1). In this election, the Liberals were widely expected to win as they had done in the previous contest. We can model the intention to turn out as a simple function of some standard demographic factors such as age, education, or dissatisfaction with the economy. We can also include terms for loser status (did not vote for the governing Liberal party in 1997) and also a term for the expectation that the respondent's preferred party will win in the riding (district). We see that, generally

TABLE 9.1. *Predicting the intention to abstain on election day*

	Unstandardized coefficients		Standardized coefficients
	Beta	Std. error	Beta
Did not vote Liberal 97	−0.102***	0.025	−0.097
Chance of preferred party winning seat	0.001*	0.000	0.061
Personal finances better or worse	0.018	0.029	0.015
Female	0.027	0.024	0.026
French language	0.039	0.026	0.036
Strong partisanship	0.032	0.029	0.026
High education	0.057*	0.027	0.052
High school dropout	−0.084*	0.036	−0.057
Age	0.017***	0.004	0.539
Age squared	0.000**	0.000	−0.411
Constant	3.228***	0.129	
R^2	0.05		
N	1,805		

***$p < 0.001$.
**$p < 0.01$.
*$p < 0.05$.

Notes: Dependent variable: 'On election day are you certain to vote, likely, unlikely, or certain not to vote?' (coded so that 1: will not vote; 2: unlikely; 3: likely; 4: certain).

Source: Canada (2000) Pre-Election Poll.

speaking, losers are somewhat less enthusiastic about being willing to vote, but also that expectations play an important role. The better the chance of the voter's preferred party winning in the riding (electoral district), the more likely it is that the respondent will express a willingness to vote. Or, turning this around, if respondents see little chance of their preferred party of winning the district they become less likely to say they intend to vote. At least in this simple example, expectations of loss dampen the willingness to engage.

POLITICAL EFFICACY

While losing may decrease voters' willingness to turn out and vote, does it also diminish their sense of confidence that they can influence the political system? Or does losing translate into a decreased willingness to participate in elections but no change or even an increase in voters' psychological engagement with the political process? To examine whether losing leads not only to exit in terms of voting participation but also a diminished sense that participation has an impact, we examined whether losing translates into lower levels of efficacy:

Political efficacy is the feeling that individual political action does have, or can have, an impact upon the political process, ... the feeling that political and social change is possible, and that the individual citizen can play a part in bringing about this change. (Campbell, Gurin, and Miller 1954: 187)

This concept is not so literally tied to electoral prospects as the level of party competition within the district but does speak to the general expectations of the possibility of success—defined in terms of influencing the political system—that voters may have. To have a sense of influence on the political process, an individual has to believe that they have the means to affect the process (internal efficacy). Moreover, citizens have to believe that the political process must be open and responsive to such influences (external efficacy) (Lane 1959; Balch 1974). Citizens who understand the political process and believe that their participation can influence policy-making are likely to take a more positive view of democratic governance.

Table 9.2 shows the results of multivariate regression models that estimate the impact of loser status (measured by a vote recall question) on people's sense of political efficacy, controlling for a number of individual-level factors, such as age, education, and employment. The data presented here come from surveys collected as part of the International Social Survey Program (ISSP) in 1996. The results show that there are only a few countries where winning and losing affects voters' sense of efficacy. That is, in most countries, being an electoral loser does not appear to diminish people's confidence in their ability to influence the political process in the same way that it reduces their faith in the political system (as shown in previous chapters). At the same time, there are some countries that exhibit a significant gap in the direction

TABLE 9.2. *The effect of political loser status on political efficacy*

Country	Efficacy
Canada	−0.096
Czech Republic	−0.395***
Germany	0.057
Great Britain	−0.201***
Hungary	0.053
Ireland	−0.021
Italy	−0.408***
Japan	0.147*
Latvia	0.031
New Zealand	0.025
Norway	0.025
Russia	0.006
Spain	−0.081*
Sweden	−0.124**
United States	0.117
All countries	−0.042**

***$p < 0.001$.
**$p < 0.01$.
*$p < 0.05$, one-tailed.

Notes: Unstandardized OLS regression coefficients. Coding of loser–winner status, losers: 1; winners: 0. Based on multivariate estimation models controlling for age, sex, education, employment, social class, and having voted.

Source: International Social Survey Program 'The Role of Government' (1996).

of decreasing efficacy (the Czech Republic, Great Britain, Italy, Spain, and Sweden)—that is, five of the fifteen countries included here. In these countries, losing reduces people's sense of efficacy, and this effect is particularly strong in the Czech Republic and Italy. However, it is worth noting that most countries either do not have an efficacy gap or even have a gap in the opposite direction (e.g. Japan) where those in the minority express a more efficacious attitude. While losing, overall, thus tends to either reduce political efficacy or at least fail to consistently increase it, this effect is neither as consistent nor as strong across countries as it was shown to be with regard to people's general evaluations of the political system earlier in this book (see also Vetter 2000). Thus, while losing holds the potential for diminishing people's confidence that their actions in the political system matter, this effect is not automatic or omnipresent.

These results hold some interesting, albeit at this point suggestive, implications. Specifically, the finding documented in earlier chapters that the political losers hold more negative attitudes toward the political system combined with the current result that they, by and large, feel just as efficacious as the winners may imply that losers are less likely to exercise the patience so critical for democratic survival. Because efficacious losers are most likely to push for changing the political status quo and because democracies are by their very nature amenable to deliberate change—a number of them maintain ongoing experiments with structural traits such as electoral systems and parliamentary structures—we examine this demand for change in the following section.

LOSING AND SUPPORT FOR INSTITUTIONAL CHANGE

Other than exhibiting some sense of frustration or of resignation, what, if any, are the consequences of losing? A standard expectation, due to Riker, is that losers will try to become winners. For political parties this can simply mean changing their party platform in order to appeal to a different, and hopefully larger, set of voters. This may involve parties changing their policy positions. The rightward drift of socialist parties in contemporary Europe, for example, can be seen as a search for more voters in order to achieve government as much as it represents a rethinking of socialist ideology in the post-cold war era. In a multidimensional setting, parties may simply emphasize different, and hopefully more popular, policy dimensions and issues. As both Riker (1986) and Miller (1983) note, losers thus are a continual source of new issues being raised to the agenda in hopes of becoming winners.

Another approach is for losers to attempt to change the rules of the game. If one set of institutions—electoral rules or parliamentary procedure—makes it hard to become a winner, then losers may try to propose alternative rules. Of course, this may be somewhat harder than simply raising new issues. Institutions are, and in many cases should be, resistant to change, acquiring their legitimacy, in part, through their longevity. Moreover, if losers cannot win on an issue in a given political arena they are unlikely to be able to have the ability to change the rules governing the arena themselves since changing institutions typically requires an even larger majority than changing policy.

Nevertheless, elite support for a variety of institutional changes is strongly influenced by status as a loser (Bowler, Donovan, and Karp 2002). Losers' agitation has, for example, been used to explain legislative choice about voting rules in Korea (Brady and Mo 1992), Poland (Benoit and Hayden 2004), Germany (Bawn 1993), and the European Parliament (Garrett 1992). Similar portraits of elite preference have been offered to explain support for new electoral rules in Spain (Gunther 1989) and British Columbia (Angus 1952), or in changes to electoral systems to ward off possible losses (Boix 1999; but see Andrews and Jackman n.d.). And, as Nancy Bermeo points out, in extreme cases elites play an important role in the breakdown of democracy (Bermeo 2003).

Self-evident and less extreme examples of elite-led institutional change are found in gerrymandering efforts where, in districted systems, redistricting is used in order to solidify the shares of legislative seats of one party typically at the expense of another (Cox and Katz 2002). During 2003, for example, Republican legislators in the US state of Texas introduced a new districting plan that would increase the number of Republican members of Congress coming from the state from fifteen to twenty-two and reduce the number of Democratic districts to ten. Complaints about the unfairness of this new plan were met with the reply that the previous—Democratic—plan gave Republicans fifteen out of thirty-two Congressional seats (46 percent of the total number of seats) despite the fact that the Republicans obtained 57 percent of the vote. At one point, in order to forestall a vote on the new districts by denying a quorum, Democratic legislators literally ran away into neighboring states in order to avoid a legislative quorum on the issue. While this may be an extreme (and entertaining) example, and questions of fairness to one side, repeated examples of redistricting clearly show elites manipulating rules in order to change the balance of winners and losers.

In each of these cases competing elites are seen to press for rules that will benefit them. When we do see times of institutional change, winning and losing have thus motivated a variety of rule changes at the elite level. For citizens, however, we suspect that issues of institutional change must appear to be an even more remote possibility than for elite level losers. In the main, citizen support for institutional change may often amount to receptivity to claims made in the platforms of parties that seek a new institutional deal. But survey results shown in Table 9.3 illustrate that there are instances where citizens who see themselves as losers are more supportive of major institutional

TABLE 9.3. *Losers' support for institutional reforms: United States, 2003*

	Self-identified losers (percent)	All respondents (percent)
Proportional representation to elect the US Congress	59	48
Eliminate the Electoral College/for direct election of President	68	53

Notes: $N = 689$. Losers are those who indicated they expect candidates who they support to lose 'most of the time' in future elections.

Source: Survey conducted for authors by Indiana University Center for Survey Research. Fall 2003.

changes—even changes that are not advocated by major parties. In this particular case, Americans who expect candidates they might support to lose 'most of the time' in future elections are much more likely to embrace changes in how Congress and the President are elected. Specifically, in a survey of American voters conducted in 2003, we found that majorities of voters who expect to lose were significantly more likely to embrace proportional representation electoral rules to elect the US Congress (59 percent, compared to 48 percent for the all respondents) and to support doing away with the Electoral College to elect the President (68 percent, compared to 53 percent).

When we examine voter opinions towards such proposals for institutional change in greater detail, we see a strikingly similar pattern of attitudes to those of elites. Following the controversial 2000 US election, for example, there was discussion concerning people's willingness to change the US Constitution to abolish the Electoral College and adopt a system of direct election of the president. Table 9.4 presents some results from a very simple model of opinions towards retaining the Electoral College or changing the Constitution 'and elect as President whoever gets the most votes in the whole country' (CBS/*New York Times* Poll November 2000). Alongside from standard, and not terribly interesting, demographic controls the main variables of interest are those that capture stances towards the two candidates, Bush and Gore. In addition to (recalled) vote preference for those candidates we also include a measure of whether, at the time the survey was taken, the respondent thought their candidate was ahead in the popular vote or not—that is, the expectation of how one's preferred candidate will have done as the recount proceeded. In the first column of Table 9.4 both candidates are included together, in the second column we break out Bush and Gore voters. Because the coefficients of probit models are difficult to interpret, we present changes in the probability of being willing to change the US constitution by key variables of interest in Table 9.5.

As can be seen, believing that one's candidate is ahead in the popular vote has a powerful impact upon support for direct election of the president. That is, even though Republican identifiers and Bush voters are generally very unsupportive of a change in the direct election of the President, this is most definitely not the case for those Bush voters who thought George Bush ahead in the popular vote. As both Hirschman and Miller suggested, we see that expectations of loss colors responses to considering future institutional changes.

Citizen attitudes toward institutions and institutional change, even to the point of being willing to change a 200-year-old constitutional practice can thus be seen to be shaped by winning and losing (and the expectation of winning and losing). To be sure, citizen views are shaped not only by losing but are affected by other factors, too: everything else being equal, one consistent finding in this literature is that a respondent undergoing economic bad times is typically more willing to consider change than one who has a well paying job. Similarly, there may be ideological considerations at work or simple demographic ones

TABLE 9.4. *Probit models of willingness to adopt direct election of President in the United States*

	Model 1	Model 2
Respondent's preferred candidate judged ahead in popular vote	0.473*** (3.75)	
Bush voter	−0.622*** (3.30)	
Gore voter	−0.200 (0.94)	
Bush voter * Bush being seen to be ahead in popular vote		0.423*** (2.66)
Gore voter * Gore being seen to be ahead in popular vote		0.592*** (4.79)
Nader voter	0.776 (1.64)	1.157** (2.55)
Democratic identifier	0.054 (0.43)	0.112 (0.94)
Republican identifier	−0.313*** (2.67)	−0.449*** (4.01)
Did not vote	0.067 (0.35)	0.471*** (3.86)
Age	−0.040 (0.81)	−0.041 (0.83)
Education	−0.237*** (5.94)	−0.245*** (6.11)
Anglo	−0.314** (2.36)	−0.360*** (2.72)
Latino	0.282 (1.42)	0.257 (1.31)
Florida resident	0.105 (0.52)	0.086 (0.43)
Female	0.189** (2.07)	0.203** (2.22)
Pseudo R^2	0.15	0.13
Constant	1.389*** (5.17)	1.063*** (4.46)
N	929	929

*$p < 0.1$.
**$p < 0.05$.
***$p < 0.01$.

Notes: *T*-values in parentheses. Dependent variable: keep the electoral College (0); amend the Constitution (1).

Source: CBS News/*New York Times* Monthly Poll #6 November 2000.

(young voters being more willing to consider change; better educated ones being more reluctant). But the point here is that, even after controlling for several other possible and powerful explanations, it is possible to see large effects of winning and losing status on the willingness to change institutions.

TABLE 9.5. *Probability of willingness to change constitution*

	Model	Probability	Difference
Preferred candidate is *not* ahead in the polls	1	0.53	
Preferred candidate *is* ahead in the polls	1	0.71	+0.19
Bush voter	1	0.44	
Gore voter	1	0.55	
Bush voter who thinks Bush is *not* ahead in popular vote	2	0.58	
Bush voter who thinks Bush *is* ahead in popular vote	2	0.74	+0.16
Gore voter who thinks Gore is *not* ahead in popular vote	2	0.53	
Gore voter who thinks Gore *is* ahead in popular vote	2	0.74	+0.21

Notes: Based on data and coefficients from Table 9.4.

Plainly, the willingness to change the Electoral College in the United States is an example of people supporting hypothetical reforms over which they have very little actual say. In fact, voters are only very rarely allowed a direct say in institutional changes. But at certain times voters are allowed an actual say either through a referendum or, even more directly, through the initiative process. Instances of institutional change via direct democracy thus provide examples of cases to see whether, when real institutional change is at stake, the status of losers shapes voter responses to the proposal or whether responses such as those exhibited by Gore supporters amount to 'cheap talk'. Hence we next consider some examples of actual change in institutions in New Zealand and the United States.

Among the established democracies, one of the biggest changes in the recent past has been New Zealand's decision to abandon first past the post (FPP) electoral rules and move to a mixed member proportional system (MMP). Thus, New Zealand, once the archetypical case of Lijphart's 'majoritarian' system moved firmly towards a more consensus-based model. The story of the events leading to electoral system change in New Zealand has been told in numerous places (Jackson and McRobie 1998 is the most comprehensive source, but see also Vowles 1995; Boston et al. 1997).[1] Among the accounts, partisan self-interest was considered to be one of the major factors responsible for shaping attitudes about electoral system change. The summary judgment of the research team working on public opinion during this crucial period is worth quoting at some length:

As they did in 1993, when they expressed a collective verdict on FPP [first-past-the-post], the jurors, the New Zealand people, could be expected to make their judgements of MMP on the basis of a mixture of considerations (Lamare and Vowles 1996). Among the first of these is partisanship—that is, what appears to be in the best strategic interest of a person's favoured party. People tend to make their assessments not necessarily

---

[1] The following discussion relies heavily on Jeffrey Karp (personal communication) summer 2003.

on the basis of a sophisticated understanding of electoral systems, but more likely because they are cued by positions taken by party elites—the party's leaders, MPs and candidates. At first, Labour supporters were more likely to embrace the new electoral system than their National counterparts. Historically, National had benefited more than Labour from FPP. By 1993, Labour had held office for only twelve of the previous 44 years, and in 1978 and 1981 National succeeded in winning a majority of seats even though Labour had received more votes. As a result, Labour set up the Royal Commission that recommended MMP. Conversely, National's success in retaining government goes far to explain why there was little support for abandoning FPP within the National party and among its voters. (Vowles et al. 2002: 160)

Supporters of the smaller parties in the New Zealand party system were consistent supporters of the change to proportional representation. This pattern should not surprise us: 'first past the post' systems work against the interests of small parties while proportional representation systems typically increase the number of seats going to small parties. In comparing the current system—under which small parties lose out—to a proportional system supporters of small parties should, therefore, support the change much more readily than supporters of larger parties.

The initiative process in the American states provides an even more direct means for voters to make meaningful choices on institutional changes. Not only can voters have a say on institutional changes proposed by elites—as in the case of the New Zealand referendum—the initiative allows non-elites to propose changes. Here we see several examples in the way in which voters have repeatedly sought to amend existing legislative and electoral institutions. Two recent examples stand out—the introduction of term limits and the introduction of changes to the primary system—both of which sought changes in the way of conducting elections that had partisan consequences.

Term limits were introduced by initiative in both Colorado and California. At the time of their introduction, Republicans dominated Colorado's legislative politics; Democrats did so in California. Absent any other theory, we might reasonably expect the same kinds of voters to support the measure in both states. Yet, in both states, the out-party supported term limits: Democrats supported them in Colorado and opposed them in California. The pattern was reversed for Republicans (Donovan and Snipp 1994). These patterns were confirmed in a third state, Utah, where the legislature imposed limits on itself. There, too, supporters of term limits were those opposed to the majority party (Magleby and Patterson 1998). Thus, given these reversals of party support, the backing for term limits cannot be cast in simple ideological terms. Rather, support is more readily explainable in terms of loser status defined in terms of minority party affiliation: supporters of minority (losing) parties are likely to support changes in rules in order to help unseat the current winners.

We see similarly self-interested motivations of losers when we consider the literature on reform of the primary election process in the United States.

TABLE 9.6. *Predicted probabilities of voting yes on proposition 198 to allow all California voters a say in primary elections*

Baseline probability	0.51
Minor party registration	0.63
Strong Democratic identification	0.39
Activist	0.48
Strong Democratic identification activist	0.36
Strong Republican dissatisfied w/Republican candidates	0.48
Strong Republican satisfied w/Republican candidates	0.38

Source: Based on Bowler and Donovan (2003*a*).

Attempts to open up the primary process to voters other than partisans of the two major parties via the so-called open primary of California's 1996 Proposition 198 show a straightforward pattern of support for the proposition that expectations of winning and losing matter. In this instance, those who would lose out by passage of the measure would be partisans of the two major parties. After all, if the measure passed, any registered voter would be allowed to vote in the primary of their choice for each office. The net effect of this would be, as those who proposed the measure intended, to allow more centrist and moderate candidates to win primaries with the support of less ideologically committed voters (see Gerber and Morton 1998). The grip of party activists upon the nomination process would be seriously weakened or, at best, watered down. Hence, party activists and strong partisans could reasonably expect to lose out under proposed changes while those with weaker—or non-existent— attachments can expect to get a better deal.

Table 9.6 reproduces some of the results from a study of California voters' support for Proposition 198. Here we simply report predicted probabilities from the model.[2] As can be seen, the overall baseline probability of voting for the proposal was 0.51. Given the intent of the ballot proposition, we would expect party activists and those who have strong party identifications to have lower probabilities of voting for the measure. Similarly, minor party registrants should be more supportive of the measure since it would allow them to vote in the primaries of the two big parties. As we see from Table 9.6, all these patterns appear in the data. One further pattern is of interest. Republicans not happy with the outcome of their primary (the Democratic primary was not contested) were more likely (0.48 as opposed to 0.38) to support opening up the process relative to those who were happy with the process. Clearly, those not happy with the outcome favored changing the process.

---

[2] For details of the model, estimation, specification, and measurement please see the original source (Bowler and Donovan 2003*a*).

In the instances of institutional reform in the United States and New Zealand outlined earlier, the status of loser shaped voter response to actual questions of institutional change. Along similar lines, Britain's Liberal Democrats provide an example where institutional reform is not subject to direct popular vote; instead, the party platform favoring reform is an important component of the party's identity and one that resonates with its vote base. Both voters and candidates of Britain's Liberal Democrats are, for example, staunch supporters of a move towards proportional representation electoral rules. The 2001 party manifesto for the Liberal Democrats noted that, 'ultimately, we wish to see the Single Transferable Vote (STV) used for Westminster elections'. This kind of commitment to institutional reform was echoed at the level of voters. Over the course of three surveys in 1997, 1998, and 2001, on average 59 percent of those who voted Liberal Democrat in the 1997 election favored a change in the electoral system to proportional representation compared to 35 percent of those who voted Labour and only 23 percent of those who voted Conservative (*British National Election Study* series; see also Wenzel, Bowler, and Lanoue 2000). Such a high level of support among Liberal Democrats should not be surprising, since the first past the post system means that small parties, like the LibDems, are persistently under-represented in terms of seats relative to their vote share. For example, in the 2001 election the Liberal Democrats gained approximately 8 percent of the seats in the House of Commons on the basis of approximately 18 percent of the vote, while Labour gained over 60 percent of the seats on the basis of a 40 percent vote share. Britain's Liberal Democrats, then, provide an example of a set of losing voters who are receptive to the claims of institutional change made by political parties, even if they do not get to vote on the institution directly.

But not all proposals for institutional reforms are as clear-cut in their likely consequences of winning and losing for parties and partisans as the example of electoral reform, and even proposed electoral reforms may have uncertain consequences. In fact, the Liberal Democrats, whose predecessors, the Liberals, were the biggest party by far in Britain's Parliament in the period prior to the First World War, were caught in a miscalculation of the likely effects of changing electoral rules at one time. During the period from roughly the end of the First World War to the mid-1920s, the question of reforming Britain's electoral system came to the fore. It was not entirely clear whether the Liberals should support electoral reform or, rather, rely on the properties of single member simple plurality (SMSP) to help provide a barrier to the electoral threat of the newly formed Labour party. Absent poll data from that period we cannot establish whether voters were confused or uncertain about the possibility of reform, but the data suggest that the Liberal parliamentary party—that is, a set of self-interested highly aware actors—was certainly uncertain. As Table 9.7 (taken from Andrews and Jackman n.d.) shows, the Liberals were decidedly uncertain of the consequences of the reform until 1924. By then

TABLE 9.7. *UK parliamentary votes on proportional representation*

	June 1917		November 1917		May 1918		May 1924	
	Yes	No	Yes	No	Yes	No	Yes	No
Conservative	38	85	29	125	43	104	8	147
Liberal	77	53	57	70	61	55	107	1
Labour	13	11	15	8	7	9	28	90
Irish National	14	0	25	0	0	0	0	0
Other	1	1	2	1	1	1	3	2
Total	143	150	128	204	112	169	146	240

Source: Andrews and Jackman (n.d.).

the damage of the SMSP system was becoming clearer (as were the benefits to Labour), and the party delegation became strongly supportive of proportional representation. By then, however, it was too late.

These kinds of uncertainties and second thoughts are also seen in the better documented case of New Zealand. The hopes for power of the Labour party subsequent to 1993 were either dashed or buried under the necessities of coalition government. Indeed, the realities of coalition politics—the new importance of small and extreme parties such as the populist New Zealand First party acting as 'kingmakers'—seemed to startle the electorate. Support for the electoral change dropped markedly, especially among Labour supporters, as the new system did not live up to their—quite possibly unrealistic—expectations. Supporters of both major parties continued to register dissatisfaction with the new more proportional electoral system (MMP) and expressed increased support for single party government and, hence SMSP/FPP. In contrast, supporters of smaller parties remained committed to the proportional system (Karp and Bowler 2001). Table 9.8 provides some evidence in which public and candidate opinion towards MMP is tracked over the period from 1993 to 2001. As Vowles et al. comment, '[i]n all years, and consistent with partisan self-interest, people voting for the smaller parties exhibit the highest degree of support for MMP, though their levels of support also declined before recovering in 2001. ACT [liberal party] voters are the major exception' (Vowles et al. 2002: 164). Again, then, expectations of winning and losing proved key to shaping responses to institutions and support for institutional change.

The experience of the New Zealand Labour party and the British Liberals illustrates that, despite the confidence of institutional engineers, the effects of many institutional changes are frequently uncertain. Some institutional effects are likely to be unclear to voters and hence do not generate much support. Moreover, some institutions have more clear-cut consequences than others. In Tsebelis' term, 'distributional' institutions are ones that generate clear winners and losers and, hence, are likely to generate clearer responses from voters in

TABLE 9.8. *Vote to retain MMP New Zealand, 1993–2001: voters/intending voters and party candidates*

		1993 (percent)	1996 (percent)	1999 (percent)	2001 (percent)
Labour	Voters	68	59	44	59
	Candidates	72	57	56	
National	Voters	24	25	23	30
	Candidates	15	18	22	
Alliance	Voters	82	75	56	81
	Candidates	100	96	82	
NZ First	Voters	69	66	58	71
	Candidates	95	88	69	
ACT (Liberals)	Voters		47	27	46
	Candidates		54	64	
Green	Voters			62	77
	Candidates			90	

Source: Vowles et al. (2002: 164).

terms of winning and losing. This is especially the case when winners and losers are readily defined in terms of party, and actors can develop expectations over whether their party will do better or worse under a proposed institutional change. By contrast 'efficient' institutions are ones that do not generate winners or losers but, rather, make all participants better off (see also Colomer 2001). While all institutions are inherently distributional in some way, within the theoretical literature on institutions there is a debate over the extent to which efficient institutions may be said to exist. These debates to one side, we can consider institutions in abstract as simply having more or less clear impacts on who wins and who loses; hence, for our discussion, not all institutional reforms are likely to generate public support.

As Wenzel, Bowler, and Lanoue (2000) show, some proposed reforms— notably those relating to the electoral system—prompt much clearer partisan responses than others. For others, and those more like Tsebelis' 'efficient' institutions, it is harder to establish winners and losers in very general terms. Clearly, being able to identify and, of course, self-identify as a loser is a necessary precondition for losing to have an impact. If institutions muddle this issue then, clearly, the impact of losing will also be muddled. The kinds of institutional changes we have looked at so far have had quite clear distributional effects in making winners and losers and, in some cases, making current losing parties lose less badly or even turn them into winners. The notion of efficient, as opposed to distributional, institutions can be somewhat difficult to see in a real world political context. Everyday examples, such as whether we drive on the right- or the left-hand side of the road or stop when the light shows green as opposed to red, do show that there are some kinds of institutional arrangements that do not necessarily involve winners and losers. Political equivalents of the rules of the road are somewhat harder to find. The Wenzel et al. study of attitudes towards institutional reform in Britain categorizes questions of whether Britain should have a written Bill of Rights or, if such a Bill were introduced, should there be a right to a trial by jury as being more 'efficient' than 'distributive'. These questions, as opposed to ones on electoral reform, should and, as their results show, do, in fact, generate much less clear responses in terms of winners and losers simply because the institutions themselves have less clear cut effects in making winners and losers. One consequence of this finding is that institutions which mitigate or otherwise obfuscate losing are, everything else being equal, therefore much less susceptible to change than those which make clear winners and losers.

Small parties, such as the Liberal Democrats in Great Britain, remain something of an oddity. Despite having no chance of winning more than a few seats, and notwithstanding the pressures of Duverger's Law, the Liberal Democrats still compete and attract sizable support. In part, of course, their electoral appeal is that they are a party of protest. But the willingness of LibDems, and similar parties elsewhere, to play the game speaks of an extraordinary commitment to getting back into the electoral ring despite being losers. In fact, California's Republicans stand in stark contrast to Britain's Liberal Democrats. Only a few months after a Democrat won a regularly scheduled election for Governor of the state in 2002, the state Republican Party launched an effort to recall the Governor that resulted in another—special—election in October 2003 and the selection of Republican Arnold Schwarzenegger as the new Governor. The Democratic governor who won in 2002 was not alone in calling the Republicans 'sore losers'. While the recall is a legitimate constitutional procedure that is frequently used in US local elections, the image was of one party, having lost a free and fair election, using the recall to replay the election until it produced a more satisfactory result. For the most part, however, losers in democratic systems act more like Britain's Liberal Democrats than California's Republicans.

DISCUSSION

Over and above providing yet more evidence of the attitudinal consequences of losing, the findings reported above show the potential seriousness for a political system mishandling losers' consent. One of the more desirable goals for political institutions is that citizens see them as legitimate. If an institution is seen as legitimate, there would seem little justification for replacing it with an alternative. The more people who are willing to countenance change in political institutions, or the more changes in those institutions that people are willing to consider, the less legitimate those institutions can be said to be.

Some caveats are in order at this point. The kinds of changes we have examined in this chapter do not show disappointed citizens supporting the end of the democratic system, only that losers are motivated to support changes in that system. Moreover, the changes they consider are those that concern fundamental aspects of the electoral process. Voters on the losing side of a political contest are willing to consider quite sweeping changes and do so in pretty much the same terms as elites who consider rule changes in terms of partisan self-interest. While we should be careful not to overstate the importance of these results we should be careful not to understate them either. Citizens' support for the institutions that govern them is generally held to be crucially important for the effectiveness and survival of the regime (see, for example, Easton's 1965, 1975 classic work on 'diffuse' and 'specific' support). In a very basic sense, lack of change in institutional arrangements can be viewed as an indicator of legitimacy (provided some basic human rights are protected).

Having said this, we should not expect losers to support any and every attempt at institutional reform. As we saw from the New Zealand and British examples, some institutional changes may be too unclear or the effects of the change too uncertain to generate support, even among losers. Nevertheless, the findings in this chapter help to demonstrate that losing is an important part of the motor that drives institutional change even after controlling for a variety of other causal explanations The experience of losing remains one of the engines that keep the democratic machine running. And while, in most cases, losing does not presage a disaster or an abrupt end to democratic practices, it does seem to be one of the first steps in the direction of change and reform. One of the difficulties facing the design of democratic institutions is to have institutions that make losers, but not permanent losers, and to allow current losers some reasonable chance of winning in future periods.

10

Conclusion: Graceful Losers and the Democratic Bargain

This book examines the impact of election outcomes on people's attitudes about government. It traces the differences in attitudes between those on the winning side of an election and those on the losing end. And it does so from a variety of perspectives—across countries and individuals as well as over time. It also examines different dimensions of support for democratic governance in order to see if some attitudes are more strongly affected by how an election comes out than others.

Our book is driven by a concern with electoral losers because the consent of the losers is critical to the maintenance of any political system and because it shapes the dynamics of politics in myriad ways. As a result, understanding what drives losers and leads them to accept their loss is essential for understanding what makes democratic systems function the way they do. And because losers have strong incentives to withhold consent, the question of what makes them acquiesce to a political system run by those they disagree with is a primary question that motivates our analyses and that has important implications for the study of democracy.

To understand the contours and structure of losers' consent and subsequently to answer the question of why losers go along, we focus on citizens who experience defeat on election day and react to this loss in different ways. Employing data on attitudes about government collected in some forty countries at different points in time, we examined the 'winner–loser gap' in attitudes toward the political system across these countries. We also traced the dynamics of losers' attitudes toward government over time—before and after elections, over the course of electoral cycles, and over long periods of historical time. Moreover, we examined how individual predispositions to react to losing in particular ways lead some voters to react more strongly and others less so. Moreover, we argued that losing is experienced in different institutional and historical contexts, all of which help shape losers' responses to election outcomes. Thus, we paint a picture of democratic legitimacy that portrays losers as critical actors whose experience is shaped both by who they are as individuals as well as the environment in which loss is given meaning.

We developed a model that views the making of democratic legitimacy as driven by the consequences of democratic elections. Losers are less willing to bestow legitimacy upon a political system that produced an outcome they actively sought to avert. However, the negative impact of losing (and the positive impact of winning) is conditional—some losers in some contexts translate loss into significantly more negative attitudes toward government than others. As a result, losers' incentives to disagree with the election outcome and accord low levels of legitimacy to the political system is significantly affected by a country's political context as well as voters' own attitudes such that both citizens and institutions have a role in blunting the rougher edge of losing. Thus, in thinking about and examining losers' consent, we followed two major avenues of inquiry. The first revolves around citizens themselves—that is, who they are—and how their predispositions may mold their reaction to loss. The second avenue is focused on the role that political context and institutions play in moderating citizens' sense of loss.

WHAT WE FIND

Our investigation of differences in views about the political system between election winners and losers reveals that being in the political majority generally translates into more positive attitudes toward government, while losers tend to exhibit significantly more negative attitudes toward the political system. We find that there commonly exists a gap in winners' and losers' sense of whether elections are fair, their evaluations of the performance of the political system as well as feelings about whether government is responsive. Moreover, losing elections has the potential to diminish people's support for democratic principles overall, while at the same time heightening their propensity to engage in political protest. However, the evidence also suggests that this gap is not ubiquitous, nor is it of equal size across countries or even within countries over time.

For the winner–loser gap to shape political legitimacy beyond the immediate aftermath of an election and, by implication, the functioning of democratic systems in systematic and fundamental ways, the gap should be observable over time. To examine the dynamics of losers' and winners' attitudes about the political system, we therefore traced support for the political system along three dimensions: immediately before and after an election; over the course of electoral cycles; and, in cases where voters lose repeatedly, over long periods of time. Our results show that winning and losing, once it occurs, has both immediate and lasting effects. When elections reshuffle the cards of the political game, the new losers—that is, those who used to be the winners—become less content with the political system. Conversely, the new winners who used to be the losers become significantly more positive about a political system that produced a favorable outcome.

What is more, these effects persist over the course of an electoral cycle and beyond as losers remain consistently less satisfied than winners between elections. Finally, we show that repeated losing serves to increasingly undermine losers' attitudes toward the political system—while losing once does not immediately serve to undercut losers' attitudes toward government, losing twice starts a process that leads to a gradual erosion of support for a system that consistently fails to make them winners. Consistent with the idea that context matters, these analyses also show a relatively smaller winner–loser gap when elections cause a change of hands between long-term incumbents and opponents.

We then turn our attention to the question of whether and how voters' own political predispositions may help to mediate the impact of winning and losing on attitudes toward government. Specifically, we focus on how two prominent individual-level differences—partisanship and ideology—affect what makes some winners and losers more likely to have strong reactions to being in the majority and minority, and how they make others less likely to translate the experience of winning and losing into positive or negative attitudes about the political system.

Our results suggest that political predispositions do have a mediating effect; however, individual-level differences in terms of strength of partisanship or ideological extremism do not universally affect levels of winners' and losers' consent. When such mediating effects do exist, however, they point to such predispositions acting as amplifiers rather than muting the winner–loser effect. Specifically, we find that strength of partisan attachment colors and modifies evaluations of the political system's legitimacy among winners and losers such that winners who are strongly attached to their political party offer significantly more positive appraisals of the political system's performance than other winners, for example. However, such effects are somewhat less apparent among losers. This suggests that winners' feelings toward their own party more commonly help color their feelings toward the political system, while losers' attitudes toward their own party matter a bit less for their feelings about the political system.

When it comes to ideological extremism, we found that extremism also adds to the strain of losing and heightens the pleasure of winning. That is, ideologues are particularly prone to view the system through the lens of winning and losing. However, as in the case of partisanship, while these effects can be documented, they are not universal. Moreover, the substantive impact of such effects is only moderately strong. Taken together, then, the evidence suggests that individual-level predispositions act as mediators of the winner–loser effect, but that they do not do so in all circumstances. However, when they do, they serve to magnify the impact of winning and losing.

We then turn to an examination of the contextual influences on losers' consent. Initially, we focus on the difference between established democracies and newly established ones. Specifically, we developed the idea that losing has stronger negative effects in new democracies relative to mature democracies since losers have not yet learned to lose in countries where democratic governance is of recent vintage and losing elections is a novel experience. Moreover, we investigated how the transition from dictatorship to democracy in Eastern Europe affects political support for the new political system among supporters of the hegemonic Communist parties of the past who frequently find themselves in the opposition under the new system. The results of this analysis demonstrate that political losers have lower support levels than winners across all the dimensions of political support that we investigate, including beliefs in core principles of democracy. Moreover, we find that the winner–loser gap is more prominent in newly democratized and democratizing states.

In addition, our analyses revealed that the supporters of the old Communist parties exhibit significantly lower levels of support for the democratic system than voters for other parties, in particular if they are not in power. This is not unexpected since the followers of these parties are the big losers in the sense that democracy replaced a system where winning was guaranteed for them. In an amendment to these core results, we found that voters for Communist parties are at least as confident in parliament as supporters of non-communist parties. We speculate that this may be explained by the fact that Communist parties in some of the new democracies have been able to use parliament as a forum that allows them to continue to fight for their cause.

Thus, our cross-national and cross-temporal investigation into the winner–loser gap reveals that context matters—that is, winning and losing are experienced in differently structured historical and political environments, and these differences help to mute or amplify the impact of losing on beliefs about the legitimacy of government. Aside from such historical—and one might even say path-dependent—differences, there also are identifiable and relatively stable features of democratic life that serve to organize and constrain citizens' political experiences, and which affect the development of particular attitudes about the workings of the political system. Specifically, because citizens form attitudes about politics in systemic contexts whose institutional structures affect the expression of preferences, define the choices that are available, and provide citizens with opportunities to be heard in the political process, we next turned to the question of whether and how responses to losing are mediated by political institutions and, further, how specific institutions, and not just combinations of institutions, help to shape the response of losers. Our analyses show that the winner–loser gap in attitudes about the system is smaller when electoral rules are more proportional, when the political system has a greater number of veto players and hence makes it more difficult to bring about wholesale policy change, and when power is shared within the political system. We also show that federalism, as an institution that can be part of either a majoritarian or consensus bundle of institutions, is effective in allowing losers some say in the system, and therefore helps reduce the winner–loser gap as well. Put simply, then, having a say and sharing in power at some level of government, even when in the opposition at the national level, enhances losers' consent.

We then turned to a comparison of losers with losers in order to identify the factors that affect their evaluations of electoral democracy across countries and across types of losers. For one, we find that, overall, more losers are satisfied with the functioning of democracy than are dissatisfied, that an overwhelming majority believes that the most recent election was fair, and more losers say that parties and politicians care what ordinary people think than the opposite. Thus, we uncovered little evidence of widespread distress among losers across a widely divergent set of countries.

Following the book's theme that both context and individual characteristics help determine the level of losers' consent, we also found that losers' evaluations are more positive in established democracies than in non-established democracies, and that losers' evaluations of the electoral process and the responsiveness of the political system are more positive in countries with more proportional electoral systems. Our results also indicate that losers in developed countries are more satisfied with the performance of democracy and express greater faith in the responsiveness of the political system but also are less positive in their assessments of the fairness of the most recent election.

When we looked at differences across losers' evaluations of electoral democracy with an eye toward the kinds of parties they supported, we found that supporters of losing parties that had never been in government were the most critical of representative democracy, while supporters of the major losing party that formed the government prior to the election felt most positive. Moreover, the data show that such differences between types of losing parties are more pronounced in less developed countries.

Regarding differences across losers' responses that may be driven by individual-level factors, our analyses show that more highly educated losers are more satisfied with the functioning of democracy, more positive about the fairness of the election in less developed democracies, and more sanguine about responsiveness in more developed countries. Aside from levels of education, our results also show that losers' ideology matters: while those who are on the 'extreme' right are not more critical towards representative democracy—in fact, they tend to be slightly more positive—voters on the extreme left expressed more negative evaluations of the political system. This latter effect is particularly pronounced in less developed democracies, where losers who are on the extreme left are more negative than similar losers in more developed countries.

Finally, we consider whether losing translates into lower levels of legitimacy by looking at a variety of behavioral implications of losing. The more people are willing to countenance change in political institutions, or the more changes in those institutions that people are willing to consider, the less legitimate those institutions can be said to be. As it turns out, voters on the losing side are willing to consider quite sweeping changes in the electoral process, and they do so in terms similar to elites who consider rule changes in terms of partisan self-interest. New Zealand and Great Britain furnish vivid examples of countries where voters are quite willing to support institutional changes, even when the effects of the changes are not entirely clear. Clearly, we find that losing is an important part of the motor that drives institutional change in democracies even after controlling for a variety of other causal explanations.

IMPLICATIONS FOR UNDERSTANDING LEGITIMACY AND DEMOCRATIC POLITICS

Depending on one's perspective, these findings can be taken to be good news or bad news. They are good news for those interested in developing a more systematic understanding of political legitimacy because they confirm the existence of the winner–loser effect with regard to people's attitudes toward the political system in a variety of countries and with regard to different dimensions of legitimacy. Moreover, they provide corroborative evidence that the effect exists in countries as different as the Czech Republic or Japan. The findings are bad news were we to insist that the winner–loser distinction provides empirical and conceptual leverage for every kind of attitude toward politics and unfailingly across all countries or at every point in time. Clearly, the results show that this is not the case.

But it is this lack of uniformity that opens up the opportunity of investigating why this gap does not exist at all times for all types of voters. Our findings regarding differences in individual predispositions—partisanship and ideology—suggest several conclusions for understanding the winner–loser gap at the level of individual voters. First, voters bring political predispositions to the table that heighten the effect of winning and losing. Second, however, because such effects are far from omnipresent and because their substantive impact is modest, they cannot serve as the sole explanation for the sometimes sizable and sometimes more modest winner–loser gap in attitudes toward the political system.

While we believe that understanding how election outcomes affects political attitudes more generally is a critical issue for the study of comparative political behavior, our findings also hold implications for students of comparative politics and democratization more generally. Our results regarding the deteriorating effects of repeated losing on attitudes toward government suggest that long periods without alternation in power lead to progressively less positive views about the political system among those on the losing side and may well produce a breeding ground for significant change in the political system. This is also consistent with the finding that supporters of parties that have never been in power are most critical of electoral democracy. Thus, even apparently stable countries with political cultures that value stability possess the inherent potential for significant upheaval when losers, instead of tuning out, ask for the political system to address their grievances.

But even in the short run, the relative stability of the winner–loser gap we observe during the course of electoral cycles regardless of who is in power has obvious implications for democratic governance. Unhappy (or at least, relatively unhappy) voters are unlikely to be as cooperative as happy ones when it comes to evaluating policy outcomes positively or supporting government policies or abiding by the rules of the game. And, by democratic design, governments time and again face a sizable and comparatively less happy segment of voters who are liable to view their actions through the lens of losing. Such a dynamics is of obvious relevance for understanding the politics of both established and newly emerging democratic systems.

Put simply, a sizable winner–loser gap makes things difficult for the winners, even if democracy does not automatically fail when it is particularly large. While failure is the worst outcome from the perspective of democratic legitimacy, it is not the only one. Large winner–loser gaps or really unhappy losers also mean that there is likely to be friction that may impede the efficient and proper functioning of democracy during the course of normal business because this gap may well affect the incentives of those in and out of power. When winners are particularly happy, those who represent them have little incentive to push for reform, even if sorely needed. Conversely, particularly unhappy losers have diminished incentives to play by the rules.

Thus, winning and losing are both short-term and long-term based phenomena and they affect high stakes politics—should we keep this political system as is?—and mundane decisions of compliance—should I pay a fine to a government I do not like? In the short run, losers feel bad about a system that did not favor them in the most recent election. In the medium term, the initial disappointment gives way to viewing the political system in ways that are consistent with the initial disappointment and the reality of being out of power.

Knowing that the political losers hold more negative attitudes toward the political system and generally are more willing to engage in political protest activities may mean that they will be less likely than the political winners to exercise the patience so critical for democratic survival. Because unhappy losers are most likely to push for changing the political status quo and because democracies are by their very nature amenable to deliberate change, research into the winner–loser effect and how institutional arrangements determine who ends up in the majority or the minority has direct implications for policy-makers (cf. Huntington 1991; Lijphart 1994; Guinier 1998).

The finding that support for democratic principles is affected by the loser–winner distinction, and particularly so in new democracies, is sobering as it points to inexperienced losers as a particularly weak link in the chain of stable democratic governance. Not only do electoral losers in new democracies express particularly negative attitudes toward regime institutions and processes, they also are less likely to endorse democracy as a good way of governing their societies. Perhaps unsurprisingly, these negative views are especially evident among supporters of the old regime—in the case of the Central and East European countries, the old, unreformed communist parties, for example. These results point to the need to pay particular attention to this group of disaffected democrats among those concerned with the stability and legitimacy of the new democratic system. Moreover, they suggest that the path to successful democratic consolidation is hazardous during election time and, in large part, a function of the behavior of the electoral losers (see also Casper and Taylor 1996). Thus, efforts to win over the old-winners-turned-new-losers without dampening the enthusiasm of the new winners may be a particularly wise strategy in light of the findings we report in this book.

Although not a primary focus of this study, our findings may have some normative implications for the nature of representative democracy. They suggest that levels of citizen satisfaction in contemporary democracies may not stem from the capacity to process the demands put on the system by citizens who seek to have more input. Thus, asking for more opportunities for citizen input into the system may not be a panacea for perceived inadequacies of democratic governance. Instead, the findings appear to indicate that systems could become unstable if a significant minority is *consistently* excluded from the political process. Because institutions mediate how minorities are treated by the system and, by implication, how these minorities feel about the political process, it may therefore not matter so much that too many people want too many things from their governments but whether everyone gets a hearing at least and a seat at the table every once in a while.

Although it is clear that those who are dissatisfied with the outputs provided by the system are less satisfied with that system, it may matter more what kinds of people want things from the government, given the differences across countries in how inclusive and consensual the democratic process is. Our results show that minorities are more likely to be satisfied with the way democracy works—despite their minority status—if there are mechanisms that provide for procedural justice in the democratic process and opportunities to have an input into the decisions made by the government. Institutional reforms that go in the direction of allowing those citizens who are in the minority more access to the political process, while ensuring that winning elections is still meaningful and allows for the implementation of policies preferred by the majority, may go a long way toward increasing citizen satisfaction with democracy, and toward ensuring the viability of democratic systems in the long term.

Whether citizens evaluate the functioning of their democracy based on the recent performance of their electoral institutions and organization or based on the more lasting institutions, such as electoral laws, holds importance for the broader scholarly debate about the design of democratic institutions. Specifically, political theorists have debated whether it is more important that the institutions produce superior outcomes or that the institutions are designed in a way that produces maximum process fairness to all participants. One of the difficulties facing the designers of democratic institutions is the need to have institutions that make losers without producing permanent losers, and that allow current losers some reasonable chance of winning in future periods. Put simply, the democratic bargain calls for winners who are willing to ensure that losers are not too unhappy and for losers, in exchange, to extend their consent to the winners' right to rule (see also Weingast 1997).

THE STUDY OF ELECTIONS AND COMPARATIVE POLITICAL BEHAVIOR

Aside from pointing to the importance of a critical variable for understanding political legitimacy—being an electoral loser—this book also seeks to contribute to and broaden our understanding of comparative political behavior more generally. That is, we are interested in mapping out a research agenda that promises to generate insights into mass political behavior that are generalizable across individuals and countries and beyond specific historical experiences and political cultures. As such, our agenda is, at least in part, about more than simply examining an interesting effect; instead, it is meant to reorient, to the extent possible, the study of comparative political behavior more fundamentally. To place our study in the proper context of research on political behavior, therefore, it may be useful to take a brief look at the evolution of behavioral political science and how our study fits into the bigger scheme of things.

While the early 1940s do not mark the beginning of time, they certainly constituted the period during which behavioral political science experienced its take-off phase in terms of becoming a modern social science. At the outset, the early survey-based studies of political attitudes and behavior undertaken during this period were explicitly motivated by long-standing normative questions political theorists have posed regarding the prerequisites of stable and well-functioning democracy (e.g. Campbell et al. 1960; Almond and Verba 1963). By placing individuals' behaviors and attitudes in the broader context of understanding how democracy works and the role citizens play in its success, researchers during the initial phase of the behavioral revolution sought to confront classic assumptions about democratic ideals with the reality of systematic empirical inquiry (Miller 1994).

Before too long, it became abundantly clear that most people do not live up to the Aristotelian ideal of the well-informed and enlightened citizen (cf. Berelson, Lazarsfeld, and McPhee 1954; Campbell et al. 1960; Converse 1964). Instead, the picture that emerged was one of democratic citizens who appeared ill-informed and largely uninterested in politics as well as perhaps naïvely trusting of those who exercised control over the levers of national political institutions. One by-product of these seemingly disappointing findings about citizens' competence to function as envisioned in normative theory may have been the subsequent lack of attention given to developing insights into political behavior that were expressly grounded in theories about how democracy does or should work more generally.[1] Instead, scholars increasingly turned their attention toward somewhat technical issues of methodology and measurement and away from democratic theory (Weatherford 1992; see also Miller 1994).

Part of this shift was fostered by the institutionalization of the *National Election Studies* in the United States and similar efforts in a number of advanced industrial societies, which continue to produce rich and lasting founts of data for understanding mass political behavior. In their wake, issues of survey design and measurement had considerable influence on theory development and seem to have become as important to the science of politics as normative concerns about the proper and ideal functioning of democracy. We suspect that this development was necessary—after all, it is difficult to draw inferences about the world when the data we base them on are inadequate or deficient. Or, as one colleague remarked to one of us at one point during a conversation in the hallway: 'Without good data, you're just another guy with an opinion'.

And hardly coincidentally, the development and analysis of survey items and strategies for improving the collection and quality of reliable data frequently was based on theories imported from psychology, sociology, or economics rather than conceptualizations that were generated from within political science. In particular, among students of political behavior an explicit concern with establishing a connection between individuals and the macro-political (i.e. democratic) environment in which they functioned as citizens became sporadic. Thus, all the while scholars debated the proper measurement of particular concepts, there regularly existed a disconnect between experiences people have—*sui generis*—as participants in the political process and how they interact with the constraints any particular political system or situation provides.[2] Politics, and the behavior of citizens, it seems, existed in a vacuum.

---

[1] Naturally, there have been notable exceptions to this rule over the years. In recent years, for example, we note the path-breaking work on how citizens with limited information can make reasonable and rational choices in elections (cf. Lupia and McCubbins 1998).

[2] There were notable exceptions to the rule of survey research in a vacuum. Most notably, scholars working in the sociological tradition were willing to explore the multifaceted and notably more realistic world of citizens acting in particular social and political environments. An example of such efforts was the South Bend study by Huckfeldt and Sprague (1995), which explored people's richly textured, and difficult to measure, micro-political environment in which they experience politics. In a comparative setting, the contributions in van der Eijk and Franklin (1996) are an example of research aimed at integrating electoral institutions and mass political behavior. Moreover, several scholars have investigated the impact of political participation—in particular voting—on people's sense of political efficacy (Ginsberg and Weisberg 1978; Finkel 1985; Clarke and Acock 1989; Mutz 2002a, b). These efforts are important conceptually because they

And this, we would argue, had implications for the role of political (democratic) institutions in studies of political behavior as well as the acceptance of the importance of explaining election outcomes.

Political Institutions and Political Behavior

Turning first to the issue of how political context affects political behavior, the general finding in this book that contextual variation is an important mediator of public opinion toward political authorities confirms that political behavior cannot be understood in a vacuum. This is important and it should require a rethinking of how we postulate what shapes individuals' political behavior, in particular as it pertains to the role of political institutions. As recent research on government support has shown, institutional variation is an important element for understanding citizens' ability to assign credit and blame to incumbents for economic performance (Powell and Whitten 1993; Anderson 1995). Regarding the study of democratic institutions, our analyses also document important and systematic consequences of different kinds of democracies at the level of mass publics. Aside from affecting policy outcomes (Lijphart 1994; Crepaz 1996), cabinet stability and conflict (Powell 1986), or the congruence of elite and mass policy preferences (Huber and Powell 1994), different forms of democratic organization also have consequences for public attitudes toward democracy as a form of government.

What we have done in this volume, then, is to bring a discussion of institutions explicitly into models of mass opinion and behavior. We know from the study of electoral systems that formal details—of how votes are aggregated, for example—can have sizable impacts on how people behave (see, for example, the contributions in van der Eijk and Franklin 1996). But our concern with institutions has not centered so much on those kinds of details but on the consequences and incentives associated with making winners and losers. In that sense we have built the fundamental consequences of institutions into explanations of mass attitudes and behaviors. For us, institutions are not simply disembodied objects external to voters but, rather, are factors that help shape and give meaning to political attitudes. In a way, then, institutions are both endogenous and exogenous to political behavior.

The gap in opinions between winners and losers has been seen across a varied set of attitudes and behaviours. We have shown that it is important to take account of how citizens stand in relation to those institutions. By building institutions into our models, we have taken account of just what it is that institutions do to and for voters. Institutions make winners and losers and

have sought to redirect scholars' attention to understanding political behavior in the context of constraints shaped by the environment they live in and the experiences they have as active participants in the political process.

those two conditions imply very different sets of attitudes and behaviors for voters, not least of which is that they also create very different sets of attitudes towards the institutions themselves. One lesson to be drawn from this work, then, is that institutions do indeed matter so far as mass opinions are concerned. Institutions matter in part because they create losers and do so in a way that either amplifies or dampens that sense of loss.

Focusing on Understanding the Outcomes of Elections

Perhaps as importantly, another by-product of the institutionalization of behavioral political science via national election studies and other large-scale survey and data collection efforts has been a predominant concern with explaining election outcomes rather than understanding the consequences of elections for how voters behave. This made enormous practical sense. If elections are the most common forum for citizen participation in a democracy, why not try and understand why they come out the way they do and why citizens make the choices they make?

In part, this tendency to focus on election outcomes also can be viewed as a function of the heavy influence of sociology and social-psychology (two fields that were fairly unified at the time of the behavioral revolution) on early studies of political behavior. Given that the behavioral paradigm in these fields, in particular in social-psychology, led scholars to focus on attitudes as independent variables, which were used to explain political behavior (such as electoral choice) or other attitudes (such as partisanship), it should not come as a surprise that much of electoral research, both in the United States and in comparative perspective, has long focused on explaining the behavior of voters with the help of attitudes or people's demographic characteristics. Thus, among the most common research questions in electoral research has long been this: how do we explain wins and losses? That is, what are the underlying determinants of why parties won or lost, increased their share of the vote, and how people came to choose one party or candidate over another?

Given the crucial role elections play in a democracy, this is both proper and unsurprising. Yet, such an approach, in all likelihood unintentionally, led electoral researchers to emphasize winners and winning at the expense of losers when thinking about the functioning of democracies. It also established the dominance of a theoretical paradigm that privileged behavior (such as vote choice) as the outcome of interest (that is, the dependent variable), and attitudes as explanatory factors (independent variables). Regrettably, such a focus on explaining election outcomes made it difficult to imagine that the causal arrow could be reversed and that we should focus on explaining attitudes with the help of behavior. In fact, reviewing the state of the scholarly literature on political participation in the mid-1970s, Robert Salisbury (1975) argued that scholars had made considerable progress toward explaining political behavior

with the help of attitudes, but that it would be a long time before political science would understand the impact of political behavior and its consequences
on attitudes (see also Finkel 1985). As it turned out, Salisbury's argument was
strikingly prescient; in the ensuing three decades, few scholars have sought
to understand how voting behavior and election outcomes affect people's attitudes and behaviors.

In our view, the general lack of attention to questions of democratic governance and institutions in studies of political behavior and the specific lack of
attention to how elections affect behaviors and attitudes has limited progress
in behavioral research because there are good theoretical reasons for assuming that such influences carry important implications for understanding how
democracies work. Thus, to help correct this imbalance and contribute to our
understanding of the nexus between citizens and their governments, and in
some small part refocus the study of political behavior in democracies, we
argue for the importance of understanding what drives the losers of democratic elections and how losing affects their attitudes and behaviors. In a way,
then, we are suggesting that future research on political behavior incorporate
both the strategic behavior of voters and the impact of institutions as well as
the psychological mechanisms at work. To put it in statistical terms, we propose that students of political behavior focus on the outcomes of elections as
the independent variable and attitudes—such as trust in the political system
or opinions on public policy—as the dependent variables in order to create
and test theories that are truly political, inherently dynamic, and that promise
leverage for understanding political conflict and its resolution in a wide variety of contexts. Such a strategy would allow for a (re)integration of the study
of political behavior with the study of democratic institutions and democratic
stability, and it would have the potential to integrate what we know across
vibrant yet all-too-frequently separate subfields of the study of politics.

Appendix: Data Sources and Survey Items

The data used in this book come from several survey projects, including the Eurobarometer (EB) surveys (various years), the 1996 International Social Survey Program (ISSP) surveys conducted as part of a study called *Role of Government III*; the Comparative Study of Electoral Systems (CSES) election surveys conducted between 1996 and 2000; the 1999 European Values Surveys (EVS), which are part of a larger project on World values, as well as the American and Canadian National Election studies surveys, which have been conducted for a number of years. These survey programs are continuing regular programs of surveys covering topics important to social science research. The ISSP, CSES, and EVS jointly develop modules dealing with important areas in the social sciences, and they usually field these modules in supplements to national surveys undertaken by the members. All surveys usually include an extensive common core on background variables, and project members make the data available to the social science community. The Eurobarometer data are collected twice a year by the European Commission and made available to the scholarly community via data archives, including the Inter-university Consortium for Political and Social Research (ICPSR) at the University of Michigan. Additional data used in our analyses come from a variety of stand-alone surveys, including surveys conducted by news organization (such as CBS News) and the authors.

CHAPTER 3

Evaluations of political system performance. 'All in all, how well or badly do you think the system of democracy in (country) works these days?' It works well and needs no changes (4), it works well but needs some changes (3), it does not work well and needs a lot of changes (2), it does not work well and needs to be completely changed (1).

External political efficacy (system responsiveness). Average of four items derived from two internal efficacy items and two external efficacy items that range from 1 to 5, with 1 denoting strongly agree and 5 strongly disagree. Question wording: 'How much do you agree or disagree with each of the following statements: (a) People like me have no say about what the government does; (b) The average citizen has considerable influence on politics; (c) Elections are a good way of making governments aware of the important issues facing our country; (d) People we elect as members of parliament try to keep the promises they made in the election'. Respondents' answers were coded such that five constituted the most efficacious response.

Protest potential. Based on factor scores of five survey items. Question wording: 'Would you or would you not do any of the following to protest against a government action you strongly oppose?' (a) Attend a public meeting organized to protest against the government; (b) go on a protest march or demonstration. Respondents could choose from definitely would (scored 4), probably would (3), probably would not (2), and definitely would not (1). In addition, respondents were asked: 'There are many ways people or organizations can protest against a government action they strongly oppose. Please show which one you think should be allowed and which one should not be allowed'. (a) Organizing public meetings to protest against the government; (b) organizing protest marches and demonstrations; and (c) organizing a nationwide strike of all workers against the government. Respondents could choose from definitely allowed (4), probably allowed (3), probably not allowed (2), and definitely not allowed (1).

Difference in evaluations of current political system versus previous regime. (Items were coded such that high values mean positive political support.) 'People have different views about the system for governing this country. Here is a scale for rating how well things are going: 1 means very bad, 10 means very good. Where on this scale would you put the political system as it was ...'

in former communist countries: under communist regime
in countries where recently a change of regime xx has taken place: under xx
    regime
in countries where no regime change has taken place: ten years ago?

Confidence in parliament. 'How much confidence do you have in parliament, is it a great deal, quite a lot, not very much or none at all?' A great deal (4); quite a lot (3); not very much (2); none at all (1).

Support for democratic principles. Additive index of the following items:

1. 'Would you say that having a democratic political system is a very good, fairly good, fairly bad or very bad way of governing this country?' Very good (4); fairly good (3); fairly bad (2); very bad (1).
2. 'Could you please tell me if you agree strongly, agree, disagree, or disagree strongly?' Democracy may have problems but it's better than any other form of government. Agree strongly (4); agree (3); disagree (2); disagree strongly (1).
3. 'I'm going to read off some things that people sometimes say about a democratic political system. Could you please tell me if you agree strongly,

agree, disagree or disagree strongly, after I read each of them?' Agree strongly (1); agree (2); disagree (3); disagree strongly (4).

- In a democracy, the economic system runs badly
- Democracies are indecisive and have too much squabbling
- Democracies aren't good at maintaining order.

4. 'I'm going to describe various types of political systems and ask what you think about each as a way of governing this country. For each one, would you say it is a very good, fairly good, fairly bad or very bad way of governing this country?' Very good (1); fairly good (2); fairly bad (3); very bad (4).

- Having a strong leader who does not have to bother with parliament and elections?
- Having experts, not government, make decisions according to what they think is best for the country?
- Having the army rule the country?

CHAPTER 4

Satisfaction with democracy. 'On the whole, are you very satisfied, fairly satisfied, not very satisfied, or not at all satisfied with the way democracy works in your country?'

Trust in government. 'Generally speaking, can the [federal] government, that is, the government in Washington DC, be trusted to do the right thing?' Just about always (4); most of the time (3); only some of the time (2); never (1).

CHAPTER 5

Partisan attachment. 'Do you feel very close to this (party/party block), somewhat close, or not very close?' Very close; somewhat close; not very close.

Ideology. 'In politics people sometimes talk of left and right. Where would you place yourself on a scale from 0 to 10 where 0 means the left and 10 means the right?'

CHAPTER 6

Difference in evaluations of current political system versus previous regime. See Chapter 3.

Confidence in parliament. See Chapter 3.

Support for democratic principles. See Chapter 3.

Old communists. (See chapter Appendix 6A.1 for list of reformed communist parties.) Voting for an old communist party (1); voting for other any other party (0).

Reformed communists. (See chapter Appendix 6A.1 for list of reformed communist parties.) Voting for a reformed communist party (1); voting for other any other party (0).

CHAPTER 7

Veto players. Number of parties in government (range: 1–6).

Veto players squared. Square of veto players measure.

Federalism. Dummy variable, where 1 if Austria, Belgium, Germany, or Spain.

New Democracy. Dummy variable, where 1 if Portugal, Spain, Greece, East Germany.

Electoral system. List proportional representation (PR) with closed list (Netherlands, Portugal, Sweden) (1); PR with preferential system (Australia, Belgium, Denmark, Finland, Luxembourg, Spain) (2); PR with voting for individual candidates (Greece, Germany) (3); individual districts (France, Ireland, Italy, and UK) (4).

Satisfaction with democracy. 'On the whole, are you very satisfied, fairly satisfied, not very satisfied, or not at all satisfied with the way democracy works in NAME OF COUNTRY?' Very satisfied (4); fairly satisfied (3); not very satisfied (2); not at all satisfied (1).

Confidence in parliament. 'To what extent can you rely on your National Parliament?' Ten point scale, ranging from 'cannot' (1) to 'can' (10).

Confidence in national government. 'To what extent can you rely on your National Government?' Ten point scale, ranging from 'cannot' (1) to 'can' (10).

Trust in state government. 'How often do you trust [your] state government?' Always (1); mostly (2); sometimes (3); never (4).

CHAPTER 8

Satisfaction with democracy. See Chapter 4.

Fairness of the electoral process. 'In some countries, people believe their elections are conducted fairly. In other countries, people believe that their elections are conducted unfairly. Thinking of the last election in (country), where would you place it on this scale of one to five, where ONE means that the last election was conducted fairly and FIVE means that the election was conducted unfairly?'

Responsiveness of the political system. Additive index based on three items. (1) 'Some people say that members of Parliament know what ordinary people think. Others say that members of Parliament don't know much about what ordinary people think. Using the (one to five) scale, where would you place yourself?'; (2) 'Some people say that political parties in (country) care what ordinary people think. Others say that political parties in (country) don't care what ordinary people think. Using the (one to five) scale, where would you place yourself?'; (3) 'Some people say it makes a difference who is in power. Others say that it does not make a difference who is in power. Using the (one to five) scale, where would you place yourself?'

CHAPTER 9

Efficacy. Additive index of two items. (1) 'People like me don't have any say about what the government does'; (2) 'Elections are a good way of making the government pay attention to the important political issues facing our country'. Answer categories included: strongly agree, agree, neither agree nor disagree, disagree, and strongly disagree, with 4 denoting a more efficacious attitude.

Proportional representation to elect Congress. 'Some people suggest we should use proportional representation to elect Congress. This would probably mean that three or more parties would be represented in Congress. Would you support such a proposal?' Yes (1); no (0) (Table 9.3).

Direct election of President. 'When it comes to electing the President, some suggest we get rid of the Electoral College and simply elect the candidate who most people voted for. Would you support or oppose such a proposal?' Yes (1); no (0) (Table 9.3).

Support for constitutional change (US). 'Presidents are elected by the Electoral College, in which each state gets as many votes as it has members of Congress and can cast all of them for whoever wins in that state. Do you think we should keep the Electoral College, or should we amend the Constitution?' Amend the Constitution (1); other answer (0) (Table 9.4).

Support for Prop. 198 in California. 'As you know Prop. 198 would create a single primary election ballot on which the names and party affiliations of all candidates would be placed. Candidates' names would not be grouped by political party. Any registered voter, including those not affiliated with a political party, would be able to vote for any candidate regardless of party. If the election were being held today, would you vote yes or no on Proposition 198?' Yes (1); no (0).

References

Abelson, Robert P. (1968). *Theories of Cognitive Consistency: A Sourcebook* (Chicago: Rand McNally).

——, and Milton J. Rosenberg (1958). 'Symbolic Psycho-Logic: A Model of Attitudinal Cognition'. *Behavioral Science* 3(1): 1–13.

Almond, Gabriel A., and Sidney Verba (1963). *The Civic Culture* (Princeton: Princeton University Press).

Anderson, Christopher J. (1995). *Blaming the Government: Citizens and the Economy in Five European Democracies* (Armonk, NY: M. E. Sharpe).

—— (1998). 'Party Systems and Satisfaction with Democracy in the New Europe'. *Political Studies* 46(4): 572–88.

—— (2000). 'Economic Voting and Political Context: A Comparative Perspective'. *Electoral Studies* 19(2–3): 151–70.

—— (2002). 'Good Questions, Dubious Inferences, and Bad Solutions: Some Further Thoughts on Satisfaction with Democracy'. Binghamton University, Center on Democratic Performance Working Paper No. 116, Binghamton, NY.

——, and Christine A. Guillory (1997). 'Political Institutions and Satisfaction with Democracy'. *American Political Science Review* 91(1): 66–81.

——, and Andrew J. LoTempio (2002). 'Winning, Losing and Political Trust in America'. *British Journal of Political Science* 32(2): 335–51.

——, and Kathleen M. O'Connor (2000). 'System Change, Learning, and Public Opinion about the Economy'. *British Journal of Political Science* 30(1): 147–72.

——, and Yuliya V. Tverdova (2001). 'Winners, Losers, and Attitudes about Government in Contemporary Democracies'. *International Political Science Review* 22(4): 321–38.

——, and Yuliya V. Tverdova (2003). 'Corruption, Political Allegiances, and Attitudes Toward Government in Contemporary Democracies'. *American Journal of Political Science* 47(1): 91–109.

——, Silvia Mendes, and Yuliya V. Tverdova (2004). 'Endogenous Economic Voting: Evidence from the 1997 British Election'. *Electoral Studies* 23(4): 683–708.

Andrews, Josephine, and Robert Jackman (n.d.). 'Strategic Fools; Electoral Choice Under Extreme Uncertainty'. *Electoral Studies*, in press.

Angus, H. F. (1952). 'Note on the British Columbia Election in June 1952'. *Western Political Quarterly* 5(4): 585–91.

Atkinson, John W. (1957). 'Motivational Determinants of Risk-Taking Behavior'. *Psychological Review* 64(4): 359–72.

Balch, George I. (1974). 'Multiple Indicators in Survey Research: The Concept Sense of Political Efficacy'. *Political Methodology* 1(1): 1–43.

Barber, Benjamin (1984). *Strong Democracy* (Berkeley: University of California Press).

Barnes, Samuel, and Max Kaase et al. (1979). *Political Action: Mass Participation in Five Western Democracies* (Beverly Hills, CA: Sage).

Bartolini, Stefano, and Peter Mair (1990). *Identity, Competition, and Electoral Availability* (New York: Cambridge University Press).

Bawn, Kathleen (1993). 'The Logic of Institutional Preferences: German Electoral Laws as a Social Choice Outcome'. *American Journal of Political Science* 37(4): 965–89.

Beggan, James K., and Scott T. Allison (1993). 'The Landslide Victory That Wasn't: The Bias Toward Consistency in Recall of Election Support'. *Journal of Applied Social Psychology* 23(8): 669–77.

Benoit, Kenneth, and Jacqueline Hayden (2004). 'Institutional Change and Persistence: The Evolution of Poland's Electoral System, 1989–2001'. *Journal of Politics* 66(2): 396–427.

Berelson, Bernard, Paul F. Lazarsfeld, and William V. McPhee (1954). *Voting: A Study of Opinion Formation in a Presidential Campaign* (Chicago: University of Chicago Press).

Bermeo, Nancy (2003). *Ordinary People in Extraordinary Times* (Princeton: Princeton University Press).

Blais, André, and Mathieu Turgeon (2004). 'How Good are Voters at Sorting Out the Weakest Candidate in their Constituency?' *Electoral Studies* 23(3): 455–61.

——, Elisabeth Gidengil, Richard Nadeau, and Neil Nevitte (2001). 'Measuring Party Identification: Britain, Canada, and the United States'. *Political Behavior* 23(1): 1–22.

——, and Louis Massicotte (2002). 'Electoral Systems', in *Comparing Democracies: New Challenges in the Study of Elections and Voting*, ed. Lawrence LeDuc, Richard G. Niemi, and Pippa Norris (London: Sage).

Boix, Carles (1999). 'Setting the Rules of the Game. The Choice of Electoral Systems in Advanced Democracies'. *American Political Science Review* 93(3): 609–24.

Booth, Alan, Greg Shelley, Allan Mazur, Gerry Tharp, and Roger Kittock (1989). 'Testosterone, and Winning and Losing in Human Competition'. *Hormones and Behavior* 23(4): 556–71.

Boston, Jonathan, Stephen Levine, Elizabeth McLeay, and Nigel S. Roberts (1997). *From Campaign to Coalition: New Zealand's First General Election Under Proportional Representation* (Palmerston: Dunmore Press).

Bowler, Shaun, and Todd Donovan (2000). 'Public Opinion about Democratic Institutions: Constituencies for Change'. Paper presented at the annual meeting of the American Political Science Association, Washington, DC, August.

——, and —— (2002). 'Democracy, Institutions and Attitudes about Citizen Influence on Government'. *British Journal of Political Science* 32(2): 371–90.

——, and —— (2003a). 'Political Reform Via the Initiative Process: What Voters Think about when they Change the Rules', in *Voting at the Political Fault Line: California's Experiment with the Blanket Primary*, ed. Bruce E. Cain and Elisabeth R. Gerber (Berkeley: University of California Press).

Bowler, Shaun, and Todd Donovan (2003*b*). 'The Effect of Winning and Losing on Attitudes about Political Institutions and Democracy in the United States'. Paper presented at the annual meeting of the Midwest Political Science Association, Chicago, IL, April.

Bowler, Shaun, Todd Donovan, and Jeffrey Karp (2002). 'When Might Institutions Change? Elite Support for Direct Democracy in Three Nations'. *Political Research Quarterly* 55(4): 731–54.

Brady, David, and J. Mo (1992). 'Strategy and Choice in the 1988 National Assembly Election of Korea'. *Comparative Political Studies* 24(4): 405–29.

Brehm, Jack W. (1956). 'Postdecision Changes in the Desirability of Alternatives'. *Journal of Abnormal Social Psychology* 52(3): 384–89.

——(1962). 'Motivational Effects of Cognitive Dissonance', in *Explorations in Cognitive Dissonance*, ed. Jack W. Brehm and Arthur R. Cohen (New York: Wiley & Sons).

Brent, Edward, and Donald Granberg (1982). 'Subjective Agreement with the Presidential Candidates of 1976 and 1980'. *Journal of Personality and Social Psychology* 42(3): 393–403.

Brittan, Samuel (1975). 'The Economic Contradictions of Democracy'. *British Journal of Political Science* 5(1): 129–59.

Brody, Richard A., and Benjamin I. Page (1972). 'Comment: The Assessment of Policy Voting'. *American Political Science Review* 66(2): 450–8.

Brown, Jonathon D., and Keith A. Dutton (1995). 'The Thrill of Victory, the Complexity of Defeat: Self-Esteem and People's Emotional Reactions to Success and Failure'. *Journal of Personality and Social Psychology* 68(4): 712–22.

Budge, Ian, Ivor Crewe, and Dennis Farlie (1976). *Party Identification and Beyond: Representations of Voting and Party Competition* (London: John Wiley).

Cain, Bruce, Russell J. Dalton, and Susan E. Scarrow (2003). *Democracy Transformed: Expanding Political Opportunities in Advanced Industrial Democracies* (New York: Oxford University Press).

Campbell, Angus, Philip Converse, Warren Miller, and Donald Stokes (1960). *The American Voter* (New York: Wiley and Sons).

——, Gerald Gurin, and Warren E. Miller (1954). *The Voter Decides* (Evanston, IL: Row, Peterson).

Casper, Gretchen, and Michelle M. Taylor (1996). *Negotiating Democracy: Transitions from Authoritarian Rule* (Pittsburgh: University of Pittsburgh Press).

Cigler, Allan J., and Russell Getter (1977). 'Conflict Reduction in the Post-Election Period: A Test of the Depolarization Thesis'. *Western Political Quarterly* 30(3): 363–76.

Clarke, Harold D., and Alan C. Acock (1989). 'National Elections and Political Attitudes: The Case of Political Efficacy'. *British Journal of Political Science* 19(4): 551–62.

——, and Alan Kornberg (1992). 'Do National Elections Affect Perceptions of MP Responsiveness: A Note on the Canadian Case'. *Legislative Studies Quarterly* 17(2): 183–204.

——, Marianne C. Stewart, and Paul Whiteley (1997). 'Tory Trends: Party Identification and the Dynamics of Conservative Support since 1992'. *British Journal of Political Science* 27(2): 299–319.

——, Euel Elliott, William Mishler, Marianne Stewart, Paul Whiteley, and Gary Zuk (1992). *Controversies in Political Economy: Canada, Great Britain, The United States* (Boulder: Westview Press).

Colomer, Josep M. (2001). *Political Institutions: Democracy and Social Choice* (New York: Oxford University Press).

Converse, Philip E. (1964). 'The Nature of Belief Systems in Mass Publics', in *Ideology and Discontent*, ed. David E. Apter (New York: Free Press).

Cox, Gary W., and Jonathan N. Katz (2002). *Elbridge Gerry's Salamander: The Electoral Consequences of the Reapportionment Revolution* (New York: Cambridge University Press).

Crepaz, Markus M. L. (1996). 'Consensus Versus Majoritarian Democracy: Political Institutions and their Impact on Macroeconomic Performance and Industrial Disputes'. *Comparative Political Studies* 29(1): 4–26.

Daalder, Hans, and Peter Mair (eds.) (1983). *Western European Party Systems* (Beverly Hills, CA: Sage).

Dahl, Robert A. (1971). *Polyarchy* (New Haven: Yale University Press).

——(1989). *Democracy and its Critics* (New Haven: Yale University Press).

——(2002). *How Democratic is the American Constitution?* (New Haven: Yale University Press).

Dalton, Russell J. (2002). *Citizen Politics: Public Opinion and Political Parties in Advanced Industrial Democracies*, 3rd edn. (New York: Chatham House Publishers).

——(2004). *Democratic Challenges, Democratic Choices: The Erosion in Political Support in Advanced Industrial Democracies* (Oxford: Oxford University Press).

Dennis, Jack (1966). 'Support for the Party System by the Mass Public'. *American Political Science Review* 60(3): 600–15.

Donovan, Todd, and Joseph R. Snipp (1994). 'Support for Legislative Term Limitations in California: Group Representation, Partisanship and Campaign Information'. *Journal of Politics* 56(2): 492–501.

Duverger, Maurice (1954). *Political Parties: Their Organization and Activity in the Modern State* (London: Methuen).

Easton, David (1953). *The Political System: An Inquiry into the State of Political Science* (New York: Knopf).

——(1957). 'An Approach to the Analysis of Political Systems'. *World Politics* 9(2): 383–400.

——(1965). *A Systems Analysis of Political Life* (New York: Wiley).

——(1975). 'A Re-Assessment of the Concept of Political Support'. *British Journal of Political Science* 5(4): 435–7.

Eijk, Cees van der, and Mark N. Franklin (eds.) (1996). *Choosing Europe? The European Electorate and National Politics in the Face of Union* (Ann Arbor, MI: University of Michigan Press).

Erber, Ralph, and Richard R. Lau (1990). 'Political Cynicism Revisited: An Information-Processing Reconciliation of Policy-Based and Incumbency-Based Interpretations of Changes in Trust in Government'. *American Journal of Political Science* 34(1): 236–53.

Evans, Geoffrey, and Stephen Whitefield (1993). 'Identifying the Bases of Party Competition in Eastern Europe'. *British Journal of Political Science* 23(4): 521–48.

Evans, Geoffrey, and Stephen Whitefield (2001). 'The Dynamics of Cleavage Formation in Conditions of Economic Transformation: Comparing Cleavages in Russia, Ukraine, and Lithuania'. Paper presented at the annual meeting of the American Political Science Association, San Francisco, CA, September.

Festinger, Leon (1957). *A Theory of Cognitive Dissonance* (Stanford, CA: Stanford University Press).

——(1964). *Conflict, Decision, and Dissonance* (Stanford, CA: Stanford University Press).

Finkel, Steven E. (1985). 'Reciprocal Effects of Participation and Political Efficacy: A Panel Analysis'. *American Journal of Political Science* 29(4): 891–913.

——(1987). 'The Effects of Participation on Political Efficacy and Political Support'. *Journal of Politics* 49(3): 441–64.

——, Edward N. Muller, and Mitchell A. Seligson (1989). 'Economic Crisis, Incumbent Performance and Regime Support: A Comparison of Longitudinal Data from West Germany and Costa Rica'. *British Journal of Political Science* 19(2): 329–51.

Fiorina, Morris P. (1981). *Retrospective Voting in American National Elections* (New Haven: Yale University Press).

Franklin, Charles H., and John. E. Jackson (1983). 'The Dynamics of Party Identification'. *American Political Science Review* 77(4): 957–73.

Freedom House (2001). *Freedom in the World: Country Ratings 1972–73 to 2000–01* (New York: Freedom House).

Freeman, Jonathan L., and David O. Sears (1965). 'Selective Exposure', in *Advances in Experimental Social Psychology*, Vol. 2, ed. Leonard Berkowitz (Orlando, FL: Academic Press).

Frenkel, Oden, and Anthony Doob (1976). 'Postdecision Dissonance at the Polling Booth'. *Canadian Journal of Behavioral Science* 8(4): 347–50.

Fuchs, Dieter (1993). 'Trends of Political Support', in *Political Culture in Germany*, ed. Dirk Berg-Schlosser and Ralf Rytlewski (New York: St. Martin's).

——, and Hans-Dieter Klingemann (1989). 'The Left–Right Schema', in *Continuities in Political Action*, ed. M. Kent Jennings and Jan W. van Deth (New York: de Gruyter).

——, Giovanna Guidorossi, and Palle Svensson (1995). 'Support for the Democratic System', in *Citizens and the State*, ed. Hans-Dieter Klingemann and Dieter Fuchs (New York: Oxford University Press).

Funder, David C., and C. Randall Colvin (1991). 'Explorations in Behavioral Consistency: Properties of Persons, Situations, and Behaviors'. *Journal of Personality and Social Psychology* 60(5): 773–94.

Gabel, Matthew J., and John D. Huber (2000). 'Putting Parties in their Place: Inferring Party Left–Right Ideological Positions from Party Manifestos Data'. *American Journal of Political Science* 44(1): 94–103.

Gabriel, Oscar W. (1989). 'Regierungswechsel und politische Unterstützung: Implikationen des Parteienwettbewerbs für die Struktur politischer Unterstützung in der Demokratie'. *Politische Vierteljahresschrift* 30(1): 75–93.

Gallagher, Michael (1991). 'Proportionality, Disproportionality, and Electoral Systems'. *Electoral Studies* 10(1): 33–51.

Gamson, William A. (1968). *Power and Discontent* (Homewood, IL: Dorsey Press).

Garrett, Geoffrey (1992). 'International Co-operation and Institutional Choice: The European Community Internal Market'. *International Organizations* 46(2): 533–60.

Gerber, Elizabeth, and Rebecca Morton (1998). 'Primary Election Systems and Representation'. *Journal of Law, Economics, and Organization* 14(2): 304–24.

Gibson, James L. (2002). 'Becoming Tolerant? Short-Term Changes in Russian Political Culture'. *British Journal of Political Science* 32(2): 309–34.

——, Gregory A. Caldeira, and Lester Kenyatta Spence (2003). 'The Supreme Court and the US Presidential Election of 2000: Wounds, Self-Inflicted or Otherwise?' *British Journal of Political Science* 33(4): 535–56.

Ginsberg, Benjamin (1982). *The Consequences of Consent: Elections, Citizen Control, and Popular Acquiescence* (New York: Random House).

——, and Robert Weisberg (1978). 'Elections and the Mobilization of Popular Support'. *American Journal of Political Science* 22(1): 31–55.

Granberg, Donald (1993). 'Political Perception', in *Explorations in Political Psychology*, ed. Shanto Iyengar and William J. McGuire (Durham: Duke University Press).

——, and Edward Brent (1983). 'When Prophesy Bends: The Preference–Expectations Link in U.S. Presidential Elections, 1952–1980'. *Journal of Personality and Social Psychology* 45(3): 477–91.

Green, Donald, Bradley Palmquist, and Eric Schickler (2002). *Partisan Hearts and Minds: Political Parties and the Social Identity of Voters* (New Haven: Yale University Press).

Guinier, Lani (1998). *Lift Every Voice* (New York: Simon & Schuster).

Gunther, Richard (1989). 'Electoral Laws, Party Systems, and Elites: The Case of Spain'. *American Political Science Review* 83(4): 835–58.

Habermas, Jürgen (1975). *Legitimation Crisis* (Boston: Beacon Press).

Harmel, Robert, and John D. Robertson (1986). 'Government Stability and Regime Support: A Cross-National Analysis'. *Journal of Politics* 48(4): 1029–40.

Harvey, John, and Judson Mills (1971). 'Effect of a Difficult Opportunity to Revoke a Counterattitudinal Action Upon Attitude Change'. *Journal of Personality and Social Psychology* 18(2): 201–9.

Held, David (1987). *Models of Democracy* (Cambridge: Polity Press).

Hetherington, Marc J. (2004). *Why Trust Matters: Declining Political Trust and the Demise of American Liberalism* (Princeton, NJ: Princeton University Press).

Hirschman, Albert O. (1970). *Exit, Voice, and Loyalty: Responses to Decline in Firms, Organizations, and States* (Cambridge: Harvard University Press).

Hofferbert, Richard I., and Hans-Dieter Klingemann (1999). 'Remembering the Bad Old Days: Human Rights, Economic Conditions, and Democratic Performance in Transitional Regimes'. *European Journal of Political Research* 36(2): 155–74.

Holmberg, Sören (1999). 'Down and Down We Go: Political Trust in Sweden', in *Critical Citizens,* ed. Pippa Norris (New York: Oxford University Press).

—— (2003). 'Are Political Parties Necessary?' *Electoral Studies* 22(2): 287–99.

Huber, John (1989). 'Values and Partisanship in Left Right Orientations: Measuring Ideology'. *European Journal of Political Research* 17(5): 599–621.

——, and G. Bingham Powell (1994). 'Congruence Between Citizens and Policymakers in Two Visions of Liberal Democracy'. *World Politics* 46(3): 291–326.

Huckfeldt, R. Robert, and John D. Sprague (1995). *Citizens, Politics and Social Communication: Information and Influence in an Election Campaign* (New York: Cambridge University Press).

Huntington, Samuel P. (1968). *Political Order in Changing Societies* (New Haven: Yale University Press).

——(1974). 'Postindustrial Politics: How Benign will it be?' *Comparative Politics* 6(1): 163–91.

——(1991). *The Third Wave: Democratization in the Late Twentieth Century* (Norman, OK: University of Oklahoma Press).

Huseby, Beate (1999). 'Government Economic Performance and Political Support', in *Challenges to Representative Democracy: Parties, Voters and Public Opinion*, ed. Hanne Marthe Narud and Toril Aalberg (Bergen: Fagbokforlaget).

Hyman, Herbert, and Charles R. Wright (1979). *Education's Lasting Influence on Values* (Chicago: University of Chicago Press).

Inglehart, Ronald, and Hans-Dieter Klingemann (1976). 'Party Identification, Ideological Preference and the Left–Right Dimension among Western Mass Publics', in *Party Identification and Beyond*, ed. Ian Budge, Ivor Crewe, and Dennis Farlie (New York: Wiley).

Jackson, John E. (1975). 'Issues, Party Choices, and Presidential Votes'. *American Journal of Political Science* 19(2): 161–85.

Jackson, Keith, and Alan McRobie (1998). *New Zealand Adopts PR* (Aldershot, UK: Ashgate).

Jacoby, Willam G. (1988). 'The Impact of Party Identification on Issue Attitudes'. *American Journal of Political Science* 32(3): 643–61.

Jennings, M. Kent, Jan W. van Deth, Samuel Barnes, Dieter Fuchs, Felix Heunks, Ronald Inglehart, Max Kaase, Hans-Dieter Klingemann, and Jacques Thomassen (1990). *Continuities in Political Action: A Longitudinal Study of Political Orientations in Three Western Democracies* (New York: de Gruyter).

Joslyn, Mark R. (1998). 'Opinion Change After the Election'. Paper presented at the annual meeting of the American Political Science Association, Boston, MA, September.

Kaase, Max (1988). 'Political Alienation and Protest', in *Comparing Pluralist Democracies*, ed. Mattei Dogan (Boulder, CO: Westview Press).

——(1995). 'Demokratie im Spannungsfeld von politischer Kultur und politischer Struktur', in *Jahrbuch für Politik*, Vol. 5, ed. Werner Link, Eberhard Schuett-Wetschky, and Gesine Schwan (Baden-Baden: Nomos).

——(1999). 'Interpersonal Trust, Political Trust, and Non-Institutionalized Political Participation in Western Europe'. *West European Politics* 22(3): 1–21.

——, and Kenneth Newton (1995). *Beliefs in Government* (New York: Oxford University Press).

Kahneman, Daniel (1994). 'New Challenges to the Rationality Assumption'. *Journal of Institutional and Theoretical Economics Zeitschrift Für die Gesamte Staatswissenschaft* 150(1): 18–36.

——, Peter P. Wakker, and Rakesh Sarin (1997). 'Back to Bentham? Explorations of Experienced Utility'. *Quarterly Journal of Economics* 112(2): 375–405.

Karp, Jeffrey A., and Shaun Bowler (2001). 'Coalition Politics and Satisfaction with Democracy: Explaining New Zealand's Reaction to Proportional Representation'. *European Journal of Political Research* 40(1): 57–79.

Klingemann, Hans-Dieter (1979). 'Ideological Conceptualization and Political Action', in *Political Action: Mass Participation in Five Western Democracies*, ed. Samuel Barnes and Max Kaase (Beverly Hills: Sage).

——(1999). 'Mapping Political Support in the 1990s: A Global Analysis', in *Critical Citizens*, ed. Pippa Norris (New York: Oxford University Press).

Knight, Jack (1992). *Institutions and Social Conflict* (Cambridge: Cambridge University Press).

Kornberg, Allan, and Harold D. Clarke (1992). *Citizens and Community: Political Support in a Representative Democracy* (New York: Cambridge University Press).

Krosnick, Jon A. (1990). 'Americans' Perception of Presidential Candidates: A Test of the Projection Hypothesis'. *Journal of Social Issues* 46(2): 159–82.

Küchler, Manfred (1991). 'The Dynamics of Mass Political Support in Western Europe: Methodological Problems and Preliminary Findings', in *Eurobarometer: The Dynamics of European Public Opinion, Essays in Honor of Jacques-Rene Rabier* ed. Karlheinz Reif and Ronald Inglehart (New York: St. Martin's).

Lagos, Marta (1997). 'Public Opinion in New Democracies. III. Latin America's Smiling Mask'. *Journal of Democracy* 8(1): 125–38.

Lamare, James W., and Jack Vowles (1996). 'Party Interests, Public Opinion and Institutional Preferences: Electoral System Change in New Zealand'. *Australian Journal of Political Science* 31(3): 321–46.

Lambert, Robert D., James E. Curtis, Steven D. Brown, and Barry J. Kay (1986). 'Effects of Identification with Governing Parties on Feelings of Political Efficacy and Trust'. *Canadian Journal of Political Science* 19(4): 705–28.

Lane, Robert E. (1959). *Political Life. Why People Get Involved in Politics* (New York: The Free Press).

Lasswell, Harold (1953). *Politics: Who Gets What When and How* (New York: McGraw Hill).

Lewis-Beck, Michael S., and Richard Nadeau (2000). 'French Electoral Institutions and the Economic Vote'. *Electoral Studies* 19(2–3): 171–82.

Lijphart, Arend (1984). *Democracies* (New Haven: Yale University Press).

——(1994). *Electoral Systems and Party Systems. A Study of Twenty-Seven Democracies, 1945–1990* (New York: Oxford University Press).

——(1999). *Patterns of Democracy* (New Haven: Yale University Press).

Linde, Jonas, and Joakim Ekman (2003). 'Satisfaction with Democracy: A Note on a Frequently Used Indicator in Comparative Politics'. *European Journal of Political Research* 42(3): 391–408.

Lipset, Seymour Martin (1959). 'Some Social Requisites of Democracy: Economic Development and Political Legitimacy'. *American Political Science Review* 53(1): 69–105.

——(1960). *Political Man: The Social Bases of Politics* (New York: Doubleday).

Listhaug, Ola (1995). 'The Dynamics of Trust in Politicians', in *Citizens and the State*, ed. Hans-Dieter Klingemann and Dieter Fuchs (New York: Oxford University Press).

Listhaug, and Bernt Aardal (2003). 'Support of Democracy in Europe'. Paper presented at the Conference on Democracy in the New Europe, Center for the Study of Democracy, University of California, Irvine, February.

——, and Kristen Ringdal (2004). 'Civic Morality in Stable, New, and Half-hearted Democracies', in *European Values at the Turn of the Millennium*, ed. Wil Arts and Loek Halman (Leiden: Brill).

Listhaug, Ola, and Matti Wiberg (1995). 'Confidence in Political Institutions', in *Citizens and the State*, ed. Hans-Dieter Klingemann and Dieter Fuchs (New York: Oxford University Press).

——, Bernt Aardal, and Ingunn Opheim Ellis (2002). 'Institutional Variation and Political Support: An Analysis of CSES Data from 23 countries'. Paper presented at Comparative Study of Electoral Systems, WZB Berlin, February.

Lopez Pina, Antonio, Peter McDonough, and Samuel H. Barnes (1994). 'The Nature of Political Support and Legitimacy in Spain'. *Comparative Political Studies* 27(3): 349–80.

Löwenberg, Gerhard (1971). 'The Influence of Parliamentary Behavior on Regime Stability'. *Comparative Politics* 3(1): 177–200.

Lupia, Arthur, and Mathew D. McCubbins (1998). *The Democratic Dilemma: Can Citizens Learn What They Need to Know?* (New York: Cambridge University Press).

MacKuen, Michael, W. Russell Neuman, and George E. Marcus (2000). 'Affective Intelligence, Voting, and Matters of Public Policy'. Paper presented at the annual meeting of the American Political Science Association, Washington, DC, September.

Magleby, David B., and Kelly D. Patterson (1998). The Art of Persuasion: Consultants and the Rise of Direct Democracy. Paper presented at the annual meeting of the American Political Science Association, Boston, MA, September.

Markus, Gregory B., and Philip E. Converse (1979). 'A Dynamic Simultaneous Equation Model of Electoral Choice'. *American Political Science Review* 73(4): 1055–70.

McAuley, E., D. Russell, and J. B. Gross (1983). 'Affective Consequences of Winning and Losing: An Attributional Analysis'. *Journal of Sport Psychology* 4(1): 167–76.

McCaul, Kevin D., Brian A. Gladue, and Margaret Joppa (1992). 'Winning, Losing, Mood, and Testosterone'. *Hormones and Behavior* 26(4): 486–504.

McClelland, David C. (1987). *Human Motivation* (New York: Cambridge University Press).

McClosky, Herbert, and John Zaller (1984). *The American Ethos: Public Attitudes Toward Capitalism and Democracy* (Cambridge: Harvard University Press).

McDonald, Michael D., Silvia M. Mendes, and Ian Budge (2004). 'What are Elections For? Conferring the Median Mandate'. *British Journal of Political Science* 34(1): 1–26.

McGann Anthony J. (2002). 'The Tyranny of the Super-Majority: How Majority Rule Protects Minorities'. Working Paper, Center for the Study of Democracy, University of California, Irvine, CA.

McGuire, William J. (1968). 'Theory of the Structure of Human Thought', in *Theories of Cognitive Consistency: A Sourcebook*, ed. Robert P. Abelson (Chicago: Rand McNally).

Miller, Nicholas (1983). 'Pluralism and Social Choice' *American Political Science Review* 77(3): 734–46.

Miller, Warren E. (1994). 'An Organizational History of the Intellectual Origins of the American National Election Studies'. *European Journal of Political Research* 25(2): 247–65.

Miller, Arthur H., and Ola Listhaug (1990). 'Political Parties and Confidence in Government'. *British Journal of Political Science* 20(3): 357–86.

Miller, Arthur H., and Ola Listhaug (1999). 'Political Performance and Institutional Trust', in *Critical Citizens: Global Support for Democratic Governance*, ed. Pippa Norris (New York: Oxford University Press).

Mishler, William, and Richard Rose (1996) 'Trajectories of Fear and Hope: Support for Democracy in Post-Communist Europe'. *Comparative Political Studies* 28(1): 553–81.

——, and —— (1997). 'Trust, Distrust and Skepticism: Popular Evaluations of Civil and Political Institutions in Post-Communist Societies'. *Journal of Politics* 59(2): 418–51.

——, and —— (2001). 'Political Support for Incomplete Democracies: Realist vs. Idealist Theories and Measures'. *International Political Science Review* 22(4): 303–20.

——, and —— (2002). 'Learning and Re-learning Regime Support: The Dynamics of Post-Communist Regimes'. *European Journal of Political Research* 41(1): 5–36.

Morrell, Michael E. (1999). 'Citizens' Evaluations of Participatory Democratic Procedures: Normative Theory Meets Empirical Science'. *Political Research Quarterly* 52(2): 293–322.

Mutz, Diana C. (2002*a*). 'The Consequences of Cross-Cutting Networks for Political Participation'. *American Journal of Political Science* 46(4): 838–55.

—— (2002*b*). 'Cross-Cutting Social Networks: Testing Democratic Theory in Practice'. *American Political Science Review* 96(2): 111–26.

Nadeau, Richard, and André Blais (1993). 'Accepting the Election Outcome: The Effect on Participation on Losers' Consent'. *British Journal of Political Science* 23(4): 553–63.

Neilson, William S. (2000). 'Victory and Defeat in a Model of Behavior in Games and Toward Risk'. Working Paper, Department of Economics, Texas A&M University, College Station, TX.

Nicholson, Stephen P., and Robert M. Howard (2003). 'Framing Support for the Supreme Court in the Aftermath of Bush v. Gore'. *Journal of Politics* 65(3): 676–95.

Noelle-Neumann, Elisabeth (1974). 'The Spiral of Silence: A Theory of Public Opinion'. *Journal of Communication* 24(2): 43–51.

Norris, Pippa (1999). 'Introduction: The Growth of Critical Citizens?' in *Critical Citizens*, ed. Pippa Norris (New York: Oxford University Press).

North, Douglass (1981). *Structure and Change in Economic History* (New York: W. W. Norton).

Paldam, Martin, and Peter Skott (1995). 'A Rational-Voter Explanation of the Cost of Ruling'. *Public Choice* 83(1–2): 159–72.

Paskeviciute, Aida, and Christopher J. Anderson (2004). 'Political Parties, Partisanship, and Attitudes Toward Government in Democracies'. Paper presented at the annual meeting of the Midwest Political Science Association, Chicago, IL, April.

Pateman, Carol (1970). *Participation and Democratic Theory* (New York: Cambridge University Press).

Pedersen, Mogens (1983). 'Changing Patterns of Electoral Volatility in European Party Systems, 1948–1977: Explorations in Explanation', in *West European Party Systems: Continuity and Change*, ed. Hans Daalder and Peter Mair (London: Sage Publications).

Pempel. T. J. (1990). *Uncommon Democracies: The One-Party Dominant Regimes* (Ithaca, NY: Cornell University Press).

Pitkin, Hanna (1967). *The Concept of Representation* (Berkeley: University of California Press).

Plutzer, Eric (2002). 'Becoming a Habitual Voter: Inertia, Resources, and Growth in Young Adulthood'. *American Political Science Review* 96(1): 41–56.

Powell, G. Bingham, Jr. (1982). *Contemporary Democracies: Participation, Stability, and Violence* (Cambridge: Harvard University Press).

Powell, G. Bingham (1986). 'Extremist Parties and Political Turmoil: Two Puzzles'. *American Journal of Political Science* 30(1): 357–78.

—— (1989). 'Constitutional Design and Citizen Electoral Control'. *Journal of Theoretical Politics* 1(1): 107–30.

—— (2000). *Elections as Instruments of Democracy* (New Haven: Yale University Press).

——, and Guy Whitten (1993). 'A Cross-National Analysis of Economic Voting: Taking Account of the Political Context'. *American Journal of Political Science* 37(3): 391–414.

Przeworski, Adam (1991). *Democracy and the Market: Political and Economic Reforms in Eastern Europe and Latin America* (New York: Cambridge University Press).

—— (2001). Democracy as an Equilibrium. Working Paper, New York University, Department of Politics, New York, NY.

Putnam, Robert (1993). *Making Democracy Work: Civic Traditions in Modern Italy* (Princeton: Princeton University Press).

Rae, Douglas (1967). *The Political Consequences of Electoral Laws* (New Haven: Yale University Press).

Regan, Dennis T., and Martin Kilduff (1988). 'Optimism About Elections: Dissonance Reduction at the Ballot Box'. *Political Psychology* 9(1): 101–7.

Richardson, Bradley M. (1991). 'European Party Loyalties Revisited'. *American Political Science Review* 85(3): 751–75.

Riker, William H. (1965). *Democracy in the United States*, 2nd edn (New York: Macmillan).

—— (1976). 'The Number of Political Parties: A Reexamination of Duverger's Law'. *Comparative Politics* 9(1): 93–106.

—— (1982). *Liberalism Against Populism: A Confrontation Between the Theory of Democracy and the Theory of Social Choice* (San Francisco: W. H. Freeman).

—— (1983). 'Political Theory and the Art of Heresthetics', in *Political Science: The State of the Discipline*, ed. Ada W. Finifter (Washington: American Political Science Association).

—— (1986). *The Art of Political Manipulation* (New Haven: Yale University Press).

Rohrschneider, Robert (1999). *Learning Democracy: Democratic and Economic Values in Unified Germany* (New York: Oxford University Press).

Rosenberg, Milton J. (1956). 'Cognitive Structure and Attitudinal Affect'. *Journal of Abnormal Social Psychology* 53(4): 367–72.

Salisbury, Robert (1975). 'Research on Political Participation'. *American Journal of Political Science* 19(2): 323–43.

Sanders, David, and Malcolm Brynin (1999). 'The Dynamics of Party Preference Change in Britain, 1991–1996'. *Political Studies* 47(2): 219–39.

Scarbrough, Elinor (2003). 'On the Shoulders of Giants: A Tribute to Warren E. Miller'. *Electoral Studies* 22(2): 197–216.

Schickler Eric, and Donald P. Green (1997). 'The Stability of Party Identification in Western Democracies: Results from Eight Panel Surveys'. *Comparative Political Studies* 30(4): 450–83.

Seligson, Mitchell A. (1993). 'Political Culture and Regime Type: Evidence from Nicaragua and Costa Rica'. *Journal of Politics* 55(3): 777–92.

Shepsle, Kenneth A. (1979). 'Institutional Arrangements and Equilibrium in Multi-dimensional Voting Models'. *American Journal of Political Science* 23(1): 27–59.

—— (2003). 'Losers in Politics (and How They Sometimes Become Winners): William Riker's Heresthetic'. *Perspectives on Politics* 1(2): 307–15.

Stevenson, Randolph T. (2002). 'The Cost of Ruling, Cabinet Duration, and the "Median-Gap" Model' *Public Choice* 113(1 2): 157–78.

Stokes, Susan C. (1996). 'Introduction. Public Opinion and Market Reforms: The Limits of Economic Voting'. *Comparative Political Studies* 29(4): 499–519.

Stricker, George (1964). 'The Operation of Cognitive Dissonance on Pre- and Post-Election Attitudes'. *Journal of Social Psychology* 63(1): 111–19.

Strom, Kaare (1984). 'Minority Governments in Parliamentary Democracies: The Rationality of Nonwinning Cabinet Solutions'. *Comparative Political Studies* 17(2): 199–227.

Thaler, Richard (1994). *The Winner's Curse: Paradoxes and Anomalies of Economic Life* (Princeton, NJ: Princeton University Press).

Thompson, Dennis (1970). *The Democratic Citizen* (New York: Cambridge University Press).

Torcal, Mariano, Richard Gunther, and Jose Ramon Montero (2002). 'Anti-Party Sentiments in Southern Europe', in *Political Parties: Old Concepts and New Challenges*, ed. Richard Gunther, Jose Ramon Montero, and Juan J. Linz (Oxford: Oxford University Press).

Tsebelis, George (2003). *Veto Players* (Princeton: Princeton University Press).

——, and Jeannette Money (1997). *Bicameralism* (New York: Cambridge University Press).

Tversky, Amos, and Daniel Kahneman (1992). 'Advances in Prospect Theory: Cumulative Representation of Uncertainty'. *Journal of Risk and Uncertainty* 5(4): 297–323.

Tyler, Tom R. (1990). *Why People Obey the Law* (New Haven, CT: Yale University Press).

—— (1999). 'Trust and Democratic Governance', in *Trust and Governance*, ed. Valerie Braithwaite and Margaret Levi (New York: Russell Sage Foundation).

Vetter, Angelika (2000). 'Frischer Wind in einer alten Beziehung? Political Efficacy und die Bundestagswahlen 1998', in *Wirklich ein Volk? Die politischen*

Orientierungen von Ost- und Westdeutschen im Vergleich, ed. Jürgen W. Falter, Oscar W. Gabriel and Hans Rattinger (Opladen: Leske & Budrich).

Vowles, Jack (1995). 'The Politics of Electoral Reform in New Zealand'. *International Political Science Review* 16 (1): 95–115.

Vowles, Jack, Jeffrey Karp, Susan Banducci, and Peter Aimer (2002). 'Public Opinion, Public Knowledge, and the Electoral System', in *Proportional Representation on Trial*, ed. Jack Vowles, Peter Aimer, Jeffrey Karp, Susan Banducci, Raymond Miller and Ann Sullivan (Auckland: Auckland University Press).

Weatherford, M. Stephen (1987). 'How Does Government Performance Influence Political Support'. *Political Behavior* 9(1): 5–28.

—— (1991). 'Mapping the Ties that Bind: Legitimacy, Representation and Alienation'. *Western Political Quarterly* 44(2): 251–76.

—— (1992). 'Measuring Political Legitimacy'. *American Political Science Review* 86(1): 149–66.

Weingast, Barry R. (1997). 'The Political Foundations of Democracy and the Rule of Law'. *American Political Science Review* 91(2): 245–63.

Wenzel, James, Shaun Bowler, and David J. Lanoue (2000). 'Citizen Opinion and Constitutional Choices: The Case of the UK'. *Political Behavior* 22(3): 241–65.

Westle, Bettina (1989). *Politische Legitimität: Theorien, Konzepte, empirische Befunde* (Baden-Baden: Nomos).

Whitefield, Stephen, and Geoffrey Evans (1994). 'The Russian Election of (1993): Public Opinion and the Transition Experience'. *Post-Soviet Affairs* 10(1): 38–60.

Wilson, George V., and John H. Kerr (1999). 'Affective Responses to Success and Failure: A Study of Winning and Losing in Competitive Rugby'. *Personality and Individual Differences* 27(1): 85–99.

Wright, Gerald C. (1993). 'Errors in Measuring Vote Choice in the National Election Studies, 1952–88'. *American Journal of Political Science* 37(1): 291–316.

Yoshinaka, Antoine (2002). 'Participants and By-Standers: The Effect of Turnout on Individuals' Levels of Satisfaction with Democracy in the United States'. Paper presented at the annual meeting of the Midwest Political Science Association, Chicago, IL, April.

Zaller, John R. (1992). *The Nature and Origins of Mass Opinion* (New York: Cambridge University Press).

Index

Made in the USA
Lexington, KY
12 May 2011